RHYTHM, MUSIC,
AND THE BRAIN

Studies on New Music Research

SERIES EDITOR:

Mark Leman, Institute for Psychoacoustics and Electronic Music, Department of Musicology University of Ghent, Belgium

RHYTHM, MUSIC, AND THE BRAIN

Scientific Foundations and Clinical Applications

MICHAEL H. THAUT

ROUTLEDGE
NEW YORK AND LONDON

Published in 2005 by
Routledge
Taylor & Francis Group
270 Madison Avenue
New York, NY 10016

Published in Great Britain by
Routledge
Taylor & Francis Group
2 Park Square
Milton Park, Abingdon
Oxon OX14 4RN

© 2005 by Taylor & Francis Group, LLC
Routledge is an imprint of Taylor & Francis Group

Printed in the United States of America on acid-free paper
10 9 8 7 6 5 4 3

International Standard Book Number-10: 0-415-97370-8 (Hardcover)
International Standard Book Number-13: 978-0-415-97370-0 (Hardcover)
Library of Congress Card Number 2005006731

Library of Congress Cataloging-in-Publication Data

Thaut, Michael H.
   Rhythm, music, and the brain : scientific foundations and clinical applications / Michael H. Thaut
       p. cm. -- (Studies on new music research ; 7)
   Includes bibliographical references and index.
   ISBN 0-415-97370-8 (hardback : alk. paper)
   1. Music and science. 2. Musical meter and rhythm. 3. Music--Physiological aspects. 4. Music--Psychological aspects. I. Title. II. Series.

ML3800.T44 2005
781'.11--dc22   2005006731

Taylor & Francis Group
is the Academic Division of T&F Informa plc.

Visit the Taylor & Francis Web site at
http://www.taylorandfrancis.com

and the Routledge Web site at
http://www.routledge-ny.com

Contents

Introduction

Music has received an unprecedented research focus in the brain sciences over the previous two decades. This came as a surprise to many artists and scientists alike; it was an unlikely development for music, as an aesthetic medium and art form, to become a focus of many serious brain scientists' major research efforts. Furthermore, music received an almost exclusive and privileged position in brain research compared to other artistic fields. No other art form has received anything close to this level of attention.

Music, as a highly abstract and non-representational art, that nevertheless seems to speak so directly and specifically to our thoughts, feelings, and sense of movement in a powerful manner, has exerted an enormous attraction on brain science. Music's effects on the human experience have always been difficult to explain in their totality, as if always keeping a shroud of mystery, never entirely opening the curtain to the stage play of the forces on the human mind. Philosophers, scientists, artists, psychologists, and many great minds from other scholarly fields have attempted to give a full account of the role music plays in influencing emotion and cognitions, providing entertainment, shaping and preserving societal values, and playing significant roles in work, play, education, religion. The historical and cultural account of music's influences is large and takes time to fully grasp and record. However, the question of "how" music moves us, stimulates our thoughts, feelings, and kinesthetic sense, and how it can express and reach the human experience in such profound ways, continues to puzzle and intrigue.

With the advent of modern cognitive neuroscience and its new tools of studying the human brain, "live," music as a highly complex, temporally ordered and rule-based sensory language quickly became a fascinating topic of study, probably driven by the quiet hope that these new tools and paradigms would bring us closer to an understanding of the function and role of music and its mechanisms to attract our minds. In parallel to these aspirations, however, another highly significant development in studying music scientifically occurred, which was possibly less foreseen by many researchers. We now know that by studying the physiology and neurology of brain function in music we can actually obtain a great deal of knowledge about general brain function, in regard to the perception of complex auditory sound stimuli, time and rhythm processing, differential processing of music and language as two aural communication systems, biological substrates of learning versus innate talent in the arts, and processing of higher cognitive functions related to temporality and emotion. Music has become a very useful model for brain research in perception and cognition.

It has become quite clear in recent years that one of the most interesting and provocative suggestions coming out of these efforts in music and brain science is the realization of music as a biologically deeply ingrained function of the human brain. The brain has neural circuitry that is dedicated to music. Music is associated with a specific yet complex brain architecture. Sensitivity to music plays a critical role in the development of all children regardless of the presence or absence of later artistic achievement. Music is ubiquitous in all known historical and present cultures. It is safe to say that music is much more than cultural artifact, an icing on the cake of human evolution after basic biological needs and developments were adaptively satisfied. This will be discussed further in this book in relationship to a new paradigm of a neuroscience of aesthetics.

This book has a specific focus within music. It deals predominantly with rhythm. Rhythm is, in many scholars' and artists' view, one of the two big "pillars" in music that hold the auditory temporal architecture of music together. Rhythm and polyphony, sequentiality and simultaneity, create temporal order whereby one may offer the argument that polyphony, i.e., the vertical simultaneity of sound in multiple melodies, intervals, and harmonies, is still nested within the larger "beam" of rhythm, when one defines rhythm in the broadest sense as structure of temporal distribution and organization. That a book on music and science can be at least seriously attempted—successfully or not—with a fairly exclusive focus on one of the many components of music, is a testimony to the breadth and depth of a virtual explosion in research of music and the brain sciences in the past 20 years.

The main goal of the book is to provide an attempt—which should be timely for the current state of interest—to bring the knowledge in the arts and the sciences together and review systematically our current state of study about the brain and music, specifically in rhythm. Underneath that overarching goal, the book was written with three supporting goals in mind, each considered a stepping stone to help along the progress in elucidating the main goal:

1. To create a theoretical and structural framework for understanding the nature and structure of rhythm as a critical building element in music, and how rhythm shapes critical features in the way the brain perceives time and music.
2. To review the current state of research on rhythm and brain function.
3. To introduce a historically new paradigm for biomedical applications of music to therapy and medicine and critically examine their scientific and clinical evidence. The biomedical applications, presented in detail in the last four chapters of the book, flow directly from the theory and science discussed in the previous chapters.

Chapters 1 and 2 provide discussions of the nature of rhythm and of the relationship between music and psychobiology. With an understanding of the critical function of time and rhythm in music, and a background in regard to how a new "biological aesthetics" may guide our understanding of music, behavior, and brain function, the book proceeds to the second part laid out in Chapters 3, 4, and 5. Here the emphasis is on reviewing and appraising the research findings about the neurobiological foundations of rhythm and the brain, as well as focusing on the new research that shows how music and rhythm can affect non-musical brain and behavior function in profound ways. Chapter 5 is a special chapter among these, highly mathematical in nature, showing how one can use the parameters of mechanical physics and the language of mathematics to understand the critical influence rhythm and music can have on kinesthetics, the control of movement, through providing time information to the brain. Finally, Chapters 6, 7, 8, and 9 introduce the clinical building, i.e., the new therapeutic methodology of Neurologic Music Therapy, that has been erected on the research foundations in rhythm, music, and the neurological sciences. These last chapters deal quite extensively with clinical techniques and implementations in rehabilitation. However, one must remember that these techniques are the clinical derivatives of the scientific and theoretical knowledge presented earlier. They cannot be read or understood in isolation or separation from the rest of the book. Those final chapters lay a new evidence-based, quantifiable, and functional foundation for the profession of music therapy.

We hope that the book will be of interest and good use for the interested lay and professional readers in the sciences and arts, as well as the professionals in the fields of neuroscientific research, medicine, and rehabilitation. It is also hoped that it may help stimulate more discussion, exchange, and mutual understanding in order to serve progress in linking aesthetics, music, and the brain sciences. A special interest and recognition of importance has been invested in this book to the discipline of music therapy. The book was written in a way so as to also serve as a foundational or advanced text to train music therapists in the art and science of Neurologic Music Therapy.

1

The Structure of Rhythm:
The Essence of Time in Music

1.1 Rhythm, Time, and Communication in Music

Throughout human history, music has been considered a form of communication. However, the nature of *what* and *how* music communicates has been the subject of long-standing and fascinating inquiries in philosophy, religion, the arts, and the sciences. Music has been frequently described as a language-like form of human expression, although musical sounds do not carry designative meaning, as speech sounds do. Communication —defined in the broadest terms as the process involving any exchange of meaningful information between two or more participants (Gillam et al. 2000)—requires signs and symbols to exchange information between the originator and the recipient. Signs are frequently defined as anything that stands for something, usually with rather specific references, whereas symbols, as subforms of signs, evoke less specified meanings and are much more subjective. They must have significance for the originator producing them (cf. Kreitler and Kreitler 1972; Berlyne 1971).

In submitting music to communication analysis, the comparison with speech and language is intriguing and has been invoked many times (cf. Aiello 1994). Speech and music have structural similarities in regard to prosodic features: pitch, duration, timbre, intensity, accents, and inflection patterns built from those elements. Music can also be studied in analogy to phonological analyses of single speech sounds. A case could also be made for possible morphological analogies in regard to an analysis of the smallest sound units that convey meaning. One of the most important overlaps in comparative analysis between music and speech occurs within syntax and pragmatics. Music and speech both are built on syntactical systems that organize sound patterns into rule-based structures. Parallels between music and speech from this point of view have been made, for example, by comparing Noam Chomsky's linguistic model of deep and surface structure in language with structural analyses in music, such as Heinrich Schenker's *Ursatz* (Schenker 1935; Bernstein 1976; Sloboda 1985). Although the common existence of syntactical systems in music and speech is undisputed, the exact function and meaning of these systems within them, however, are not necessarily viewed as common (cf. Deutsch 1979).

Furthermore, the pragmatic elements of communication—meaning that is shaped and conveyed by social and cultural context, learning and enculturation, as well as communicative intent of the participants in the communication process—also play important roles in music and speech (Merriam 1964; Kraut 1992). Speech and music both take on meaning within the cultural background, the social context, and the intents and expectations of the situation in which the communication takes place.

However, most likely the most important difference between speech and music lies in the lack of explicit semantic or referential meaning in music. Musical sounds and sound patterns communicate themselves in abstract fashion. They do not intrinsically denote or refer to extramusical events, objects, concepts, or cognitions. Musical meaning is embodied, and its nondiscursive symbols cannot be translated directly into referential denotations. One must note, of course, that attempts at infusing direct referential systems into music have been attempted throughout history. Consider, for instance, the doctrine of affections in the Baroque period or the program music of the nineteenth century, which used associative prescriptions to develop the expression of dramatic plots in music.

Another very clear distinction between music and speech is found in the differences in the neurological bases of processing speech and music. Whereas expressive and receptive speech functions can be localized in a relatively constrained and lateralized neural network, the neuroanatomical basis of music is widely distributed neurologically and quite dependent on subfunctions of music processing.

Dowling and Harwood (1986) have proposed a system of terms that comprehensively summarizes the different ways in which music is thought to communicate meaning (Peirce 1935; Langer 1942; Meyer 1956; Berlyne 1971): indexically, by learned association with extramusical material; iconically, by likeness or resemblance to extramusical events or experiences; and symbolically, by communicating the role and value of its symbols (i.e., musical events) within the structure of musical patterns. Arguably, the symbolic, embedded form of communication has been often called the core function of musical communication because this is what the listener or performer actually hears, and without meaningful and salient perception of musical structure, little associative learning value or iconic representation would be possible (Meyer 1956).

Considering the nonreferential embodied meaning as a core function in musical communication, an understanding of the major organizing syntactical elements in music (i.e., those which create meaningful sound patterns) is of utmost importance. Musical "grammar" is obviously very complex, has undergone significant historical developments, and manifests itself in great diversity across different cultures. However, a somewhat reductionistic conceptualization will provide us with a fundamental understanding of the essential nature of musical grammar and syntax. One of the most important characteristics of music—also when compared with other art forms—is its strictly temporal character. Music unfolds only in time, and the physical basis of music is based on the time patterns of physical vibrations transduced in our hearing apparatus into electrochemical information that passes through the neural relays of the auditory system to reach the brain. Within this temporal basis, two core dimensions emerge: sequentiality and simultaneity. Music's particular nature permits it to express both at once. This is a unique feature among art forms and communication systems. Language is sequential but monophonic. Visual art has analogies of time dimensions expressed in its works within the physical essence of the spatial dimension, although the observer and the creator in the visual arts experience the work in time. Yet this remains a segregated process in contrast to music. For further expositions on these fascinating issues one may consult, for example, the brilliant writings and paintings of Kupka, Klee, Delauney, or the Cubists (Shaw-Miller 2002). Music's whole physical and cognitive-perceptual nature, however, rests solely within this two-dimensional temporality. Translating them into musical terms, we may speak of rhythm and polyphony as the two core dimensions of music. Rhythm and polyphony contain the two dimensions that organize sounds sequentially and simultaneously into meaningful patterns and structures, creating "the language" of music.

However, distinct from speech, music is not a referential, associative language—it is initially a perceptual language whose intrinsic pattern structure conveys meaning to the human brain. The significance and meaning of the musical symbols within that pattern structure depend on their place and role in the pattern, relative to the other symbols in a syntactical network that is organized sequentially and simultaneously in time. Within such context, rhythm becomes one of the most important structural elements to build the expression of formal meaning in music. In music, the human brain creates and experiences a unique, highly complex, time-ordered, and integrated process of perception and action. Rhythm in music is the core element that binds simultaneity and sequentiality of sound patterns into structural organizational forms underlying what we consider musical language. In this function, rhythm assumes a critical syntactical role in communicating symbolic, as well as associative, meaning in music.

1.2 Rhythm in Aesthetic Perception

In aesthetics, as in language usage in daily life, the term "rhythm" has both a broad and a more narrowly defined sense. Rhythm, as Berlyne (1971) states, is frequently used to refer to patterns of temporal distribution of events, objects, symbols, or signs in general. Order and pattern in discernible temporal organization may be the key to understanding rhythm in this broader sense. Rhythm, in the narrower sense, refers to explicit divisions of time or space into intervallic time systems, recurrent and often (but not always) characterized by periodicity. Components of musical time divisions such as pulses, beats, and meter systems are relevant in this understanding of rhythm.

In the broader sense, every work of art possesses rhythm. Because rhythm deals with the discernible structure of temporal organization of an artwork's "building blocks" into an arrangement of its physical elements into form-building patterns, rhythm is one of the most important components of an artwork. In music, the critical role of rhythm in building musical forms and communicating meaning has already been discussed, based on the notion that music unfolds exclusively in the time dimensions of sequentiality and simultaneity. But the structure and function of rhythm can also be transposed to visual-spatial elements, for example, by organizing patterns of deflections in lines, by patches of distinct coloring, or by arranging similarly shaped objects in spatial configurations. The rhythms of speech and the rhythms of statements and dialogues, in conjunction with movements, can express dramatic rhythms in theatrical plays. The distribution of syllables and inflection points in poetry and the distribution of elements of motion of the human body in dance are examples of rhythms in other art forms.

In the narrower sense, rhythm carries two core aspects of temporal organization: periodicity and subdivision into similarly structured groupings. Periodicity refers to the grouping of events into successive sequences of equal temporal and spatial extent. These groupings are often hierarchical, as is easily illustrated in the metric and phrase structure of music, with equal groupings containing smaller subunits of equal groupings. The subdivision of groupings, on the other hand, refers to the similarity of internal structures among these groups, such as intensity via language, durations via music, or kinematic shapes via dance (Berlyne 1971). As Berlyne states, these rhythms determine and guide many of the acts by which all artists—painters, musicians, poets, sculptors, dancers—form and generate their works.

Rhythm can access and powerfully influence some core elements of the perceptual mechanisms that drive patterns of meaning in symbolic communication of artworks. First, discernible temporal distribution and organization of events in groupings imposed by a rhythmic structure allow for better perceptual gestalts to emerge, minimizing conflict and difficulty in perception, such as being confronted with stimuli that are hard to distinguish. Both Gestalt psychology of perception and perceptual neuroscience emphasize innate drives to search for pattern structures that allow the emergence of larger units of events, a way of imposing order and meaning onto the perceptual process. Rhythm determines, assigns, and builds time relationships between events in the perceptual process. Because all efforts in perception must fundamentally include a multidimensional temporal process, regardless of sense modality, rhythm assumes a critical role in the shaping and modulating of meaning in perception.

Second, rhythm as temporal ordering process—especially in its narrower sense as cyclical, periodic phenomenon—creates anticipation and predictability. Prediction and anticipation are key terms in certain theories of emotion and meaning (Dewey 1934, Mandler 1984) that have been extrapolated to the theories of emotion and meaning in music (Meyer 1956). Temporary violations of expectations or predictions (e.g., in compositional structures in music) have potential and opportunity for arousal increments that are related to the search for meaningful resolutions in the process of violating expectations. A suspended fourth chord, an unexpected modulation to a new key, or a deceptive cadence may create a temporary violation of musical predictions, which in turn leads to a heightened state of arousal to search for a meaningful resolution of the musical tension. This process of tension release in perception of music has been mentioned by many theorists as the basis for the affective experience in music (Meyer 1956; Berlyne 1971; Harwood and Dowling 1986; Kreitler and Kreitler 1972), unfolding in the continuous interplay between expectation and temporary suspense, tension and release, arousal and de-arousal, arsis and thesis, throughout the patterns of a well-crafted musical composition. Periodic structures in rhythm can become drivers of a process of dialectical communication of meaning in artworks, helping to build theses and antitheses and new syntheses, assuming thesis function, in the temporal shaping of melody, harmony, and counterpoint in music or the shaping of lines and colors in paintings, sculptures, or architecture.

Third, rhythms can form and shape memory. It has been known since the work of G. E. Mueller and Schumann (1894)—and has been impressively confirmed by recent research in psychology and neuroscience—that metrical organization makes it easier to remember verbal material. All processes of perception and meaning in artworks—like all cognitive operations in attention, executive function, or emotion— require some form of memory function, from working memory to short and long forms of long-term memory, in order to appreciate and understand form-building components in artworks, such as variation and development, contrast and repetition, statement and restatement. In that context, rhythm—as metrical-temporal organizer of events in artworks—facilitates aesthetic (i.e., sensory-related) memory as a prerequisite for meaningful comprehension, appraisal, analysis, and appreciation of artistic forms.

The presented analysis has given us a framework for understanding the core function of rhythm in music and aesthetic perception in regard to form and meaning. In a second step, we have also taken a look at some of the broader distinctions in understanding the structure and definitions of rhythm. In the next section, we turn our attention to the precise building blocks that constitute the "grammar and syntax" of rhythm in music.

1.3 Elements of Rhythm

Rhythm organizes time. In music, as a time-based acoustical language, rhythm assumes a central syntactical role in organizing musical events into coherent and comprehensible patterns and forms. Thus, the structure of rhythm communicates a great deal of the actual, comprehensive "musical meaning" of a musical composition. At the other end of the musical communication process, rhythm also modulates the attention of the listener in relationship to the perception of musical events. Rhythm guides the ear and brain to make sense of acoustical patterns and shapes by directing focus to important moments in the unfolding of the music.

The study of rhythm perception traditionally uses metric components as fundamental events with clear demarcations and temporal ratios. However, as we will see, the perception of rhythm and formation of rhythm may be biologically based more on the entrainment of oscillatory circuits in the brain than on actual acts of measurement in terms of timekeepers that are often conceptualized and modeled as clocks, pulse counters, or stopwatches in the brain. The entrainment of different oscillatory circuits that respond individually to different periodicities in the amplitude spectrum of a complex rhythmic pattern (such as a Fourier analysis) would give the brain considerably more temporal flexibility and temporal stability to perceive, process, form, and modulate rhythms than would a counting process involving duration measurements. As such, periodicities of rhythms would be determined not by the measurement of discontinuous time elements, but by categorical entrainment of interval-based time modules, coded in the neural firing rates of the auditory system and projected into other resonant brain tissue. Such modules could serve more effectively as synchronization references to flexible time adaptations that are crucial for musical expression, such as the well-known bending of time through techniques such as rubatos, accelerandos, or decelerandos; metric modulations; or simple, minute variances in time to add nuances of emphasis in phrasing and expression. Within such a framework of entrainment, faster and slower time adaptations would not eventually run away in time or distort the perception of an overall coherent temporal structure, but would always be rescalable to the basic time structure.

Parncutt (1994), in a highly influential paper, has suggested that such basic temporal structure in music is uniquely based on felt pulse patterns. The perception of pulses, formed as a sequence of acoustic events created by amplitude modulations, is based on two processes. One refers to the extreme sensitivity of the auditory system to such fluctuations in the sound source to establish the sensation of a pulse. Pulse sensations in the visual system, as visual rhythms, are much harder or almost impossible to create. The other process is based on the sequential horizontal discrimination sensitivity of the auditory system to compute periodicities (i.e., repetition rates that establish the sensation of a regular, cyclical pulse sequence). Based on the evidence for periodicity entrainment and discrimination, however, it follows that the perception of rhythms is not an event-based process, but an interval period-based process, with pulses simply serving as event markers demarcating rhythmic intervals.

Pulse perception, creating interval templates, must then be considered as a fundamental component in rhythm formation. It is a universal characteristic of music, forming the basis for the temporal organization of music in virtually all cultures. Pulses serve as isochronous, equidistant time points generated by interval or period durations. Pulses divide the flow of time into regular reference points. They serve as critical frameworks for the essential function of synchronization, which is the fundamental building process of rhythm. Rhythmic events are referenced and synchronized against underlying sensations of pulse patterns. Any perception or production of metrically structured rhythms in music—even irregular rhythms—would be based on some process of synchronization against underlying pulse structures. Pulses are, therefore, crucial components in music. They are, as already pointed out, inferred from and constructed upon time intervals, and ultimately depend on them for their continued existence. Pulses serve another important function in rhythm perception that has tremendous implications for the control of cognitive functions and motor performance: They establish anticipation and predictability, two components that—as we will discuss in later chapters—have tremendous influence on the regulation of nonmusical temporal processes in perception, cognition, and motor control. However, pulses also serve as constraints and limitations in rhythm formation in music. Pulses do not change in a given sequence. Musical-rhythmic events that are identical to the underlying pulse pattern are inevitably perceived as of little information value, and cause habituation. They express little in themselves in complexity of time structure, although they serve as important underlying references without which the building of rhythmic complexities via synchronization would be nearly impossible. They are most likely an example of primitive grouping operations in perception, because they do not require long-term memory to be constructed; they are perceived directly through echoic or short-term (immediate working) memory (Snyder 2000).

It is interesting—as well as at times confusing—to see how the terms "beat" and "pulse" have been used to refer to very similar or essentially the same concepts. Some authors, however, have suggested that it may be useful to recognize and infuse subtle differences into their meanings to characterize slightly different rhythmic events in music. Beats can be defined as audible pulse markings, which would imply marking off time units of equal duration. In that sense, beats become sequenced events, "keeping the beat." Metrical subdivisions of pulses into time measures, as we will see later, are often referred to as having a certain number of beats (e.g., the 4/4 measure has four beats, with the first and third being strong and the others weak). However, beats can also be defined even more subtly as time points often (but not always) represented by musical events (Snyder 2000). They must have precise attack points where the sound event begins to be classified as beats. They are time points of no duration, having only temporal positions. We propose here a further variance: that they can be simultaneous with the underlying pulse, but can also deviate from it in slight shifts. Beat events are perceived in relation to the steady, immutable pulse, leading, for instance, to perceptions of rushing or driving in contrast to dragging or slowing. Beat perceptions are also organized across functional positions in measures (onbeat, offbeat) or across longer rhythmic phrase groupings across measures.

Beat structures are important in metrically organized Western music in relationship to pulse templates and structures of measures (3/4, 4/4, and the like). They are even more interesting in relationship to non-Western music, which is not organized in metric, low-integer measures. For example, Indian raga modes, which consist of extended groupings of rhythmic events forming long rhythmic patterns, are built on pulse structures that are accentuated and phrased to a large extent by beat patterns.

Beats as components of the pulse structure are of considerable importance as expressive tools in music. Also, within such a framework, all rhythmic patterns can be reduced to isochronous, pulse-based prototypes that provide the essential harness of time for synchronizing more complex rhythmic events to that basic template. This view may also be supported by time-span reduction theory, which implies that true rhythm should refer only to events within the time scales of short-term (working) memory (Jackendoff and Lerdahl 1982).

The repetition rate of regularly occurring beats or pulses in a given amount of time defines the pulse speed or frequency (i.e., the tempo of music). The perception of tempo can be considered a macro organizer of time, with the detail of rhythmic pattern events embedded as micro organizers of time. Pulse rate defines, within given interval durations, how fast time, expressed through music, flows. Tempo in Western music is measured by the metronome and expressed in beats per minute (bpm). Pulse rates between 30 and 300 bpm create perceptions of tempo in streams of musical events. Outside of this region, rhythms seem to be perceived not as establishing basic pulse repetitions, but as multiples or subdivisions of another pulse rate. The region in which listeners seem to be most likely to infer tempi from basic pulse rates ranges from 60 to 150 bpm. This is also the region of tempi most frequently employed in Western music. Although tempi outside this region do exist, their salience to be heard as basic pulses diminishes relative to both their decrease and increase. Therefore, this region is called the region of greatest pulse salience.

Tempo in music—unlike the concept of felt pulse—is never completely stable and regular in reference to equidistant pulse repetition rates. However, fluctuating tempi do not seem to undermine our sense of stability in an underlying pulse. If we briefly return our attention to our opening statement about entrainment of oscillator circuits underlying rhythm coding in the brain, we may find a good physiological rationale for such apparent categorical perception of time as a basic framework for temporal organization. Some interesting evidence from anthropological research further supports a possible hardwired biological basis for categorical tempo perception. By analyzing tempo changes in live music performances of non-Western cultures, strong evidence was found that these changes occurred in proportion to each other characterized by low integer ratios (Epstein 1985). Such exact proportional tempo changes, found in very diverse musical cultures with no or little history of musical notation across a wide geographical spread, point to the universality of behavior that in turn suggests biological factors. In parallel to Chomsky's proposal of a universal language acquisition device in the human brain, then, we may ask whether we do possess intrinsic mechanisms of categorical tempo perception that produce proportional time- or tempo-keeping. If we assume the existence of oscillatory entrainment mechanisms underlying rhythm perception, such a hypothesis may find a fairly logical biological rationale.

Within the pulse, beat, and tempo structure of music, however, other elements of rhythmic form-building have arisen to create complexity in musical time structure. An important expressive device in the timing architecture of music is the accent. Accents are created by specific stress patterns on given musical events to give emphasis, to make them stand out. Such accentuations can be created by changes in loudness, timbre, duration, or pitch contour. Several different types of accents have been distinguished in descriptions by music theorists. For example, phenomenal accents are simply accentuations of a single event to make it stand out from the rest of the musical surface, regardless of any structural implication regarding phrasing, grouping, or meter. Structural accents usually occur at the beginning and ending of phrases to create rhythmic units. Metrical accents are created when phenomenal or structural accents occur at regularly spaced intervals in the rhythmic pulse pattern. Such regularly recurring accents create basic metric subdivisions in musical time patterns that are referred to as meter, such as 3/4, 4/4, or 5/8. In European music, a single cycle of a meter was eventually referred to as a measure. Such metrical frameworks, based on regular subdivisions of pulse sequences, are very common to certain music cultures, but are not found universally. Western music has employed and developed meter structures in a most predominant fashion.

Meters serve as uniform cyclical time units above isochronous pulse streams that by themselves have no defined beginning or ending point. Meters serve in the other direction as underlying metrical time units upon which an array of beat patterns can be mapped in simultaneous layers. Beat patterns can be quite simple, such as low-integral subdivisions of the existing beats in the measure. Beat patterns can also assume the most complex arrangements of time points in asymmetrical, syncopated time divisions of the basic *tactus* of the meter. However, unless hemiolas or extended polyrhythms, which consist of the superposition of different meters, are employed, all time divisions within a meter structure—no matter how complex—can be aligned or synchronized as subdivisions of the basic beat or pulse pattern. In the special case of polyrhythmic structures, different meters (i.e., different metrical subdivisions of the basic pulse sequence) are simultaneously performed against each other in sequence, creating ambiguity—through continuous phase shifts between alignments of metric beats—as to what the basic felt pulse pattern is. However, even within the same meter, shifts in accents and beat positions can create rhythmic contours that deviate quite considerably from the underlying metric pulse structure, creating rhythmical tension, although in the final analysis they remain within the same network of pulse synchronization. Such rhythmic contours can be extended into event groupings and phrasings across many measures, creating large-scale patterns of metrical tension. Such extended phrase patterns are very common compositional devices used to create large musical forms.

A brief discussion about so-called free rhythms may enhance and complement our current survey. Free rhythms emphasize that although many people equate rhythm with meter or some metrical organization, rhythms of an ametrical nature are quite possible. Ametrical rhythms are not organized within a metrical, pulse-based temporal framework. They are most frequently found in musical genres such as improvised folk music from illiterate cultures, the free jazz movements of the 1960s and 1970s, or in serial classical music of the second half of the twentieth century. Free rhythms blur the distinction between organization into metrical units and organization in rhythmic groupings. Free rhythms consist of extended or brief groups of rhythmic events that are characterized and distinguished from each other by changes in contour, timing, intervals, durations of sequences, tempo changes, or accent patterns. As such, they utilize structural organization in temporal distribution of elements to build patterns. They are not random assemblies of time events. Because even highly trained musicians are unable to correctly identify durations or time intervals without a metric or pulse framework as reference, free rhythms are processed and distinguished by nuances, by the dynamical changes in their internal structure.

In Western music, rhythmic beat patterns that are mapped onto metric units may or may not repeat themselves; it is the meter and the underlying pulse that repeat themselves. The underlying metric pulse structure creates the sense of time stability. Metric structures arose relatively early in Western music, during the Middle Ages, within complex frameworks of temporal organization that have disappeared to a large extent from classical music. Isometric rhythms became established in the twelfth and thirteenth centuries in Europe through modal rhythms. The six codified modal rhythms were called trochaic, iambic, dactylic, anapestic, spondaic, and tribrachic. They all consisted of simple rhythmic patterns that were repeated consistently in ternary meter (e.g., trochaic = long/short//; iambic = short/long//). Many attempts were made to establish fixed tempi, for example, by the *tempus* of the thirteenth century—roughly equal to 80 bpm—and the *tactus* of the sixteenth century, set at 60–70 bpm. These modes were superimposed within a metric pulse system.

In later developments these modal structures became freer and considerably more flexible, allowing for developments of polyrhythms, hemiolas, dotted rhythms, and syncopations, woven together in a flourishing style that reached its multimetric peak of rhythmic polyphony unmatched thereafter, in the fourteenth century. With the advent of accompanied melody and the slow abandoning of polyphony, isometric nonmodal organization of rhythms became pervasive and the concepts of meter and measure-dominated music became the matrix of musical development. However, the reductionistic application of short, regular, rhythmic-metric units fostered the development of long musical pieces, allowing for an enormous amount of temporal variation within a neutral time structure, and supporting the rise of tonality as a major form-building element without the immutable constraints of internally complex but self-contained and nonmodulatory units of rhythmic patterns marking time. Not until the twentieth century did broader concepts of rhythms from earlier historical developments and non-Western sources became more prominent again in Western classical music.

In non-Western music, very different rhythmic vocabularies have developed. For example, in the raga music of North India, extended rhythmic beat patterns or rhythmic modes can be as long as 128 beats before they repeat themselves. To call them "long meters" or "hypermeters" is not exactly accurate, because they are not simply long time markings whose equidistant beats subdivide 128 pulses. These models are in themselves highly complex, exhibiting a pattern structure that consists of events sequenced in different durations and syncopated shifts over the basic pulse pattern. As such, one can say that the North Indian musical term *tal*, which means "meter" or "measure," is not the equivalent of the metrically defined meter in Western music. *Tal* reflects complex beat patterns or rhythmic modes consisting of rhythmic motifs that can be anywhere from three to 128 beats long and are directly mapped onto an underlying pulse structure of a given tempo. As such, the Western metrical subdivision of pulses into meters as an in-between organizational layer between felt pulse and rhythmic pattern does not exist in raga music.

Another example from very different cultures and geographical regions further illustrates the diversity in rhythmic vocabulary. Many West African musical cultures employ very dense polyrhythmic structures or syncopations and cross-rhythms that are produced by asymmetrical accent patterns shifting across different, simultaneous rhythmic event lines, a form of rhythmic development that one may call complex rhythmic polyphony. Such rhythmic complexities are unusual in Western music. Some music analysts have found it difficult to discern an underlying synchronization framework of shared salient pulse pattern in such polyphonies. The more common explanation is that such a pulse pattern may be either highly obscured within the temporal complexity of the multilayered rhythmic events, or that the felt pulse may be perceived as implicit in the specific beat pattern of the performed rhythmic mode. An interesting dichotomy in the pulse experience may arise, depending on the level of perceptual analysis. On one hand, the pulse may be perceived as abstract with respect to the performed pattern because it is not clearly delineated in the heard lines. On the other hand, the pulse is entirely nonabstractable, because it is not extractable from the specific beat pattern. The pulse is communicated as embedded in the total sequence.

The interesting question that arises from the existence of such timing phenomena in musical rhythm is what mental representations underlie the performance of such time patterns in which the measurement of time and tempo cannot be separated or abstracted from the existence of specific beat patterns of a rhythmic mode.

Meters, defined in Western music as an inserted subdivision of pulse patterns into relatively short cyclical time units, are fairly simple metrical structures. This structural use has led to what many observers have called the metric (not rhythmic) simplicity, especially of Western classical music (Dowling and Harwood 1986). Meters, as units of uniform time shape, allow complex event elaborations to be mapped unto them. Due to the underlying constant metrical framework, the time structure of these patterns can modulate freely. In non-Western music, rhythmic complexity can evolve in much longer and denser time structures that are difficult to reconcile with short, repetitive meters built on simple metric accent structures. Polyrhythms are easy to conceive across rhythmic modes, but much harder to conceive as superimposed on meters. This may be one of the reasons why polyrhythms were very rare from 1600 to 1900 in European music, with the exception of isolated hemiola passages, which are more prominently displayed, for example, in the works of Handel and Brahms. However, the lack of the meter as a value-free subunit of timing constrains rhythmic performance to preset modes, no matter how complex they are.

There appears to be a trade-off in development of structural elements in rhythm, possibly similar to the split between scales and modes in pitch patterns and melodic and harmonic development. Major scales are uniform, stepwise patterns across the pitch spectrum, but are essentially the same in intervallic configuration, regardless of the pitch on which they start. Minor scales have retained a little more of their modal origin by maintaining three different scale patterns. The pitch scale in itself has little variety and interest, but allows for free horizontal and vertical developments in melody and harmony and for elaborate shifts of modulations from scale to scale in the same musical piece. Melodic modes, on the other hand, have preset intervallic patterns using a variable number of tones (e.g., in pentatonic or heptatonic modes). A cursory survey across musical cultures reveals a multitude of different modes with fascinating tone combinations and rich musical expressiveness due to their rich intervallic architecture. However, the trade-off lies in the fact that although the modes have considerably more complex intervallic patterns within themselves, their individual and preset structure causes them to be constrained in regard to modulation and to base harmonic or polyphonic structures on them.

Returning to the comparison between rhythmic modes and meter, the neutrality and cyclical nature of basic equidistant pulse units makes them musically uninteresting by themselves, but allows them to serve as foundations for complex and variable pattern structures. Rhythmic modes in themselves have a deep richness in expressiveness due to their individual time patterns, but are limited in their flexibility to create compositional variability due to their preset nature. And so it seems that in the development of different musical systems, what is given up in complexity on one level enables the attainment of a different complexity on another level, and vice versa.

Considering the centrality of rhythm for the structural and expressive formation of music, it comes as no surprise that varied and rich vocabularies and languages of rhythm have emerged throughout human history in different cultures. The organization of time in music has found very different ways of expressing itself as well as of being understood and conceptualized. However, there are common threads of rhythmic time organization that seem universal across cultures, suggesting biological factors as underlying mechanisms. Notions of different structural levels of rhythm have appeared in all musical cultures, making this a useful normative descriptor in cross-cultural analysis and description. Pulse and beat patterns appear to be a common concept underlying the most basic organization of time and rhythm in all cultures. Meter defined as a metrical subdivision of equidistant pulse sequences into regular, relatively short, cyclical time units is a predominantly Western (or European) development in musical syntax. Non-Western cultures have developed many very different ways of subdividing pulse sequences into regular time units. Many cultures have various concepts of patterns, or modes, that within themselves carry highly intricate time relationships. These modal beat patterns are superimposed directly on the underlying pulse. The concept or schema of an equidistant pulse grouping as a necessary intermediate level between pulse and complex rhythmic pattern elaborations is absent in many musical cultures. However, the division between basic pulse and the superposition of more elaborate rhythmic event patterns appears to be an appropriate distinction across a wide variety of musical cultures.

1.4 Coda

This brief survey of the structure of rhythm in music lays a foundation for the following discussions in regard to the neurobiological foundations of music and rhythm. It also sets a framework for the types of research questions we may ask when studying rhythm and the brain. Rhythm is a very complex phenomenon of timing, with some underlying universals that seem to function as biological constraints within human brain function and information processing. However, rhythm is a multidimensional system of temporal organization. Therefore, research questions have to be aligned with definitions of specific dimensions in rhythm. Cultural differences in rhythm formation may make it a very interesting question whether such environmental constraints are reflected in differences in brain processing of rhythmic components by individuals from different cultures. One may further argue that the multidimensionality of rhythm and the cultural diversity in conceptualization and development of rhythmic vocabulary require a relatively independent modular neural circuit system in the brain for different aspects of rhythm processing. Thus tempo, meter, pattern, duration, and pulse may be processed in specifically dedicated network modules in the brain that may be partially overlapping, but also may have to retain sufficient segregation from each other.

Time receives structure within music. Following this metaphor, one may say that music measures and marks the flow of time. The primary element in music that creates the perception of time is rhythm. Rhythm creates sound shapes within which time becomes audible. In rhythm we hear not just time marked off in the pulsating ticks of a stopwatch; we become aware that time exists in patterns that shape and unfold horizontally and sequentially in interaction with patterns of vertical simultaneity. In other words, in rhythm we become aware of a comprehensive architecture of time that is communicated to us through sound in complex motion. Different streams of time (Bregman 1990) expressed through the levels of tempo, beats, metric patterns, cyclical periodicities, or accents allow melodic and harmonic events to evolve and build meaningful relationships.

The Greek language has two words for time: *kairos* and *chronos*. *Chronos* refers to chronological time, the concept of time as a clock mode; *kairos*, on the other hand, refers to time as a temporal dimension of meaning, informing the correct understanding and interpretation of events, perceptions, actions, and cognitions. *Kairos* expresses "if this is the right time," "if time is in our favor," "if we must act now": how time orders and shapes personal and historical experience. In music, both *chronos* and *kairos* find expression in a dialectical interplay through the embedded rhythm structures that organize chronological time; they also build time patterns essential for comprehending the meaningful arrangement and composition of all musical elements into complete musical forms and pieces that can speak to us emotionally.

Spatial images through sound are common and often reported. Sound durations can express extensions and distances; rhythmic and melodic contours can express images of lines and geometric figures; vertical stacks of sound can evoke pictures of multidimensional forms and layered objects. One of the most impressive and illustrative ways to study such translations can be found in the writings and works of Paul Klee (cf. Düchting 2002). However, in music, time unfolds in the dialectical interaction between the process of perception of the music and the actual temporal dynamics of the sound structures themselves. In music, the listener's perception moves in time with the music and is shaped by time in music. Rhythm, in all its fascinating complexity in vocabulary across cultures, constitutes the major syntax and grammar of time in music. Because all mental operations and all behavior of human beings must unfold in regulated time to be purposeful, rhythm may have a profound influence on our thinking and feeling and sense of moving. Rhythm in music translates the perception of time into a sensory language that makes time visible in complex order for our brain.

The recent body of brain research shows impressively that sensory experience changes the brain. An enriched sensory environment facilitates the construction of synaptic connections and the proliferation of highly distributed networks of neuronal ensembles. Exposure, learning, and training shape and develop the complexity of the neuronal architecture, the wiring scheme of the brain, into a more and more diverse and efficient executive system. Music can play an interesting dual role in this process; on one hand, it is a part of the basic biological blueprint of the brain and, on the other hand, it is a strong environmental sensory stimulus able to influence changes in the brain. If we return briefly to the importance of temporal regulation for all our higher cognitive and motor functions, we may have very good reason to believe that rhythm in music, the element of temporal order, has a unique and profound influence on our perceptual processes related to cognition, affect, and motor function. Rhythm may enhance our brain operations through providing structure and anticipation in time. Rhythm may be one of the central processors to optimize our gestalt formation in the basic processes of learning and perception.

2
Aesthetics and Psychobiology

2.1 Berlyne's Model: A Connection Between Biology and the Art Experience

In 1971, a book was published that seemed, in retrospect, generations ahead of its time. The book, *Aesthetics and Psychobiology*, written by D. E. Berlyne, laid out in great—and possibly unprecedented—depth a framework to understand the relationship between the perception of artworks and the concept of physiological arousal as a basis for affective-aesthetic behavior. Berlyne attempted to develop an understanding of how perceptual variables in artworks can influence physiological variables (arousal) and their associated behavioral states (activation), and how such responses form the basis for an affective-aesthetic response to the artwork (i.e., a response to the artistic value and worth of a work of art). His bold attempt to fuse perception and physiology in responding to the arts was conceived at a time when psychology was still far away from the benefits of the new research models and theoretical paradigms of cognitive neuroscience.

Berlyne—whose view on how we perceive and respond to artworks was clearly influenced by gestalt theories of perception—showed (at least in principle) that artworks have profound effects on brain and behavior function, based on perceptual processes that are intrinsic to the human brain. These views have been in many ways confirmed and considerably expanded through recent developments in brain research in the arts, which has been dominated so far by music-related studies. We believe that

19

the continuing scientific pursuits of questions and models of study in music must be closely linked to a complex understanding of music and aesthetic theory. Only such linkage can yield insight into the nature and meaning of music, as well as into what we can learn about the brain from music. In support of this belief, we will first briefly analyze Berlyne's views, then put them into a larger framework of theories of art and aesthetics, and finally relate his theories to current approaches in the cognitive neuroscience of music.

A comprehensive and fully satisfying exposition of musical aesthetics and psychobiology cannot even be attempted in a single book chapter. Also, the time may not have come for us to be able to consider a thoroughgoing basis of the theoretical foundations of a new aesthetic theory. However, since about 1985 or 1990, a new cognitive neuroscience of music has begun to develop, in basic research as well as in biomedically oriented research (e.g., Zatorre and Peretz 2001; Avanzini et al. 2003). There were also earlier, groundbreaking attempts to move music closer to the neurosciences (e.g., Clynes 1982; MacDonald, Critchley, and Henson 1977).

Aesthetic theory has shown little movement toward appropriating the new brain research in music into its foundations. Reciprocally, neuroscientists studying music have made few attempts to evaluate their findings within the frameworks of established aesthetic theory. Therefore, it seems appropriate and necessary to at least attempt to address the development of a potential future linkage. This chapter sketches out some of the territory and some possible key notions on which to build successful connections between science and aesthetic theory in music. However, to do justice to the current state of knowledge, it must remain in many ways only a sketch of a future building.

2.2 Berlyne's Theories of Art and Psychobiology

For the reader who may not be familiar with Berlyne's work, it will be helpful to summarize his theories. Although Berlyne refers to artworks in general in his theoretical considerations, we may—for the main purpose of this book—limit the discussion specifically to music. Central for Berlyne in the meaningful perception of and response to all artworks is the concept of arousal or activation. "Arousal" is a term referring to multiple processes in the nervous system relating states of heightened physiological activity expressed, for example, in the autonomic nervous system (e.g., heart rate, blood pressure), neuroendocrine system (e.g., hormones), or central nervous system (muscle activation, brain waves, sensory perception channels, increased activation in brain regions mediating attention, executive functions, motor control). The term "activation" refers to behavior states associated with physiological arousal states.

Arousal and activation states are considered to have critical regulatory functions for the brain and nervous system to interact appropriately with the environment. Arousal/activation states determine—along a continuum of different dimensions of activation—how alert, excited, wakeful, or attentive a human being is. Arousal concepts have also been extended to underlie motivational and emotional states—important concepts for approach and avoidance behavior—which stimulate reward and pleasure systems in the brain. One may say that human beings try to establish and maintain appropriate levels of arousal and activation, equilibrium points or states of homeostasis (sometimes simply defined as levels of appropriate balance), in order to optimize their mental and physical levels of functioning.

Berlyne proposes that the key to understanding how artworks induce an affective-aesthetic response lies within the arousal and activation responses. Artworks, including music, have strong stimulus properties or attributes that induce heightened states of arousal activation. The two key dimensions in the activation domain are structure and energy.

The dimension of structure is accessed by the collative variables in music. Collative variables are the structural aspects of music, its compositional syntax in melody, harmony, rhythm, and form. An experience in structure involves some simple or complex analytical process of events at different points in the continuum of time. Experiences in structure can be characterized by descriptors such as order, clarity, ambiguity, surprise, comprehension, familiarity, novelty, or stability. Meyer (1956), in his landmark work *Emotion and Meaning in Music*, conceived that this understanding and experience in music are based on the expectations that are built rapidly (and sometimes subconsciously) during the listening process relative to how musical events follow each other, based on the proper application of syntactical rules in the compositional language. Activation or arousal is achieved in the compositional process by infusing a carefully crafted scheme of delays and suspensions of immediate resolutions of expectations. During the suspense process, arousal is triggered, which in turn leads to a search for the proper resolution. The satisfying resolution is eventually reached (or not), leading to an emotional response of a particular quality. Meyer's specific account of emotion and meaning in music is based on Dewey's (1934) conflict theory of emotion. Berlyne's model is driven by principles of Gestalt perception (cf. Koffka 1935). Regardless of the difference in models, both theorists share the concept of activation and the critical role of the subdimension of "experience in structure" as key elements for the affective-aesthetic response in music.

The second dimension, the dimension of energy, involves a simultaneous and holistic processing of the stimulus material. Berlyne emphasizes the psychophysical attributes or properties of the music as drivers of the experience in energy, frequently described in terms of excitement, intensity, activation behavior, energy, or stimulation. The stimulus attributes that contain the energy dimension are tempo, intensity, waveform, color (timbre), and rate change (Berlyne 1971; McMullen 1999).

Taken together, these experiences in activation/arousal, within the subdimensions of structure and energy, lead to an affective-aesthetic response that is characterized by a specific evaluative response in regard to hedonic tone. Hedonic tone is the state of pleasure or reward experienced in the stimulus. The hedonic tone of the affective-aesthetic response can be located within a two-dimensional framework consisting of the dimensions of activation and evaluation. On the x-axis, the level of activation progresses from low to high, originating in the zero position. The evaluative level is plotted on the y-axis, moving from rejection to acceptance (also from zero). Theorists in experimental aesthetics propose that these two dimensions, which determine the quality of the affective-aesthetic response, are related to one another in an inverted U-function. As activation levels become increasingly complex, the evaluative response moves toward acceptance until activation becomes too complex (past the midpoint of the x-axis) and evaluation reverses toward rejection.

Such a two-dimensional framework has also been used as one of the major approaches to examine and classify emotional states in general, outside of music and the other arts. The other major approach to describe emotional states has traditionally used lists of basic categories of emotion and affective response such as fear, happiness, or anger (cf. Plutchik 1962; Watson 1925; McDougall 1908). The dimensional approach, however, based on Wundt's (1874) dimensional classifications of affective states, shows agreement quite consistently across the literature of many decades on the existence of a dimension of activation/excitement and an evaluative dimension of acceptance/rejection.

Berlyne clearly advocates that the dimensional approach is the more appropriate and fruitful way to describe the affective-aesthetic response to works of art. His two main reasons for this advocacy are based on his particular view of the role and function of art. First, he maintains the centrality of the perception of patterns and structures in the artwork as determining our experience. Music does not represent intrinsically extramusical concepts and ideas. It cannot directly represent an emotional category, such as love, that is similar to semantic expressions in verbal language. Second, the stimulus properties in the artwork in itself (i.e., the collative and psychophysical elements) have arousal-inducing potential.

The perception of music's compositional architecture, in its melodic, harmonic, rhythmic, and polyphonic patterns, as well as its large and small organizational forms, induces and determines arousal. The induction and experience of arousal and activation, however, lead to affective-aesthetic responses. In other words, for Berlyne, music is an autonomous art whose primary purpose is to express the realization of its intrinsic principles, structures, and ideas. As such, the affective-aesthetic response in music cannot be classified as expressing a basic emotional state directly, and therefore the categorical approach to the understanding of emotional states is of little value for music (and other forms of art).

Most advocates of the autonomous theory acknowledge that music can express extramusical ideas and concepts, but only through a process of learned associations, such as defined, for example, in classical conditioning, in which music would assume the role of an emotionally salient conditioning stimulus. However, for this process to take place—for music to function meaningfully in a heteronomous fashion—it needs to bring intrinsic emotional value and saliency to the learning process in order to be an effective conditioning stimulus for associative learning to take place.

By examining Berlyne's bold—and in many ways prescient—attempt to reconcile the nature and purpose of the artistic-aesthetic experience with basic physiological principles, one cannot escape some very interesting suggestions. Berlyne's proposed linkage between aesthetic perception and physiology may suggest that the role of music and the arts in general is much more fundamental to the biology of human beings than is usually conceptualized in theories viewing the arts as cultural artifacts. Appropriate arousal and activation states are essential for optimal physiological and psychological functioning in human beings. The human brain is an arousal-seeking system rather than a system that operates on simple stimulus-response interactions. Human progress beyond evolutionary constraints—in all aspects of the development of culture, science, and technology—would otherwise not be fully explainable.

2.3 Early Evidence from Anthropology

Evidence for the existence of artworks and an engagement in artistic endeavors dates back much further than originally thought, and dates tens of thousands of years earlier than any evidence of written language and mathematical codes. Most archaeological evidence for the existence of artistic behavior has usually been attached to the discovery of functional utilitarian artifacts, such as tools, weapons, or paintings, depicting societal functions involving, for example, hunting or religious rituals (Hodges 1999). Tools that were shaped with more beauty than required for purely functional purposes have been found dating back 200,000 years. Cave paintings (e.g., of hunting scenes) that strike the contemporary viewer as possessing significant aesthetic quality have been dated as old as 70,000 years; flutes, rattles, whistles, and percussion instruments as old as 30,000 years have been found. Rock engravings as old as 16,000 years depict dancers, thus implying the presence of music. Discoveries of musical instruments, at times amounting in number to the size of modern-day full orchestras and created within the last 10,000 years, have been made in many parts of the world, including Egypt, Mesopotamia, Syria, South America, East Africa, and China. An ancient set of six wooden pipes discovered in Ireland—dated at 4,100 years of age, tuned in octaves, and executed in sophisticated craftsmanship beyond the normal Bronze Age levels—are considered to be the oldest wooden instruments found in Europe.

Recent discoveries, however, extend some of the significance of the previously recorded artifacts. Figurative artworks—works based on drawings or sculptures, or creating recognizable images of figures or objects—dating over 30,000 years ago have been found in Europe. The appearance of such figurines is considered a reflection of the evolutionary aspect of the ancient arts, because figurative artworks begin to embody symbolic representations that are created to stand for something else. The existence of such highly sophisticated artworks, virtually at a time when modern human beings appeared during the Ice Age in Europe, suggests that these artistic abilities did not evolve but rather existed. The discovery of wooden bagpipe-type instruments, tuned in octaves of D sharp, dated to the the Bronze Age (mentioned above), is another case in point.

These findings contradict earlier notions that artistic abilities evolved over many thousand years from simple scratchings to higher levels of depiction and sophisticated expression. They suggest that advances in the arts may have been driven more by advances in technology and materials or the purposes art was meant to serve, rather than by gradual attainments of progressively higher levels of talent. As such, we would have to consider these ancient artists to be as developed in their artistic ability as contemporary artists are, a notion that would have obvious consequences for our view on art and brain function.

Furthermore, true advances in the arts have always been difficult to classify. Very few developments have been universally accepted as advances. The development of perspective (i.e., the application of geometric principles to line drawing to create illusions of three-dimensional views on two-dimensional surfaces) may be one of the few, and is considered by many scholars to be an exception in art history. The use and understanding of perspective did not exist in the visual arts in any culture in the world, regardless of sophistication, until its discovery in the Renaissance by the Florentine artist Filippo Brunelleschi.

Evidence for the early existence of fully developed artistry on levels of sophistication, abstraction, and representation similar or close to modern art, with little evidence for incremental progression, can create some startling and provocative notions on the role and nature of artistic talent in the human brain. The notion of an evolutionary development of artistic ability and the belief about the lack of biological necessity for the arts—art as the "icing on the cake" of human brain development, after the basic needs of survival in culture and civilization are satisfied—are seriously questioned by these data. Why did art exist at such early stages of human history if it was not necessary for basic survival and societal progress relative to material needs? In light of such questions, artistic engagement as part of human behavior may appear much more fundamental to human brain function than originally conceptualized. The question of why art has emerged as human behavior and what role and function it holds in a human being's life may have more biological answers after all.

Following a triangular reasoning approach that (a) arousal and activation functions are essential regulatory systems components of human psychobiology; (b) artworks have arousal-inducing properties; and (c) the evidence for the existence of highly sophisticated levels of artistry goes far back in anthropology, we may infer a fundamental role for the arts and the human brain. We may suggest that the brain engages in the arts because the arts, including music, create a particular type of sensory input, a specific perceptual language that is necessary for the appropriate regulation of arousal and activation states. The brain needs to engage in combining forms of lines and colors, creating horizontal and vertical layers of sounds of different timbres, building physical shapes and movements of the human body in dance, in order to build, sharpen, maintain, and create order in its perceptual machinery as an essential aspect of brain function.

Human beings are perceptually driven; a large part of the neurological architecture of the nervous system is dedicated to intrinsic and extrinsic perception. Much of the plasticity of the neuronal wirings of the human brain is driven and modulated by perception. The purposeful and adaptive connection between perception and movement forms part of the essential core of all of the human brain's mental operations. Artistic expression may exercise fundamental brain functions and may create unique patterns of perceptual input that the brain needs and cannot generate through other means in order to keep its sensory, motor, and cognitive operations at optimal levels of functioning.

2.4 Views on Aesthetics Through History

To this point, we have summarized Berlyne's views and made several arguments about a putative biological role of music and the arts in human brain function. In order to extend our database for our final discussion and appraisal, we continue with a brief discussion of a variety of historical views on the theory of aesthetics and the arts, after which we will revisit our preliminary proposal regarding an intrinsic biological role of the arts and music.

A common definition for the term "aesthetics" is "the study or philosophy of beauty in the arts." It follows that musical aesthetics should be the study of beauty in music, with the ultimate goal that such study leads to accepted criteria of beauty. Such criteria should allow us to determine if and why a composition is beautiful or more beautiful than another composition. However, this definition of aesthetics has two problems. It does not concur with the original meaning of aesthetics as used in studying artistic endeavors. It also limits the function and role of artworks to expressing beauty. However, never in the history of art has beauty been considered the sole criterion to judge art, nor has the expression of beauty been ever considered the sole function of artworks. The aesthetic value of an artwork has always been considered much broader. The Greek root of the word aesthetics is *aesthesis*, meaning "sensation" or "being sensory-related." *Aesthetic* in Greek means "to perceive." Apel (1981) proposed that musical aesthetics should be defined as the study of the relationship of music to the human senses and intellect. As such, we may reformulate our definition of the study of aesthetics in music as the study of the relationship of music to perception and cognition. This definition may be more helpful and appropriate as an underpinning for the currently evolving cognitive neuroscience of music.

Music has frequently been called the most elusive and intangible of the arts. The forms and patterns in nature are often said to form the basis for the visual arts. One of the prominent roles of the visual arts has always been representational, even in abstraction, symbolism, and *Entfremdung*. Poetry and drama have the word, verbal language, as their expressive tool. Dance expresses through movements of the human body, possibly the most direct art form without intermediary tools of expressive translation such as a paintbrush and canvas or a musical instrument, yet clearly defined in its capabilities of representational structure as the expressive language of the human body. Music, however, does not build abstraction in expression from a representational base. It is purely abstract in expression, and only extramusical systems of rhetorical devices can create representational translations—which, however, can never be heard directly in the music itself. These representations can be expressed and recognized only as learned associations. Based on the recognition of this highly immaterial nature, Plato once stated that music must have privileged access to the soul.

Music anthropology—as well as the history of musicology—has given us many examples of this peculiar tension in musical aesthetics in attempting to describe how and what music actually can communicate. The record of the complex role and function of music in human history is full of examples of how certain pieces of music express certain emotions, concepts, or events for specific cultures and societies. Joy, happiness, sadness, and loss; rituals of life events such as birth, marriage, and death; social and political values and norms can all be expressed through music, though in its material sense only through associations and extramusical definitions. A painting can pictorially represent war scenes or a wedding celebration; music can express only nonpictorial aspects of such events, and even those only through learned associations. The sound patterns of music cannot depict a wedding ceremony. However, theorists have long known about the need to account for the strong and ubiquitous presence of associative responses in music. Berlyne introduced a third set of stimulus properties—in addition to the collative and psychophysical properties—in artworks to account for arousal and activation responses via these associative learning processes. He called them "ecological" properties.

Two other historical developments in Western music also illustrate attempts to reconcile the abstract nature of music with representational concepts. The "doctrine of affections" (*Affektenlehre*) of the seventeenth century developed an elaborate translation system in which structural and stylistic elements, as well as motivic figures, were designated to correspond to rhetorical devices in verbal language. One may want to visit the elaborate rhetorical language of Bach's sacred compositions, such as the chorale settings, cantatas, or oratorios, to get an impression of the flourishing application of such language concepts to music. In the nineteenth century, during the Romantic period, the concept of program music, the composition of music based on dramatic plots or allegorical concepts, arose. Much of the specific compositional subtleties in the music could be fully understood only by knowing the plot and how the musical elements were supposed to represent ideas, actions, or persons in the plot. Many attempts were made to codify the underlying principles and philosophy of program music. One of the most interesting approaches was the development of musical hermeneutics (*musikalische Hermeneutik*), trying to reinterpret music as a language art (*Sprachkunst*). Musical hermeneutics clearly tried to draw on earlier attempts, such as the doctrine of affections, to classify music elements into language analogues.

However, the referential interpretation of music as a heteronomous art form, as a codified language of expression for extramusical elements, was never truly successful in dominating music history. The inherent problem probably was always keenly felt, if not always consciously articulated, by composers and theorists.

In such a system of referential interpretation, music becomes secondary to the development of the translational code that communicates the real meaning of music. This approach constrains the creation of music in its full potential as a complex architecture of sound patterns.

Of course, composers have always used, and continue to use, allegorical or programmatic elements in music, but not as a strict foundation for the compositional process rather than as personal signatures to add expressive elements. It is also well accepted—as previously discussed—that music can attain representational status for nonmusical concepts, but only through an associative learning process that is motivated by the intrinsic affective-aesthetic saliency of the music itself. One can say, without causing much controversy, that all recent schools of aesthetic thought consider music as an autonomous art that communicates its intrinsic patterns and principles of structure. The only differences in this autonomous notion are found in the absolute expressionist position and the absolute formalist position. The former readily concedes that the perception of musical structures can generate meaningful emotional responses; the latter position considers the emotional response to music with great caution, seeing it as a secondary and not always desirable by-product of the intellectual experience in music from whose intoxicating influences musical thinking must be emancipated. Berlyne's thinking can aptly be located in the autonomous and absolute-expressionist camp.

The emphasis on the arts as carrying purely emotional value is a relatively recent development, firmly implanted only since the Romantic period of the nineteenth century. This view also was greatly influenced by literary movements of the German Sturm und Drang period, which placed great emphasis on literature as a means of expressing and inducing emotions in strong and dramatic individualized forms. That does not mean that the embodiment and expression of emotion and feelings have not been part of almost all views on the function of the arts; emotional experiences and expressions have always found aesthetic embodiment in artworks. However, the exclusive view of emotional embodiment is a Romantic view, and many writers have argued against it (Hanslick 1854; Stravinsky 1935; Langer 1942). In our current definition of musical aesthetics—and in line with our theoretical expositions based on Berlyne—the affective-aesthetic response is part of the complex perceptual and cognitive engagement that music delivers to the brain, on one hand as an intrinsic function of the human brain and, reciprocally, by shaping the human brain through its engaging in music.

Views on musical aesthetics have varied considerably across human history (for a review see Wartenberg 2002). In ancient Greece, music was considered in many ways to be a part of the natural sciences. The laws of music, especially within the psychoacoustical realm, were considered expressions of universal physical laws, especially relative to arithmetic and astronomy. The mathematics of the overtone relationships in vibrating sound bodies was considered reflective of the measurements of planetary motion. Following this view, one could study music to gain insights into important aspects of understanding the physical world. Many of these views were expressed in a complex manner for the first time by Pythagoras (550 B.C.).

Plato (428–347 B.C.) emphasized—in a way similar to Confucius in China—the educational value of music, noting its ability to offer insight into the natural sciences and also to train the mind and intellect in general. He acknowledged the power of music to stir emotions (and was deeply suspicious of this power), and therefore stated in the famous dialogues between Socrates and his young follower Glaucon—written in his great work *The Republic*—the need to include in his perfect and ideal state only music that evokes praiseworthy emotions characterized by virtue, courage, and restraint. Music, as a nonimitative art form, fared better in Plato than poetry and painting, which he considered imitative art forms. Therefore they had to be excluded from his ideal state on metaphysical grounds, as expressions of imperfect, changing forms that could not reflect the true, perfect, and immutable "Forms" (principles and ideas underlying the reality of all experiences and appearances of the material world).

Aristotle's (384–322 B.C.) views on the arts were influenced by Plato, with several noteworthy exceptions. Aristotle includes music as an imitative, representational art form that is able, like all other arts, to teach about reality exactly because it is representational and not actual. Thus, through art we can gain a clearer understanding of reality by its dramatic transformation. Aristotle's most important writings in this respect deal with the tragic drama as a powerful means to bring about catharsis, to purge the passions through pity and terror.

As can easily be seen by this brief survey, the early views on the role and nature of music encompass a considerable range of functions, creating an ambiguity that continues today in similar frameworks. Almost 900 years after Plato, Boethius (d. A.D. 524)—a philosopher living at the transition between the decline and destruction of the classical world of the Roman

Empire and the emerging period loosely described as the Middle Ages—summarized these multiple functions and understandings in his threefold division of music into *musica mundana, musica humana,* and *musica instrumentalis. Musica mundana* is the reflection of the Pythagorean notion of music as natural science with an intrinsic structure that embodies knowledge about the physical structure of the universe. *Musica humana* refers to the harmony between body and soul, perhaps a concept inspired by the educational and cathartic values ascribed to music by Plato and Aristotle. Paradoxically, the lowest role for music lies in our modern understanding of music in the form of *musica instrumentalis,* music as actual sound, sung and played. These subdivisions proved to be extremely influential in shaping a philosophical view on musical aesthetics. Boethius's notions dominated music theory for over ten centuries.

The scientific view of music was revived in the Renaissance when enormous progress and discoveries about the physical world came in the disciplines of physics and astronomy. Johannes Kepler, among the greatest scientists of all time, discovered that the elliptical orbits of the planets around the sun followed mathematical ratios that were exactly the low-integer ratios of the overtones in acoustical vibration patterns (i.e., 1:2, 2:3, 3:4, 4:5, etc.). Kepler saw the immediate analogy of planets traveling in their own trajectories, each of which could be characterized by a unique musical interval and together forming in their mathematical integer ratios the equivalent of a cyclical progression of musical chords, a "planetary composition." He was so overwhelmed by his discovery of these shared mathematical universals in music and astronomy that he titled his great work on his astronomic discoveries after this particular aspect. He named it *De Harmonis Mundi* (*Harmonices Mundi Libri,* 1619), roughly translatable as "Of the Sounding Harmonies of the Universe." Finally, the last of the great references to music as a science was made by the German philosopher, scientist, and mathematician Leibniz (1646–1716), who once stated—in reference to the exact mathematics of the waveform patterns underlying the sounds of music—that when it was engaging in music, the mind was engaging in an unconscious exercise in arithmetic.

A reversal in emphasis in the concept of musical aesthetics came through Kantian philosophy in the eighteenth century. However, we will reserve a special discussion for these highly influential—and continuously pertinent—views for later, at the conclusion of this chapter. Two philosophers of great achievement who represent this shift in approach are Schopenhauer in the early nineteenth century and Nietzsche in the latter half of the same century. Schopenhauer saw distinctions—influenced by Kantian philosophy, as well as Plato's teaching on Forms—between reality-in-itself and appearances. Everyday experiences are mere representations of underlying metaphysical principles and ideas. But whereas the Kantian view holds that these ultimate realities are unknowable, Schopenhauer believed that we have access to reality-in-itself through our own wills. This is where Schopenhauer assigned a critical role to the arts, especially music. The arts play a crucial role in this process of revelation through the will. Moreover, music is the purest incarnation of the human will for Schopenhauer. Thus, music is the embodiment and expression of human feelings (joy, love, sadness) in their abstract interpretation as metaphysical ideas. Music communicates metaphysical truth. Music represents the archetypes of feelings, the actual perfect forms of such ideas, of which real-life experiences, empirical things, are merely shadows.

Schopenhauer's metaphysical view on the nature of music influenced Nietzsche's view on art in somewhat distinct yet connected ways. Nietzsche, too, believed that the role of art is to transcend reality. However, he focused more on the redemptive function of art, which he divided into two types: the Apollonic and the Dionysiac. Whereas the Apollonic type embodies idealizations of reality, Dionysiac art is ecstatic, transcending and ultimately dissolving individuality to become one with the forces governing the universe. Because the underlying direction of all of Nietzsche's philosophy was a devastating critique of the decadence of culture at the end of the nineteenth century, paired with a call for a complete and uncompromising renewal and remaking of man, the Dionysiac type in the aesthetic experience and expression in the arts was of considerably more importance to him.

These deeply philosophical views on the nature of music were, however, taken over soon and almost in parallel by completely new developments in the sciences at the end of the nineteenth century. The most profound change in musical aesthetics arrived with the advent of psychology as an independent science of human behavior in the second half of the century. Slowly, deep and complex philosophical notions of the role of the arts and musical aesthetics were supplanted by more compartmental and structural approaches, using behavioral experiments and statistics. Since the foundations and mechanisms of human behavior now needed to be studied empirically rather than to be interpreted philosophically, the arts also could be understood as a particular form of human behavior that could be approached objectively through empirical models. The new approach that came into being was called experimental aesthetics, interestingly driven originally by many leading physicists of the day, such as Fechner, Helmholtz, and Stumpf. Early investigations dealt, for example, with the perception of dissonance versus consonance, a far cry from contemplations on the metaphysical nature of music to discern "ultimate realities." In the early twentieth century, these approaches were taken up by American psychologists, who founded a distinct American tradition of what very soon became termed psychology of music (Hodges 1999). In 1919, in an act characteristic of the new view of investigating art as human behavior, one of the first undertakings of the eminent American music psychologist, Carl Seashore, was to construct a psychological test that would enable objective measurement of musical talents and aptitudes in a research laboratory.

The brief historical survey has shown that complex ambiguities about the nature and function of music and the arts have existed since early cultural documentation in human societies. Undeniably, however, music and the other arts have also been a most pervasive phenomenon in all known cultures, an intricate part of the human experience as we know it. A review of the various approaches developed to understand, explain, and define art throughout human history reveals a great deal of variety not just in definitions, but also in basic approaches. Some of the various approaches have been presented above in our brief journey through the world of musical aesthetics. We may even mention some other views in passing here to enlarge the picture. Plato considered art by definition to be imitation. David Hume, the eminent eighteenth-century Scottish philosopher, considered art mostly as an object of taste. For Hegel (1770–1831), art was the best embodiment—along with religion and philosophy—of the Absolute Spirit revealing itself as the essence of the world. However, even in Hegel's highly metaphysical view, art—unlike religion and philosophy—was bound by sensible forms as a work experienced by perception, thus invoking some of the principles of the original meaning of the word aesthetics. Leaving deeply philosophical interpretations behind, twentieth-century views on the arts added new dimensions to the array of aesthetic approaches by emphasizing political or sociological interpretations.

2.5 Toward a New Paradigm: A New Approach to an Aesthetic of Music

What one can glean initially from these deeply diverse and at times disconnected views on the nature and role of the arts in human history is a paradoxical impression. A phenomenon as pervasive and consistent in human activity and culture as the arts can find only explanations that are highly inconsistent with each other. In the history of science and philosophy, divergent explanations of phenomena can point to the epistemological notion that underlying structures in thought or in data may not have been considered properly. Therefore, a new approach may be necessary to understand the role and nature of the arts as a fundamental human behavior. Such an approach should be able to integrate the diverse interpretations of the arts as local views—driven more by applications of artistic practice to specific societal purposes and historically determined cultural values—and not as an attempt at defining unifying principles of understanding of the role and nature of the arts in human history. A new approach may consider a differentiation between art theories as components of a surface structure of understanding and an exposition of fundamental principles of brain and behavior functions relative to the arts. Such new aesthetics may be developed from insight into the biology of human perception and cognition as fundamental elements of all human behavior: individual, societal, cultural.

The emerging cognitive neuroscience of music—since about 1990—has so far not contributed much to these questions. The neuroscience of music until now has emphasized a mostly empirical-analytical approach to establishing scientific research paradigms to investigate mechanisms underlying perception and production of music. Psychophysics, psychophysiology, neuroanatomy, and neurophysiology have been the fields of choice for experimental approaches, guided by some overarching general psychological constructs and borrowing techniques from the language of mathematics and the parameters of physics to analyze and interpret data. So far, this has been a fairly heuristic enterprise, yielding very interesting insights on anatomical and physiological detail, but few contributions to a new musical aesthetics.

Of course, in order to be able to create meaningful interpretations of the neuroscientific underpinnings of music, experiments and hypotheses about the biology of music must be informed by clear theoretical concepts of musical behavior and musical aesthetics rather than by neuroscientific questions. However, the studies in musical neuroscience have begun to contribute something entirely new and extremely valuable, an entire database that will provide an invaluable framework for the future development of a new musical aesthetics. Furthermore, the research is showing that music has clear neurobiological substrates, organized in complex and distributed neuronal networks in the brain. Music has a specific brain architecture associated with specific responses and behaviors. Sensitivity to music and spontaneous musical expression appear early in life, without conscious effort or directed learning efforts. Although we know almost nothing about music in ancient art, the ancient artworks in the parallel visual arts appear in complex, abstract, and symbolic sophistication coexisting with the appearance of modern humans, with no traces of a clear evolution of talent or progress.

We may, therefore, propose that music's roots, role, and nature lie in a biological hardwiring process. Like verbal language, music is a complex, rule-based sensory language. Using Chomsky's (1980) conceptualization of the neurological basis of language as a pre- (or hard-) wired biological system, an innate set of knowledge and information processing (Fodor 1975, 1983), we may propose in parallel that music—as an art form that requires very distinct behaviors and physiological processes in the diverse aspects of its perception and production—is based on a modular and innate system of knowledge, creating a biological basis of aesthetic perception. In music we exercise and express the aesthetic components of our biology, the logic and critical thinking of musical perception and cognition, just as we exercise motor control aspects in sports or cognitive aspects in mathematics and language.

A new musical aesthetics may then be based on a threefold division of the study of the relationship of music to the senses and intellect. This division may be envisioned as consisting of two concentric circles around a center. In the outer layer, the domain of aesthetics is concerned with the role and functions of music in society. In his pathbreaking book on the anthropology of music, Merriam (1964) has laid out basic roles and functions of music in human culture. Roles encompass applications of music to education, religion, work, and social and political rituals, among other areas. Basic functions of music evoke emotional response, entertain, traduce social knowledge and norms, or trigger physical response. In a subtle but insightful distinction, Merriam holds that roles for music have historically changed, however, while its functions have not; in other words, roles may be considered expressions—influenced by history and tradition—of underlying constant functions.

The second domain is concerned with the structural aspects of music. In it, theorists study how music is put together, how music communicates meaning in artistic form through its structural (i.e., syntactical, semantic, phonological, morphological) elements and architecture. Much of what was written about rhythm in chapter 1 refers to this domain. Critical contributions to such musical language cognition, such as those of Berlyne (1971) and Meyer (1956), have been mentioned earlier in this chapter.

The core domain for an understanding of musical aesthetics would be based on the intrinsic functions of music as an innate component of brain function. Music—to summarize our previous discussions—is an innate, modular, perceptual language of the brain that serves the purpose of aesthetic expression and communication, to engage in and create perceptual input necessary for proper sensory, perceptual, and cognitive functions. We engage in music because we can, because it is a part of our basic brain architecture.

Music, driven by the affective-aesthetic responses, is a critical input for appropriate regulation of physiological arousal. To further specify: Music communicates critical time dimensions into our perceptual processes.

The perception and comprehension of complex sound patterns is a unique attainment of sensory perception and cognition. The performance of a musical piece is a unique attainment of sensory-guided motor control, based on complex acoustical, structural, and emotional reasoning through the piece's particular style and language. Could it be that children in all cultures, during certain phases of their development, engage spontaneously in activities during play and learning that integrate singing and moving, dancing and rhyming, because the common denominator between musical play and the basic physiology of learning is the critical component of time? In other words, does music help to create better time-ordered traces in learning and perception during development? Do we need music to provide a specific type of perceptual input and a specific type of perceptual training to the brain in order to optimize its basic information-processing capabilities? Is music a perceptual template for order in time (i.e., temporal structure and organization) that helps to shape all aspects of cognitive, affective, and motor functions?

These are (admittedly) highly speculative questions. The evidence for a wide distribution of neural substrates for music rather than for focal music-dedicated regions, and the broad influence of rhythm on many extramusical motor, sensory, and cognitive functions (as we will discuss in depth later in this book), may seem to offer some intriguing conceptual support for these notions, but not yet on a level of conclusive empirical research support.

2.6 Immanuel Kant and the Psychobiology of Aesthetics

Returning to less speculative ground, we may, in conclusion, advocate for an autonomous music aesthetics that is fundamentally a biologically centered aesthetics of perception and cognition. We may draw support for such a view from an unexpected philosophical source. A new reading of Immanuel Kant's (1724–1804) *Critique of Judgment* (1790), the third of his three famous *Critiques,* within a contemporary context of an emerging cognitive neuroscience of music, makes his views surprisingly relevant for our current discussion. Kant's formulation of innate a priori knowledge—not driven by external sensory-based learning—as a basic cognitive structure and mechanism imposed on perception and reasoning is echoed by notions of innate cognitive architectures put forward by modern theorists in cognitive neuroscience, who are studying the neural substrates of cognitive processing. Kant has also laid out in very elegant and logically precise terms the limits of knowing for such mental operations.

Kant bases his aesthetic theory on notions of aesthetic judgment. Aesthetic judgment comes from a specific form of pleasure through the disinterested and objective contemplation of an art object. The pleasure is produced through the perception of the object's form. Going a step farther toward the centrality of perception and cognition, Kant states that the source of pleasurable perception is the features of the object that are uniquely suited to an individual's perception. This view entails and presumes the same a priori notion of knowledge that is laid out in his works on sensory perception, reasoning, and knowledge. In Kantian terms, the art object is created for its perception to fit the processing of one's perceptual apparatus. The imagination (i.e., the mental faculty that allows one to apprehend the art object) and the cognitive understanding (i.e., the faculty of comprehension and conceptualization) resonate in a synchronized perception-cognition process. It is as if the art object were produced in order to be heard or seen by the perceiver. This view assumes so much innate a priori aesthetic reasoning that it seems defensible nowadays only in the context of modern brain science, which would assign to art a biological basis in brain function. The traditional view of art as a cultural product, a cultural artifact, cannot support a Kantian view that makes the centrality of perception based on a priori knowledge of artistic forms the deciding issue in aesthetic judgment.

And so it seems that Kant's argument appears, in underlying structure, to be nothing but a philosophical expression of a biologically based aesthetics of perception and cognition. Berlyne's view of the arousal-inducing properties of paintings and music, mediated by complex perceptual processes, modulating hedonic tone, and affective-aesthetic response, seems clearly foreshadowed here. The perception of artworks becomes a fundamental biologically based activity because it operates on mechanisms in our brain that are built for this purpose. The brain is built to exercise its functions as an arousal-seeking and arousal-regulating system that operates on the environment to maintain its neural operating systems at optimal levels of sensory, motor, perceptual, and cognitive functions. The playful and volitional engagement in the faculties that create the aesthetic response—according to Kant—is unique to human beings and accessible to all people. It is a universal capability, again supporting the biological roots of such a process. The aesthetic judgment is for Kant a process that is based on the fundamental structures of cognitive and perceptual operations of the human mind, rather than on local knowledge, subjective impressions, or empirical generalizations that implicitly need to include exceptions in order to maintain their generalizability.

We may therefore build our case for a future psychobiological aesthetics of music on a Kantian ideal of aesthetic reasoning that sets out, in part, a framework for the modern study of cognitive neuroscience in the arts, specifically in music. The underlying purpose of music is in its attributes as a specific language of perception that engages brain and behavior. This engagement has a neurological basis and serves neurological purposes, stimulating cognitive, affective, and sensorimotor behavior in a way unique to aesthetic perception. Forms and patterns of artworks create a particular input to the brain that synchronizes perception and cognition in a satisfying and pleasurable way. In Plato's educational view, now understood within a biological framework, music trains the senses, the body, and the mind: The arts connect and exercise brain function and the discovery of the physical world through their unique modalities of aesthetic perception and aesthetic expression, in principle no different than the study of reading, writing, arithmetic, biology, or physics.

Around this core domain we can build further aesthetic domains as already laid out briefly, such as the aesthetic study of musical structure (i.e., the linguistics of music) and the study of the social and cultural functions of music. However, in structure and function these outer domains are informed, guided, and rooted in the principles of the core domain of music and brain function.

In closing—and before proceeding in the following chapters with a considerably more technical and empirically based discussion on the neuroscience of rhythm and its biomedical applications—it may be useful to think briefly about how a psychobiological musical aesthetics can inform future research in the cognitive neuroscience of music.

As a first principle, research paradigms must have thoroughly musically informed paradigms, from paradigms studying issues of sensory perception (e.g., pitch, timbre) to more structural syntactical issues (rhythms, chords, melodies, etc.). Participants in musical experiments must be asked to create explicit musical responses, not just responses to differences in stimuli.

Second, experimental models that involve complex cognitive processes related to musical thinking should be increasingly studied. Parallels and contrasts with language studies could be quite fruitful. Comparisons of language and musical conditions in the same experiments could be useful to extract underlying cognitive processes. For example, composition, improvisation, and musical imagery are fertile areas of study. So would be the experimental study of musical reasoning similar to studying syllogisms of logical thinking in verbal language.

Third, the critical element of time in music, expressed through rhythm, and its effect on temporal information processing in the brain related to music and extramusical tasks, is of critical importance. Music may be one of the best models enabling study of the temporal dimension of general cognitive processes in attention, memory, and executive functions.

Fourth, the effect of music as a complex sensory stimulus on sensorimotor, speech-language, and cognitive functions in patients may yield considerable insight not only into the neural substrates of music via lesion studies, but also into brain plasticity and rehabilitation issues via music-mediated therapy training.

Fifth, brain research using cross-cultural studies in music perception and music production could produce significant results relative to core issues of the biological foundations of music and the aesthetic perception of music. Ethnomusicological research involving brain imaging, for example, would help delineate—if studied within an appropriate theoretical framework—borders between universal constraints and cultural determinants of aesthetic perception.

Last, neuroscientific investigations into music learning—in music education as well as in music-facilitated general learning—will result in a better understanding of the principles of aesthetic perception because in such learning studies, one can track the neural basis of how musical stimuli regulate and shape perception and cognition in a context of change through training.

3

The Neural Dynamics of Rhythm

3.1 Rhythm and Temporality in Music

To paraphrase a famous quote by Igor Stravinsky, one of the most important aspects of the function of music is to communicate time. Stravinsky was not simply referring to music's timekeeping process as a purely chronological clock that counts time in subdivisions of duration units. Rather, in music the human brain creates and experiences a unique, highly complex, time-ordered, and integrated process of perception and action based on sensory events, as well as complex perceptual, cognitive, and affective operations. In music, the listener and performer experience time—in the temporal dimensions of sequence and simultaneity—as a regulated flow of sensory events, evoking associated emotions and thoughts in a time-ordered process and structuring coordinated movements in synchronized time to physically express music or create music.

One of our major research interests for several years has been in the neurological basis of these processes, especially of rhythm as one of the main elements of temporal organization in music. The capability for the perception and volitional production of rhythms is unique to the human brain and is dependent on the capacity for stable, precise, rapid, and complex time organization in the brain. Recent research efforts are beginning to elucidate the neural substrates for rhythmicity in the human brain that are not fully known or understood. However, we have always believed that the study of rhythm may yield insights not just into musical time, but also into the temporality of information processing in the human brain in general. Music and rhythm may be the source of very productive scientific models to study general brain function. Furthermore, as will be discussed in the last four chapters of this book, these investigations have also led to a fundamental need to rethink the role of music in therapy and medicine, including the capacity of music to serve as a powerful sensory stimulus, capable of engaging the brain in retraining neural and behavioral functions that can then be applied to nonmusical contexts.

Rhythm in music is the core element, as was discussed in chapter 1, that binds simultaneity and sequentiality of sound patterns into structural organizational forms underlying what we consider musical language. In this function, rhythm assumes a critical syntactical role in communicating symbolic, as well as associative, meaning in music. In the following sections, we will examine what we know about the neural basis of musical rhythm formation in the human brain. The findings contribute to understanding how one of the core elements in musical language structure is processed in the brain. Reciprocally, the findings also give us insights into how music shapes the brain that engages in music through listening, performance, composition, or improvisation.

We will examine the evidence, including data from our own research, in two sections. First, behavioral data from psychophysical studies will be presented in terms of how they give insight into assumed brain function on a theoretical systems level. Second, we will review studies using brain imaging and brain-wave recordings to shed some light on what we know about neurophysiological processes mediating rhythm perception and production.

3.2 Processes in Rhythmic Synchronization

One of the initial questions in regard to the scientific investigation of musical behavior deals with formulating study designs that have a valid relationship to the actual complexity of music's nature. This is a point widely debated between musicians and researchers. Musicians often find little use for reductionistic research approaches and the way musical elements are fitted into study designs and data gathering. Of course, the researchers' reply is that the only scientific way to understand a complex phenomenon such as music is by breaking it into small pieces. Both arguments have validity, but need to lead to acceptable compromises. One avenue to explore a "middle of the road" approach is to find underlying building principles or perceptual strategies that allow meaningful reductions of complex patterns in study designs for experimental research.

Several approaches that have been taken by researchers in rhythm studies illustrate this point. Converging evidence shows pulse-salient models underlying rhythm processing (Parncutt 1994). Conceptually, these are models that require synchronization of acoustic events, at various hierarchical levels of rhythmic organization, into perceptually identifiable pulse patterns, often metrically patterned, that function as isochronous temporal templates of a given duration. If the concept of periodic perceptual groupings—based on mapping sound events onto pulse-driven internal template structures—represents one of the most appropriate bases for a structural understanding of musical rhythm, then active rhythmic synchronization tasks are among the most meaningful experimental models to be used to study rhythm processing, in spite of their reductionistic nature in regard to their stimulus selection. The study of the neural substrates of rhythm closely reflects the process of intrinsic temporal pattern formation within synchronized pulse structures, which is the core effort in the perception and production of rhythm. Study designs using the production or recognition of sound patterns without an implicitly felt pulse structure, or tasks that rely predominantly on discrimination efforts, would be less central for rhythm processing because they rely largely on processes shared with other forms of nonrhythmic time processing.

Most researchers studying rhythm, out of methodological necessity in the controlled environment of the research laboratory, have given preference to experimental designs involving simple tasks, such as finger tapping in synchrony to metronome-like pulse beat sequences. However, time-span reduction theory supports the validity of these designs as one fruitful approach to the study of rhythm, because all rhythms can eventually be reduced to isochronic prototypes (Jackendoff and Lehrdahl 1982; Vos and Helsper 1992). In this case, certain aspects of rhythm formation and rhythm processing in the brain may thus be meaningfully studied by relatively "reductionistic" approaches.

We have conducted several experiments to investigate the neural mechanisms by which motor response may be synchronized to an auditory rhythm. Several important findings have helped to build an understanding of how rhythm formation is controlled in the brain. First, as has been shown in earlier works (e.g., Michon 1967; Hary and Moore 1987), steady and stable couplings between the rhythmic cue and the rhythmic motor response are achieved almost instantaneously, within one to two repetitions of the rhythmic stimulus interval. Furthermore, one of the big questions in rhythm research has been how rhythmic motor responses are kept synchronous to the external rhythmic beat. In a rhythmic synchronization task, two goals have to be met: to move at the same frequency (or period) of the rhythmic stimulus and with no time difference (or phase difference) between the beat and motor response events.

One of the more productive ways to study system behavior is always to disturb the normal steady-state behavior and analyze how the system responds to this interruption in trying to return to its original state. In a study employing random changes in the tempo of metronome sequences, we found an interesting nonlinear change in the response strategy employed to keep the rhythmic motor response (finger tap) synchronized to the beat. In small changes below 5 percent of the base interval—at or below the level of conscious perception—the duration or period errors (i.e., time difference between metronome *interval* and the tap *interval*) are corrected first. That somewhat counterintuitive response leads, at least temporarily, to an enlarged synchronization error (i.e., the time difference between the tap event and the beat event). That enlarged difference is then gradually adjusted back to prechange values over several tap cycles. At changes in the tempo of the rhythmic stimulus starting at around 5 percent of base interval and larger consciously perceived step changes, a new synchronization strategy becomes clearly observable. The period error is corrected by temporary overcorrection of the response period for one or two tap cycles, which leads to an immediate correction of the synchronization error within that same range of tap events (Thaut, Miller, and Schauer 1998). These observations have been confirmed by many other studies (e.g., Repp 1999; Large et al. 2002).

Of course, because there is interdependence between the period of the motor response and the synchronization errors at both ends of the tapping period, one can algebraically reformulate that the response interval is the result of adding and subtracting the synchronization errors from the stimulus interval. Although it is arithmetically correct, little of meaningful value regarding system behavior or underlying brain strategy can be extracted from such variable transformation. If the brain is capable of extracting stable interval information from a rhythmic stimulus such as a metronome sequence, then interval calculations are likely carried out independently from small and unstable secondary variables such as exact alignments of the finger tap with an external beat. In any case, we can—with good confidence—assume that there exists in the human brain a nonlinear neural control system that employs multiple synchronization strategies, the choice of which depends on the dynamic state of the synchronization system relative to the magnitude and the perceptual threshold of the tempo change. This is an important insight for musical rhythm performance that relies on intrinsic and, in any performance involving groups of musicians, extrinsic synchronization strategies to achieve temporal coherence and order. First, rhythm formation is an interval-based process. Second, small time deviations in synchronization alignments do not need to be corrected by overcorrections (i.e., deliberate short-term timing errors) of interval timing; they can be adjusted directly by frequency matching or perceived tempo matching.

These data show that auditory rhythm communicates stable and precise interval-based temporal templates to the brain, to which the motor system has privileged access even below levels of conscious awareness (Thaut, Miller, and Schauer 1998; Large et al. 2002). Evidence of such direct frequency entrainment in rhythmic synchronization suggests that rhythm in music can have a profound influence on the organization of movement in time and space. This is especially interesting, and we will discuss this influence in chapters 5, 6, and 7 in regard to applications to the rehabilitation of movement disorders (Thaut et al. 1999).

The findings of Thaut, Miller, and Schauer (1998) were replicated in a recent study by using a syncopated synchronization design in which the beat and the motor response were 180 degrees out of phase (Thaut and Kenyon 2003). Randomly presented step changes of 2 percent of the stimulus interval were immediately compensated for by the motor response adapting to the new stimulus period, even though the size of the tempo modulation was not consciously perceptible. A recursive mathematical model showed a predominant weighting factor of 5:1 in favor of correction of the period error over the synchronization error when adapting the motor response to the new tempo. Thus, the model gives further support for strong frequency- or period-based entrainment mechanisms between motor and auditory systems, similar to oscillators that become coupled in frequency to one another. In such a model, rhythmic stimulation provides a continuous time reference to the motor system throughout the entire movement period to help optimize the scaling of all movement parameters. Details of this optimization process are introduced in chapter 5.

Further evidence of subliminal coupling mechanisms between auditory rhythm and motor response was demonstrated in a study where we employed a metronome pattern with continuous modulation rates—similar to a cosine wave—with amplitudes of 1, 3, 5, and 7 percent of a base interval of 500ms (Thaut, Tian, and Azimi 1998). Response curves of the timing of the rhythmic movement followed the temporal dynamics of the modulating rhythm precisely, with continuous correction always one beat behind. This consistent lag time provided evidence for the interesting insight that the brain never recognized the periodicity pattern of the modulated rhythm, but continued to operate on a purely sensory-information-driven basis in which the time information of the immediately preceding interval was used to predict the next interval duration in a continuous anticipation-correction process.

In all studies of rhythmic synchronization, one of the more difficult and complex aspects of data analysis is that the timing of the rhythmic motor response on a level of milliseconds is not consistent from beat to beat, but exhibits considerable temporal fluctuations in relationship to the beat interval. Yet, the *averaged* response is very tightly synchronized to the rhythmic stimulus. Statistical models have tried to explain parts of these fluctuations as indicators of some ongoing correction process based on short-range correlations (Pressing 1999; Pressing and Jolley-Rogers 1997; Vorberg and Wing 1996). However, in a recent study, we used a method from mathematical physics developed by Salvino and Cawley (1994) to investigate whether the time-series fluctuations were deterministically chaotic or truly random (Roberts et al. 2000). A direct test for determinism using this powerful method failed to demonstrate the presence of determinism. Fractal analysis showed the absence of long-range correlations for the periods of the motor response but their presence for synchronization errors. Taken together, the synchronization mechanisms appear to be characteristic of a self-correcting system with stochastic noise attributes (Mitra et al. 1997; Kelso 1995), but with bounded phase errors that indicate thermostat-like set point limits of perceived simultaneity between motor rhythm and auditory rhythm (Hassan and Thaut 1999). These set point limits are most likely driven by perceptual constraints of the human brain, whereas the rhythmic entrainment mechanisms are most likely based on the strong resonant physiological attractor functions of the neural activation patterns in the auditory system that project into motor structures.

We may conclude that precise timing of rhythm is achieved in a system state of the human brain that resembles directed Brownian motion—which is random rather than chaotic, but which also contains correlations. As one can imagine, the exact nature and function of neural noise in brain information processing continues to present a challenging and difficult, yet fruitful, field of inquiry, but these data provide a range of interesting insights into some of the very complex brain mechanisms underlying time perception and the temporal control of behavior such as those found in music.

This conclusion also provides some reasonable causes for a fascinating observation in rhythmic synchronization studies regarding synchronization errors. Very quickly, after a few response cycles that are needed for synchronization adjustment, the synchronized motor responses are actually placed before the beat with which they are to be synchronized. In other words, in the auditory mode, synchronization is an anticipatory response to an event that has not yet taken place, but whose precise occurrence time is known. One of the more prevalent theories to explain this negative asynchrony was the central sensory code hypothesis (e.g., Aschersleben and Prinz 1995). It stated that because tactile information (from the finger tap) and auditory information (from the beat) have different neural conduction times, the slower response conduction (finger tap) had to be placed slighty ahead of the faster auditory conduction time system (beat) to achieve coincidence in the brain. This hypothesis is very persuasive in model form, but it did not prove all its premises and predictions. First, the conduction times are not clearly as precise in difference biophysically as is needed for this model. Second, such central sensory asynchronies, if they exist and are compensated for as proposed, would require complete and continuous shifts in all peripheral perception-action coupling. Third, peripheral asynchronies would be the same in all frequencies across the spectrum of fast and slow tempi. However, the size of the synchronization error is different for different frequencies, for example, smaller in faster rhythmic frequencies (Pressing 1999). That change in magnitude undercuts the theory that the time difference is supposedly created from differences in conduction times between two different sensory modalities.

Another view may explain these asynchronies more satisfactorily. In considering the nature of rhythm as a temporally predictable structure of timed events, responding ahead of the beat makes sense simply by maximizing the benefit of anticipation to programming the motor responses. Responding exactly at time point zero on the beat is physiologically impossible within a motor system that has some time slack and noise (i.e. built-in imprecision) in its execution. As a result of the equidistant beat sequence, it is known to the brain when the beats will occur. Responding slightly ahead of time—within the conscious perception of coincidence—turns the task into a feedforward response instead of tapping a few milliseconds after the beat occurred, which will provide feedback at a time when no correction of the response interval, if necessary, is possible. Receiving the beat feedback after the executed response gives appropriate sensory confirmation when corrections can be made for the next response cycle. This model is also supported by the findings of K. Mueller et al. (2000) showing that the electromagnetic response correlates in the sensorimotor cortex after the tap-beat sequence is executed, indicating possible sensory feedback mechanisms to scale the next beat cycle properly.

3.3 Neurophysiologcial and Neuroanatomical Evidence

Our next line of investigation was to study the physiological mechanisms underlying rhythmic synchronization behavior. In human brain research, the temporal processes of information processing can be studied by analyzing brain-wave patterns. Electro- and magnetoencephalography (EEG, MEG) are excellent techniques to study brain activations in millisecond ranges. We used MEG to answer our next research question in regard to understanding the dynamics of how neuronal activation patterns unfold in time during information processing involving rhythmic synchronization. We again utilized the step change experiment (Tecchio et al. 2000). We performed a series of MEG measurements to investigate whether the brain-wave response of the auditory cortex exhibited markers that were correlated with interval changes randomly interspersed in sequences of metronome beats. In line with our previous experiments, we again compared brain cortical responses during rhythmic tempo changes above and below levels of conscious perception. The step changes were either 2 percent or 20 percent of a base interval of 500 ms.

Results revealed that the amplitude of a specific component brain wave (M100, a specific brainwave potential that emerges 100 ms after the stimulus) of the measured magnetic field of the brain scales proportionally to changes in rhythmic interval duration, regardless of whether the tempo modulation was perceived consciously (at 20 percent) or not (at 2 percent). Amplitudes of the M100 brain wave increased systematically with increases in interval duration and decreased with decreases in duration. Our experiment was the first one to show such dependency of brainwave amplitude on interval duration. Dependency of the M100 magnitude on temporal stimulus characteristics had previously been shown (cf. Imada et al. 1997; Lu et al. 1992), but not with time measures as brief and in millisecond ranges as in our experiment.

We used a technique called dipole analysis to locate the source of this particular brain wave. The analysis showed that the M100 was generated stably in localization and latency within the supratemporal Heschl's gyrus (primary auditory cortex), where the primary analysis of all aspects of perceived sounds occurs in the cortex. Because neurons can only fire or not fire, rather than fire stronger or weaker, the change in magnitude of the brain wave in relation to the duration of the beat interval indicates that the cerebral time coding was caused by the synchronized firing of more activated neurons (within an ensemble or circuit of neurons) working together in a fixed time pattern, similar to an orchestra performing together. The experiment makes clear that such mechanisms in brain activity must be a part of the brain's way to code and process time in rhythm and music. It is of course a natural assumption that subcortical cell ensembles may also contribute to or generate the cortical activity patterns. These subcortical activations cannot be reached for measurement with MEG recordings. However, indirect evidence for this assumption—as well as support for the notion that rhythmic stimuli activate subcortical neuronal loops necessary for rhythmic motor performance (e.g., via the reticulospinal pathway in the brain stem and spinal cord)—comes from work by Rossignol and Melvill Jones (1976) and Paltsev and Elner (1967).

From this data, we can determine several interesting facets of how auditory rhythm is processed in the brain. The data demonstrate convincingly that the rapid and precise adaptations of rhythmic movements to subliminal tempo changes during our behavioral experiments have a precise neurological basis in the brain. The data show that these small time fluctuations in the range of a few milliseconds are indeed registered and coded in the brain by changes in the strength of the brainwave currents measured over the primary auditory cortex. Because changes in brainwave power are a function of more neurons firing together in synchrony, it is tempting to use the analogy of the neurons working like a rhythm band when detecting timing changes. Longer intervals require higher levels of synchronization of neuronal oscillations (i.e., more neurons are firing in more precise synchronization patterns). Furthermore, these perceived time patterns must then be projected into motor structures to generate the precise changes in temporal motor control. The exact location of these transfer points in the brain is still unclear and the subject of much debate. Within the subcortical pathways, interesting suggestions have been made—on anatomical grounds—regarding the inferior colliculus, an early brain stem nucleus in the auditory pathway, as putatively being well suited in function and localization to transduce time information into motor tissue (Casseday and Covey 1995). Auditory timing and motor maps in the inferior colliculus have been described. However, rhythmic auditory-motor synchronization is most likely a distributed and parallel process involving multiple cortical and subcortical networks that may be flexible and adapative in emerging configurations depending on the timing requirements of the specific tasks.

These studies provide some suggestive and intriguing neurological evidence for a notion that music communicates temporal order in auditory perception through its time-ordered sound structures, regardless of whether changes in rhythmic patterns are perceived consciously or subconsciously. It is an obvious conclusion that the brain takes great delight in perceiving and producing these time-ordered sound shapes within the simultaneity and sequentiality of music's syntax of rhythm and polyphony.

To build further on the psychophysical and physiological data of rhythmicity, we turned our attention to trying to identify the neuroanatomical architecture within which these processes unfold. In a series of recent brain-imaging experiments, we have begun to explore how the neuroanatomical networks of the brain are activated during rhythmic motor synchronization (Thaut 2003). Several different experimental tasks were used, such as isochronous finger tapping, tapping to random rhythms, and tapping to rhythms whose tempo fluctuations followed the pattern of a cosine wave similar to our earlier experiments (Stephan et al. 2002a). Using positron-emission tomography (PET)—measuring oxygenation changes in the brain as an indicator of activity levels of brain structures—we were able to identify the basic neural network underlying rhythmic synchronization. We found that during isochronous right-handed finger tapping, the basic network consists of a relatively simple array of auditory and sensorimotor areas. This array includes primary sensorimotor areas contralateral to the moving hand, bilateral sensory association areas, bilateral opercular premotor areas, and, subcortically, contralateral insula, putamen, and thalamus. Additional significant increases in regional cerebral blood flow were seen in right rostral ventrolateral prefrontal cortex. Within the cerebellum, right cerebellar vermis and right anterior hemispheres were activated. This network is not substantially different—with the exception of some prefrontal and cerebellar areas—from that involved in rhythmic finger tapping without tones, suggesting that the neural network underlying rhythmic motor synchronization is essentially a composite of auditory and motor areas with no specific separate brain structure dedicated to time transduction and entrainment mechanisms in the motor system.

If this suggestion is correct, it would imply that rhythmic time information coded in the auditory system may be directly projected into motor tissue entraining rhythmic motor responses, similar to a resonance function in a musical instrument (for instance, between vibrating strings). Our previous findings using MEG to study brain cortical responses in rhythmic timing (Tecchio et al. 2000) suggest that rhythmic discrimination takes place at least in part at the auditory cortex level, and as such the auditory cortex may contribute directly to synchronized motor output via common thalamic projections shared with cortical motor areas (e.g., the supplementary motor area). Furthermore, the findings in brain imaging and MEG, taken together, may support one of the two main hypotheses about the physiology of rhythm and timing in the brain. Suggestions have been made—for instance, by Buonomano and Merzenich (1995), Buonomano et al. (1997), and Buonomano (2000)—that the auditory system on brain stem and cortical levels is intrinsically capable of processing temporal characteristics of auditory input and of transducing temporal information into adjacent nervous tissue (e.g., hippocampal and motor structures). One of the other main hypotheses holds that this network needs to interact differentially with other structures, such as the basal ganglia or cerebellum, as ring circuitry (e.g., Meck 1996; Harrington and Haaland 1999; Rao et al.

2001). However, research data showing that auditory rhythm can entrain the rhythmic motor responses of Parkinsonian patients, even in off-medication states, (in gait, e.g., McIntosh et al. 1997), as well as of patients with cerebellar disorders (in finger tapping; e.g., Molinari et al. 2003), provide more evidence for the direct resonance hypothesis, at least in rhythmic auditory-motor synchronization tasks, because cerebellar or basal ganglia function can be compromised without interrupting these rhythmic processes. Similar evidence for direct motor entrainment by rhythmic cues, found when studying the effect of auditory input on spinal motor neurons, has been offered by Rossignol and Melvill Jones (1976).

These different hypotheses may not be mutually exclusive because rhythmic timing through external sensory entrainment cues or internal timing processes may be driven by quite different time generator mechanisms. Furthermore, the difference between subconscious versus conscious processing of sensorimotor information may also play a critical role in differential network activations.

Once more complex rhythmic tracking tasks beyond the basic isochronous entrainment process were introduced, the emerging neural network architecture became more complex. Prefrontal as well as cerebellar activations became more prominent and specific. When rhythmic finger tapping was executed to tempo changes in cosine-modulated as well as randomized rhythms, associated activation areas were found within additional parieto-thalamic and premotor areas, predominantly ipsilateral to the movement. Finally, primarily right prefrontal, anterior cingulate, and intraparietal areas, as a well as posterior cerebellar areas, became active specifically during cosine-modulated tapping.

An interesting pattern of an expanding network of neural activity in the prefrontal cortex was seen when people tapped to rhythms that fluctuated at different rates ranging from subconsciously to consciously perceived. Prefrontal activation, which is typically associated with higher perceptual and cognitive control functions of the brain, showed an expanding regional network depending on the magnitude of the modulation. At a 3 percent fluctuation of base interval—which was not perceived consciously by the study participants—the prefrontal cortex was already activated in the medial frontal areas. Ventrolateral areas were additionally activated during the 7 percent condition, which was associated with an awareness of an unstable beat without being able to identify the exact timing nature of the instability. Dorsolateral areas were prominently added during the 20 percent condition. A 20 percent change in base interval is an easily detectable change in interval duration. The study participants were clearly aware that the rhythmic pattern alternated between longer (slower) and shorter (faster) intervals.

Mapping the brain during these rhythmic synchronization tasks also gave some very interesting insights into the function of the cerebellum. In general, the cerebellum is thought of as being involved in many critical optimizing aspects of sensory perception and cognition functions, as well as in motor control. This complex role was reflected in very differential activation patterns during our experiments. Our analysis of cerebellar patterns (Stephan et al. 2002b) revealed three distinct neural circuits showing cerebellum and cortex being activated in concert during different aspects of rhythmic synchronization:

1. Anterior cerebellar lobe activation in vermal and hemispheric regions psilateral to the movement was present with similar strength during all conditions, regardless of whether the rhythmic task was tracking isochronous, randomized, or cosine-modulated stimuli. This activation pattern corresponded to activations in contralateral primary sensorimotor areas, caudal cingulate and contralateral thalamus.

2. Within bilateral hemispheric parts of the posterior cerebellar lobe, the magnitude of change in brain activation covaried with the magnitude of temporal change in the rhythmic stimulus interval: lowest activation for the isochronous rhythm, greater activation for stepwise increases of 3 percent and 7 percent in tempo, and highest activations during the random and the 20 percent change conditions. Changes in activation in this circuit thus were sensitive to degree of temporal change, but not to tracking strategy (randomly versus regularly modulated). Secondary sensorimotor activations, especially in right inferior parietal cortex close to intraparietal sulcus, mirrored the pattern of change in the cerebellum.

3. During the 20 percent condition, higher activations than in the other conditions were seen only in more medial parts of the left posterior hemisphere. Corresponding regions of activation were seen in the cortical regions of the right inferior parietal cortex in the deep intraparietal sulcus, lateral right prefrontal cortex (right hemispheric homologue to Broca's area), and dorsolateral prefrontal cortex. Thus, this network seemed to be activated only during conscious tracking of a supraliminally audible tempo modulation, possibly related to discerning the modulated pattern and selecting the appropriately synchronized motor response.

Two conclusions may be derived from these differential activation patterns in the cerebellum. First, the cerebellum is not a unifunctional structure; different parts of the cerebellum subserve different functions related to controlling movement and acquiring sensory information, as well as higher perceptual processes that can be mapped onto rhythmic synchronization tasks. Second, these cerebellar regions form parts of at least three distinct cortico-cerebellar networks related to different aspects of temporal control during rhythmic synchronization.

The basic neural network for isochronous rhythmic synchronization was described in a study comparing isochronous and polyrhythmic synchronization (Sanes et al. 2001). The subjects were asked to tap musical hemiola patterns (i.e., two beats against a three Hz rhythm and vice versa, at two different movement frequencies). Hemiolas belong to the most complex rhythmic patterns performed in music. The hemiola synchronization showed more activation strength compared with the isochronous condition. Faster auditory rhythm rates showed higher activation rates bilaterally in anterior portions of the superior temporal gyrus bordering on the opercular regions in the right superior parietal lobe. Faster movement did not show distinct brain activation patterns. The hemiola condition yielded more activation in bilateral supplementary motor area, as well as two small clusters in right supramarginal gyrus and left cerebellar hemisphere. Interestingly, activation in basal ganglia structures of right anterior caudate and putamen was reduced during hemiola synchronization versus isochronous tracking.

The data from this study adds another dimension to the possible functions of the cerebellum and its involvement in musical processing. Higher complexity in the rhythmic task clearly was associated with higher activation patterns in the cerebellum. As such, the cerebellum may play an important role in learning, sensory acquisition, and optimization of complex motor and perceptual functions. These roles are supported in general by current theories about cerebellar function (Schmahmann 1997) and the involvement of the cerebellum in experiments studying musical tasks (Parsons 2001).

Finally, Parsons and Thaut (2001) investigated whether distinct neural activation patterns mediate different components of rhythm. We used discrimination tasks of paired comparisons of brief rhythm motifs. We separately studied perception of differences in tempo, duration, pattern, and meter. Tempo was studied using monotone metronome sequences of dynamically increasing and decreasing rates. The meter task involved discriminations between different metric patterns (3/4, 4/4, 5/4, 5/8, 7/8, and 9/8). Rhythmic pattern discrimination was modeled after the standardized Seashore Test of Musical Aptitudes (1938). Finally, duration was tested by comparing the total time duration of monotone rhythmic sequences. All stimuli were equated on total number of tone, events, phrasing, accentuation, and so on, to make them as similar as possible in sensory structure. We tested five nonmusicans and five musicians (with academic professional music training). Task difficulty was equated across conditions and across musicians and nonmusicans to avoid confounding the task performance simply by differences in how difficult the comparisons were.

Results showed impressively that distinct and partially overlapping neural networks subserve each component rhythm; the complex nature of rhythm thus was reflected neurologically. Activations in basal ganglia and cingulate cortex were present in all tasks for musicians and nonmusicians. Nonmusicians also had strong activations in bilateral posterior lateral cerebellar hemispheres during the tempo, meter, and pattern discrimination. Tempo discrimination additionally activated predominantly right medial prefrontal cortex in nonmusicians. Pattern discrimination showed significant activation in midbrain regions, as well as bilateral posterior lateral hemispheres. Meter discrimination activated predominantly right inferior frontal cortex. All the activation patterns in the preceding condition were most pronounced for nonmusicians, and were much weaker or even absent in musicians. The reverse activation pattern was displayed during the duration discrimination task, in which musicians showed higher activations than nonmusicians in bilateral medial frontal cortex, bilateral inferior parietal cortex, and posterior lateral cerebellum. The duration task (judging the total duration of a rhythmic sequence) was considered by musicians to require a more novel or complex strategy than the other tasks, with the reverse true for nonmusicians. Musicians may have searched for cues in the number of rhythmic elements to determine the differences in total sequence duration, whereas nonmusicians may have chosen a less analytic strategy, and appeared to judge by using a more simplistic and holistic gestalt strategy. Musicians also found that task more novel than the other tasks.

The reversal of cerebellar activation patterns between musicians and nonmusicians during the duration condition points to a differential role of the cerebellum relative to task complexity and processing strategy. The more novel challenge and more analytical approaches were associated with higher cerebellar activations. These findings show a certain degree of consistency with our imaging results when tapping isochronous rhythms versus tapping in hemiola patterns. Significantly higher cerebellar activation was seen during hemiola performance. Musicians can perform hemiola rhythms without difficulty, yet hemiolas are found—as a form of polyrhythm—much less frequently than regular metric relationships in musical rhythms, and are much more complex in requiring the synchronization of time relationships between two simultaneous rhythmic patterns. The differential involvement in these rhythmical tasks helps us to understand the specific and critical role that the cerebellum plays in learning, sensory acquisition, and complexity processing.

Based on general research in prefrontal cortex function, we suggest that prefrontal activations in rhythmic discrimination are most likely supporting working memory, attention, and task-monitoring processes, whereas activations in frontal, temporal, and midbrain areas may be related to temporal pattern perception and timing.

One of the most fascinating results of this research is the affirmation of the importance of specific conceptual musical definitions of rhythm for neurobiological investigations in musical rhythm. These definitions must be consistent with theoretical concepts of rhythm in musicology to do justice to the complexity of rhythmic processes and to avoid misunderstandings or misinterpretations between musicians and neuroscientists. Furthermore, the data provides very interesting evidence for the partial neurological independence of different components of rhythm processing in the human brain.

What do we know about differential rhythm processing in the brain? Some interesting findings have begun to elucidate the neural basis of different aspects of rhythm processing. For example, research has shown that different musical elements (e.g., perception of rhythm and perception of melody) have representations in distinct neural systems (Peretz and Kolinsky 1993). The preponderance of research data suggests, furthermore, that rhythm processing is a widely distributed bilateral function and not lateralized hemispherically. A comparison of memory for familiar versus more unfamiliar rhythms—differentiated by low-integer interval ratios versus fractionated interval ratios—showed almost a lateral reversal in neural representations of rhythms (Sakai et al. 1999). The basic low-integer rhythms were supported by left frontal and parietal cortex and right anterior cerebellum, while rhythms with fractionated interval ratios were represented in right prefrontal, frontal, and parietal areas along with bilateral posterior cerebellum. Our study has taken this research a step further into differential rhythm processing in the brain by actually looking at the neuroanatomical basis of structural subcomponents of rhythm as the critical syntactical element in musical organization.

The neurological evidence of our study, taken together with other studies, would support the capability of the human brain to independently develop a large degree of syntactical diversity in rhythmic structures existent in the music of different cultures. One may think of comparisons between meter-based rhythms of Western music and Indian raga music utilizing set rhythmic modes or the very complex polyphonic layers of polyrhythmic percussion music in African cultures. The neurological data seem to put question marks after theories of rhythm that consider it natural that the structural time elements (pulse, meter, pattern, tempo, etc.) of rhythm are contingently embedded in each other in hierarchical form. Because very different neurological networks, which seem to be fairly independent of each other in circuit architecture, subserve different components of rhythm, hierarchical rhythmic structures, such as those in Western musical language systems, may be based more on particular structural developments in the syntax of musical languages specific to certain musical cultures than on a culturally independent intrinsic function of a musical biology. What would then be common to the neurological basis of rhythm formation in the human brain would be an architecture and function of neural modularity that allows the human brain to build, develop, connect, or juxtapose very different subcomponents of rhythm into complex rhythmic grammars underlying very different and culturally constrained developments of compositional and improvisational musical structures and styles.

3.4 Brain Rhythms and Musical Rhythms in Cognition

The traditional, and until recently prevalent, view on information processing in the human brain centered on the assumption that the relevant code for this processing was embedded in the neurons' firing rates of action potentials. However, this view has been challenged, initially by discoveries in perceptual neuroscience research, and has subsequently been changed —a recognition that the temporal patterns and the relative timing of action potentials among neocortical neurons carry important information. Within the context of temporal patterns as important aspects of neural information coding, the concept of synchronization of neuronal discharge—the unified temporal coherence in discharge patterns of neuronal ensembles or networks of ensembles—has received increasing attention (Singer 1993; Singer 1999; Wespatat et al. 2004). The relevance of synchronization of the oscillatory spike patterns of active neurons has been documented in learning and recall, motor performance, perceptual integration, attention, and other areas of cognitive and motor performance. During learning, evidence for cortical reorganization has been found, using brain imaging techniques. Underlying this process of brain plasticity is the emergence of new synaptical networks that are formed by repeated practice, experience, or exposure to a stimulus driving the associated neuronal populations into increasingly temporally sharpened response patterns of synchronized neuronal networks.

It has been proposed, consequently, that the synchronization of the oscillatory circuitry in specific brain systems underlies human behavior functions in cognition, learning, perception, and movement. However, if the brain indeed functions as a rhythm machine, it must operate on integrated and precisely tuned timing mechanisms in order to build such temporally coherent network structures. The question that has been raised in relationship to music is if the synchronous timing structure in music can serve as an effective timing signal to enhance learning and perception by inducing temporally sharpened neural representations in the respective brain circuitry with greater precision. Can the temporal structure of music, especially via its rhythmic components, play a critical role in entraining temporal coherence in neural ensembles in order to drive remodeled or newly emergent cell assemblies that represent newly practiced or relearned motor, cognitive, or perceptual functions?

This proposal could have specific value in rehabilitative training and learning in which one operates under the assumption that, due to brain damage, the neural systems involved have a degraded ability to generate temporal coherence in neuronal ensembles. (Merzenich et al. [1993] have posed this question separately from music in connection with developing other types of facilitative sensory input in the therapy of learning disabilities.) Several lines of investigation into brain plasticity in music have shown that cortical reorganization in music does exist. In a number of studies it has been shown that brain structures in musicians are different from those of nonmusicians. Although preexisting anatomical differences could account for this finding, some of the graded differences based on length of musical training and level of professional status point to learning and training as an important factor (e.g., Gaser and Schlaug 2003). Learning-induced cortical plasticity in music has been shown topographically in brain-imaging studies, as well as in brain-wave research and research with sensory disorders (e.g., Pantev et al. 2003; Schlaug and Chen 2001; Rauschecker 2001). The effect of instrumental (e.g., keyboard) training on cortical motor maps has been shown by Pascual-Leone (2001). A negative example of the cortical plasticity induced by musical training in motor control can be seen in the resilience to treatment of dystonia-related syndromes, which are based on maladaptive movement patterns that have been deeply ingrained through repetitive, temporally structured training of instrumental performance.

The effect of music and rhythm on brain plasticity in therapeutic training has only recently been investigated directly (Luft et al. 2004), although many studies have shown the significant effect of auditory rhythmic stimulation, compared with other forms of therapies, on the recovery of arm and gait function in, for example, stroke patients (Whitall et al. 2000; Thaut et al. 2002a; Thaut et al. 1997). However, there is evidence that sensorimotor-based therapeutic training techniques can induce cortical reorganization (e.g., Liepert et al. 2000; Nelles et al. 2001). We postulate that the well-documented functional recovery due to rhythmic training would also be reflected in cortical reorganization driven by the entrainment function of the rhythmic cue patterns. First evidence of this has been shown by Luft et al. (2004).

Recently we completed a series of preliminary experiments studying plasticity in brain-wave spectra during learning of word lists that were presented using either spoken or sung presentations (Peterson et al. 2004; Thaut and Peterson 2003). The sung condition used short songs with the word sequences set to the melody. First, behavioral learning data of the word lists showed no difference between the conditions. Pronounced increases in spectral power, indicative of increased neural oscillatory synchronization, were found during learning in both conditions, but were significantly higher for the sung condition in frontal and parieto-temporal networks. The increase in learning-related synchronization is consistent with other research (e.g., E. E. Smith et al. 1998). Second, there was a significant change in the topography of learning-related rhythmic synchronization in theta, lower and higher alpha, and gamma bands between spoken and musical conditions, providing evidence that similar behavioral performances were supported by different oscillatory networks in the brain. The study asked for spoken recall of learned words in both conditions, making a modality transfer necessary in the music-facilitated learning. Also, recall order of the words was left up to the study participants rather than asking them to recall in order of presentation. Both factors may bring out an advantage for the musical mnemonic in learning sequences of unrelated words in future studies. However, the current studies did show evidence for the type of plasticity music may induce by stimulating higher neural network synchronization and a significant topographical reconfiguration in the oscillatory learning network in certain frequency bands. To use a musical analogy, the rhythmic patterns of the musical score were redistributed with higher temporal precision across different instrumental sections of the orchestra, creating a new orchestration of the same musical piece.

Further research in the near future will most certainly continue to study brain plasticity induced by music and rhythm as an important topic in musical, as well as biomedical, applications. Behavioral evidence in certain areas of motor control and motor learning or memory point to music as a very effective stimulus to produce strong memory traces of overlearning. Rhythmic timing skills have been shown to play key roles also in speech perception and production, and related dysfunctions such as dyslexic conditions (Tallal et al. 1993; Merzenich et al. 1993; Wolff, 2002; Patel et al. 1998; Overy 2000; Overy et al. 2003; Temple et al. 2000). Furthermore, the temporal analogies in rhythm, diverse spectrality, synchronization, and entrainment between structural parameters in music and the parameters of neuronal activation patterns underlying information processing and learning will make this an interesting and fruitful field of study.

3.5 Conclusion

Through neurologic processes, music communicates information to the brain that has profound effects on learning, development, recovery of function, and aesthetic engagement. Research into the neurobiology of music has made great and unprecedented progress since the mid-1990s due to a fruitful merger of lines of investigation from neuroscience, psychophysics, and musicology, supported by other disciplines such as mathematics, physics, and engineering (Zatorre and Peretz 2001; Avanzini et al. 2003). Music, especially rhythm, can serve as a model of temporality in the human brain (Harrington and Haaland 1999; Rao et al. 2001). In support of similar views by other researchers, we may propose that music is indeed related to core functions of the biology of the human nervous system, and therefore serves adaptive evolutionary purposes beyond that of the functional interpretation of art. Music must be viewed as a biological fact, not just as a cultural phenomenon. In both arenas, the cultural and the biological, music is a powerful communicator.

Furthermore, in musical aesthetics, a great deal of emphasis in understanding musical semantics (i.e., the meaning in music) is given to the temporal nature of music as a pivotal element in conveying its rule-based language structure (Berlyne 1971). Thus, we may propose that a scientific study of music always needs to concern the various elements of music within a temporally ordered context of musical patterns.

Several key findings in rhythmic synchronization research have emerged that contribute to an understanding of the neurobiological basis of music and temporal information processing in the brain. Musical rhythm rapidly creates stable and precise internal templates for temporal organization of motor responses. The motor system is very sensitive to arousal by the auditory system. Neural impulses of auditory rhythm project directly into motor structures. Motor responses become entrained with the timing of rhythmic patterns. The entrainment process can be modeled well via resonant network functions and coupled oscillator models. The motor system has access to temporal information in the auditory system below levels of conscious perception. Rhythmic synchronization appears to emerge in a fuzzy biological system characterized by stochastic time fluctuations that are embedded in self-correcting, non-linear coupling functions. The dynamics of these processes cannot be captured by simple statistical models of local stationary corrections using, for example, variance analysis.

The neurobiology of rhythm shows a widely distributed cortical and subcortical network subserving motor, sensory, and cognitive aspects of rhythm processing (Platel et al. 1997; Penhune et al. 1998; Schlaug and Chen 2001). Consistent engagement of distinct neural circuits in the cerebellum across musical-rhythmic tasks suggests a central role of the cerebellum in the temporal organization of cognitive and perceptual processes in music (Schmahmann 1997). However, cerebellar pathology does not affect the capacity of auditory rhythms to entrain rhythmic motor responses (Molinari et al. 2001), suggesting that sensory rhythms can compensate for brain mechanisms related to timing that are dysfunctional due to disease or injury.

The basic neural network underlying isochronous pulse synchronization consists mainly of composite motor and auditory areas with no clearly designated, functionally separate brain area for synchronization. It appears that the temporal information processing in rhythm follows multiple parallel and possibly hierarchically ordered neural computation processes. Such processes may be coded on a cellular level in the emerging timing patterns of synaptic network coupling. In the case of music perception or production, these processes may originate in the auditory system and subsequently entrain other brain areas via resonant physiological network functions. Thus, the neuronal activation patterns that precisely code the perception of rhythm in the auditory system spread into adjacent motor areas and activate the firing patterns of motor tissue. One may think of it—using a nonscientific image—as a process similar to the vibrating strings of a violin that resonate with the wood molecules of the violin's body, setting them into the same vibrating motion as the strings themselves. Neuroimaging maps of rhythm (and other musical functions) suggest that on the macro level of regional brain activations, the connectivity between widely distributed brain areas in precisely timed relationships may be one of the most essential systems components in musical processing.

Further, as we will discuss in chapter 4, many clinical studies have shown striking evidence that auditory rhythm and music can be effectively harnessed for specific therapeutic purposes in the rehabilitation of patients with different neuropathologies (Thaut et al. 1999). Such findings further underscore the complex ways in which music engages and communicates to the human brain and in which the brain that engages in music can be—even in states of brain injury—changed by engaging in music (Pascual Leone et al. 1995; Peterson and Thaut, 2002; Thaut and Peterson, 2002).

In conclusion, we have reviewed new aspects of the neurological basis for key elements of musical communication. Rhythm and time are among the most eminent concepts in understanding the nature of music as an organized and rule-based sensory language. The brain is neurologically superbly sensitive to processing the time elements of music in a rapid, precise, and meaningful manner. In closing, we return to Stravinsky's famous quote that the sole function of music is to communicate time. By going beyond the obvious chronometric parameters of music and rhythm in keeping time, we may discover the dimension of time in music at the core of what we consider meaning in music. We may have reason to contemplate—if not the structured flow of time, made audible in music's temporal architecture of sound, rhythm, and polyphony—what it is that excites, moves, and gives order to our feelings, thoughts, and sense of movement when we engage in music.

4

Biomedical Research in Music

4.1 Introduction

Since about 1990, researchers have begun to elucidate the neural substrates of musical functions in the human brain. Rhythm perception and production have been a primary focus of these efforts because they form the most important organizing element in the structure or language of music. The study of rhythm has yielded insights not only into musical time, but also into temporality of information processing in the human brain in general. These investigations have led to a fundamental need to rethink the role of music in therapy and medicine, tapping the capacity of music to serve as a powerful sensory stimulus capable of engaging the brain in retraining neural and behavioral functions that can then be applied to nonmusical contexts in therapy and medicine. In this chapter, we will examine biomedical implications of music's influence on brain and behavior function by reviewing research that has driven the changing paradigm for music in therapy and medicine.

Traditionally, music in therapy has been based mostly on social science models in which the cultural role of music is interpreted as an effective facilitator for therapeutic concepts of well-being. Neuroscience research in music has created new insights into the therapeutic benefits of music, shifting the models of music in therapy from social science and interpretative models to neuroscience and perceptual models. That is, they are based on how music perception and music production engage the brain in ways that can be meaningfully translated and generalized to nonmusical therapeutic learning and training. This emphasis was very possibly intended in the original plans of the modern music therapy pioneers, at least in the United States. The writings and activities of the early leaders, such as Thayer Gaston and William Sears, show that they tried very early to connect music therapy to a medical model. Also, the research committee was the first standing committee created in 1950 by the Association for Music Therapy that had spun off from the music psychology section of the Music Educators National Conference. However, the historical context and knowledge base for a scientific understanding of music's influence on human behavior from a neurological standpoint had simply not evolved enough to significantly determine the direction of this new profession, which was trying to locate itself at the crossroads of the arts and medicine.

The study of the neurobiological basis of music is inherently linked to music's influence on brain function. In other words, the brain that engages in music is changed by this engagement. This reciprocal relationship of music and brain function—discovered in the mid-1990s within the larger context of a very fascinating line of research demonstrating the experience-dependent plasticity of the brain—is one of the most powerful motors of change in the historical paradigm of music therapy. These new findings suggest that music can stimulate complex cognitive, affective, and sensorimotor processes in the brain that can then be generalized and transferred to nonmusical therapeutic applications.

4.2 Studies in Sensorimotor Rehabilitation

The first field of inquiry in which breakthrough data emerged for a new understanding of the role and function of music in therapy came in motor-control research. Although the effect of music on physical response has always been an intricate and widely documented part of the understanding of music's cultural role in human society, the attempts to integrate music's effect on movement function in therapy were always quite ancillary and mostly informed by an overall motivational-emotional framework of well-being in music therapy. A multitude of studies conducted since the mid-1990s demonstrate impressively that rhythmic entrainment of motor function can actively facilitate the recovery of movement in patients with stroke. However, not until landmark studies by Paltsev and Elner (1967) and Rossignol and Melvill Jones (1976) was the complex basis of physiological interactions between the auditory and the motor system in clear focus. Most studies that appeared in the 1970s and 1980s and reported beneficial effects of rhythm and music on motor development and movement performance were behavioral and used a broad and very diverse array of measures— rarely including references to physiological mechanisms (for a review, see Thaut 1985). Sensorimotor research focused almost exclusively on the role of visual and proprioceptive sensory modalities in the control of movement.

It took the studies conducted by Paltsev and Elner (1967) and Rossingol and Melvill Jones (1976) to show evidence for the existence of auditory-motor pathways (e.g., via reticulospinal connections) that could influence threshold excitability of motor neurons, creating a readiness or priming effect on the segmental motor system via auditory input. Rossignol and Melvill Jones also demonstrated that this priming effect could turn into a functionally facilitating timing effect of muscle activation patterns during auditory rhythmic cuing of rhythmic leg movement.

Another indicator of the physiological effects of rhythm on motor control was reported in a physical therapy study by Safranek et al. (1982). It showed an interesting modulatory effect of auditory rhythm on muscle activation patterns during arm-reaching movements, comparing movements with no cuing against movements with cuing using both regular and irregular rhythms. Variability of muscle activations decreased with cues using regular rhythms, compared with noncued movement and movement cued by irregular rhythms.

In the early 1990s, biomedical research in music and motor control finally began to emerge in a more focused and systematic manner, including a strong biomedical emphasis. Mandel et al. (1990) were able to demonstrate that rhythmic auditory feedback was superior to electromyographic (EMG) feedback in gait training for stroke patients. After the appearance of data showing reductions in electromyographic variability of the leg muscles in rhythmically cued gait of healthy subjects (Thaut et al. 1992), a follow-up study with hemiparetic stroke patients (Thaut et al. 1993) showed significant entrainment results using auditory rhythm as pacemaker. Basic gait parameters such as velocity, step cadence, and swing symmetry all improved with rhythmic cuing. In addition, EMG variability of the gastrocnemius muscle was reduced significantly in the paretic leg, showing more economical motor unit recruitment patterns.

An in-depth kinematic study based on digital video motion analysis, published by Prassas et al. in 1997, showed significant gains in stride length symmetry, as well as reductions in lateral center of mass (COM) displacement and increases in vertical COM, indicating gait patterns closer to the norms. Similar data were found for hemiparetic stroke patients during treadmill walking (Schauer et al. 1996). Using the entrainment paradigm as the basis for a six-week gait therapy investigation, long-term training effects with rhythmic stimulation were reported that were significantly higher than for conventional gait therapy without rhythmic sensory cues (Thaut et al. 1997). Besides improvements in kinematic gait parameters, a central physiological effect of auditory rhythm on EMG patterns was found in reduction of amplitude variability of the gastrocnemius muscle.

Taken together, the clinical data began to suggest that the periodicity of the pulsed rhythmic auditory cue had a modulatory effect on motor neuron activity entraining neural activation patterns into more regular and more synchronized patterns, resulting in more consistent timing and motor unit recruitment. Because these EMG enhancements were always linked with significant kinematic improvements, one can postulate that the rhythmic cues were acting on centrally mediated mechanisms of motor control, possibly via resonance coupling of motor neuron activation patterns to the physiological coding of rhythm in the auditory pathway.

In an extension of the entrainment paradigms used for gait research, several studies used rhythmic stimulation to organize arm movements into temporally structured patterns that could be rhythmically cued. Studies by Whitall et al. (2000), Thaut et al. (2002a), and Luft et al. (2004) demonstrated that rhythmic arm training also showed significant improvements in hemiparetic stroke rehabilitation. Increases in ranges of motion were demonstrated with increases in isometric arm-joint strength and significant improvements on several standardized tests of arm function. Also, decreases in variability and increases in speed of movement times were found, as well as smoothing of trajectory variability during reaching movements.

By studying the underlying velocity and acceleration profiles during movements, a very important insight into understanding the effect of auditory rhythm on motor control was developed. There had been very strong evidence that nontemporal movement parameters, such as stride length in gait or movement trajectories of upper and lower limb joints (e.g., wrist, knee), improved during rhythmic cuing. One basic conclusion was that enhanced time stability across the duration of the movement during rhythmic cuing—by way of rhythm providing a continuous time reference based on its period information—also enhanced spatial-positional control of movement. However, a conceptual link to connect temporal cuing to spatiodynamic parameters of motor control was missing. Analyses of the acceleration and velocity profiles of joint motions during rhythmic cuing offered an intriguing explanation by linking the different parameters of movement control into an interdependent system that could be accessed and modulated by time.

The consistent evidence for smoothing of velocity and acceleration profiles of joint motions during rhythmic cuing suggests that rhythm enhances the control of velocity and acceleration by scaling movement time. Velocity and acceleration, however, are mathematical time derivatives of the spatial parameter of position. Thus, in working our theory backward, we reasoned that by fixating time through a rhythmic interval, for a movement from point A to point B the subject's internal timekeeper now had a precise reference interval, with time information present at any stage or moment of the movement. This time information allows the brain to map and scale smoother parameters of position change (i.e., velocity and acceleration) across the entire movement interval (e.g., heel strike to heel strike in gait, reaching target points in space for arm movements, etc.).

Changes in velocity and acceleration profiles, however, must be reflected in the position-time curves of the movement. This can be described mathematically as an optimization problem. If we assume that the brain uses some optimization strategy to control movement, it is possible to show, in certain cases, that such optimization implies scaling of the resulting movement over time. The immediate consequence of this assertion is that matching the period of a cyclical movement to the period of an external timekeeper will result in the regulation of the entire movement trajectory. Once the time constraint has been added, the brain is presented with a well-defined optimization problem: how to move from point A to point B in a fixed time interval while maximizing precision and minimizing some objective cost function for the body associated with making the movement. (For more detail on the fascinating effect of rhythmic timing on optimization, see chapter 5.)

The effects of rhythmic stimulation in hemiparetic stroke rehabilitation have been further studied and supported in evidence-based reviews by, among others, Jeffrey and Good (1995), Hummelsheim (1999), Mauritz (2002), Bhogal et al. (2003), and Teasell et al. (2003).

Simultaneously, a large body of auditory rhythmic research was developed through studying patients with Parkinson's disease (PD). In experiments concerning the immediate rhythmic entrainment effect on gait patterns, without extended training periods, it was found that PD patients were able to synchronize their step patterns to metronomic and musical-rhythmic cues in time-coupling ranges to a degree very similar to healthy elderly persons (McIntosh et al. 1997). Interestingly, the essential synchronization patterns were retained when PD patients went off dopaminergic medication for forty-eight hours, although variability in all gait parameters had increased. Dopaminergic medication improves basal ganglia function in the absence of normal dopamine production and uptake in the brain. The off-medication data strongly suggested that deficient basal ganglia functioning does not substantially alter rhythmic entrainment mechanisms in the brain. That is an important finding in regard to the functions of the basal ganglia, which has been implicated by many studies in important timing functions related to motor control (Rao et al. 2001). Consequently, we must assume that there must be other neural systems involved and available in time transduction of auditory information into motor tissue. The entrainment effects extended to higher step cadences as well as longer strides, resulting in higher velocities with more normalized gait parameters.

These findings have been substantiated by several studies in therapeutic training protocols of various durations, showing significant gains in gait performance after extended training periods (Thaut et al. 1996; Howe et al. 2003; Freedland et al. 2002; Pacchetti et al. 2000; Fernandez, del Olmo, and Cudeiro 2003; Morris et al. 2004). In a pilot study investigating long-term carryover effects of rhythmic gait training, after three weeks of daily training, patients maintained post-test levels for three to four weeks before significant declines set in (McIntosh et al. 1998). Stride length showed a faster decline curve than step cadence, a characteristic finding for gait pathology in PD. However, without further training, gains were sustained for an appreciable amount of time in a neurodegenerative disease. These findings will most certainly help in the design of more cost- and time-effective training schedules for patients with PD.

Further insight into facilitating auditory-motor mechanisms in Parkinsonian gait was provided in a study by Richards et al. (1992). In this study, gait patterns of groups of patients on their regular medication status, off medication, with visual cues, and with auditory metronome cues were compared. Although both sensory cues could improve gait patterns over both noncued conditions, visual cues (floor strips) increased stride length due to the spacing of the cues. Metronome cues increased both cadence and stride length, again pointing to rhythm accessing a central motor control system that—unlike the visual cues—operates independently from peripheral mediators.

The physiological effects of rhythm on motor control were also substantiated with PD patients by studying the effect of three weeks of rhythmic training on symmetry and variability of timing and amplitude of EMG patterns in the gastrocnemius, anterior tibialis, and vastus lateralis muscles (Miller et al. 1996). Those muscle groups are intricately involved in lower limb control during the gait stride cycle. Auditory rhythm increased the symmetry of muscle activation. Furthermore, the periodicity input of the rhythm significantly reduced the variability of the amplitude of the lower leg muscles but—in a reverse effect—increased the variability of the on-off timing of the lower leg muscles. Both effects brought the EMG patterns of the PD group closer to gait parameters in normal, age-matched, healthy elderly people.

Significant effects of rhythmic cuing on arm movements in PD patients relative to decrease in variability of movement time and increase in movement speed have been shown by, among others, Freeman et al. (1993) and Georgiou et al. (1993). An interesting finding emerged in the study by Georgiou et al.: where the movement times in a consecutive key-pressing task—on a board with the keys arranged in a spatially sequential order—did not improve when successful key presses activated sounds (contingent auditory feedback mode). Improvements over noncued conditions were seen only during rhythmic metronome pacing in which the cue was non-contingent on the executed movement and was presented in a rhythmic feedforward mode.

Other studies— not, however, in the areas of stroke and Parkinsonian research—have demonstrated beneficial effects of rhythmic stimulation on gait of children with cerebral palsy (Thaut et al. 1998a), patients with traumatic brain injury (TBI, Hurt et al. 1998), and patients with Huntington's disease (HD, Thaut et al. 1999). In children with cerebral palsy, the precise synchronization ability is linked to stages of motor and sensory development. However, these children do respond consistently to tempo cues even in the absence of direct, step-by-step synchronization patterns. Based on an analysis of gait control mechanisms in cerebral palsy showing strong reliance on intact temporal mechanisms, Malherbe et al. (1992) proposed the efficacy of rhythmic-musical training exercises to facilitate gait training in children with cerebral palsy. Hurt et al. (1998) found that immediate entrainment did not result in improved gait patterns for TBI patients, but a four-week training program did. Rhythmic responses by patients with Huntington's chorea differ from those of all other groups who have been reported as study subjects in the literature. Although tempo cues are translated into improved gait patterns, the temporal control of choreic gait is highly irregular. Perception of rhythmic cues is already compromised in patients who have mild or no overt disease signs, which points to an underlying pathology that affects motor functions as well as sensory perception and cognitive abilities at a very early stage.

Taken together, these research studies show strong evidence that rhythmic stimulation can influence and regulate motor control in movement disorders in complex and beneficial ways. These findings have led music therapy interventions a long way from emotional-motivational models to physiologically grounded theories and applications of how musical elements engage the brain and modulate the neural dynamics underlying learning and training in therapy. We can certainly conclude that the early findings by Paltsev and Elner (1967) and Rossignol and Melvill Jones (1976) regarding the physiological basis of auditory-motor interactions have been impressively substantiated and extended to beneficial applications in neurologic rehabilitation.

4.3 Studies in Speech and Language Rehabilitation

In the literature of aesthetics, psychology, and philosophy, we find very broad and consistent assumptions that artworks are capable of communicating meaning. Furthermore, it has been proposed that humans have acquired six symbol systems of communication—among many other symbol codes in human development—that represent unique sets of intrisic perceptual elements: the genetic code, spoken language, written language, music notation, numerals, and labanotation (a system for coding dance choreography, Premack 2004). The first two most likely evolved within the biological constraints of human evolution, while the remaining four developed as inventions within cultural and cognitive constraints. From a perspective of music anthropology, interpreting the emergence of music in human history as another auditory, symbol-based communication system, we may add as a possible seventh symbol system—in parallel with spoken language—song and musical expression on instruments. A thorough discussion of the relationship between music, speech, and language as systems of communication is not the topic of this chapter. However, these brief introductory remarks may serve as a reminder that spoken language and music have considerable overlaps, parallels, and similarities as auditory-based communication systems. There are also clear differences in communicative structure, as well as in their respective rule-based systems of constructing signs and symbols into units of meaning. (For a more detailed discussion, see chapter 1.)

From a biomedical perspective, two shared functions of music, speech, and language are important: (1) the aural and production features shared by spoken language and musical vocalization in singing and (2) the ability of both systems to embed communicative functions in the auditory modality. The suggestion that music may help language and speech functions is found in many records throughout human history. These records were often stimulated by striking—yet in earlier times unexplainable—observations that some people who suffer a stroke and lose the ability to speak can miraculously still sing. Music history includes many cases of composers who lost the ability to communicate through spoken words but could still share their feelings and stir meaningful emotional responses in listeners through their musical compositions.

One of the earliest systematic applications of music to the recovery of speech function was developed in the early 1970s by using singing with patients who suffered from expressive (Broca's) aphasia. The term "melodic intonation therapy" (MIT) was coined to describe this technique (Albert et al. 1973; Sparks et al. 1974; Sparks and Holland 1976). A large number of clinical research studies since the mid-1970s have shown the efficacy of MIT for patients with expressive aphasia (e.g., Boucher et al. 2001; Bonakdarpour et al. 2003; Goldfarb and Bader 1979; Popovici 1995; Sparks and Deck 1994; Warren et al. 2003). Lesion studies and neuroanatomical research related to encoding of spoken language versus singing have shed considerable light on the possible explanations for the facilitation of verbal output through song. In brief, original explanations centered on a simple shift of the encoding process of speech from the left hemispheric temporal-frontal speech centers to the right hemispheric homologues, thus bypassing damaged neural pathways and speech structures in the brain (Berlin 1976). The proposed neuroanatomical rerouting processes have been confirmed and extended by imaging data and lesion studies (e.g., Naeser and Helm-Estabrooks 1985; Thulborn et al. 1999; Hebert et al. 2003; Overy et al. 2004). Research has shown that expressive aphasic patients can produce undisturbed speech while singing, even when speech alone is disturbed (Yamadori et al. 1977; Cadalbert et al. 1994). More recent experiments by Stewart et al. (2001) used transcranial magnetic stimulation to disrupt speech and singing. Left hemispheric stimulation disrupted speech, but right hemispheric stimulation did not disrupt singing. These findings raise questions about the neural circuitry for singing, which may be more diffusely located and, as such, harder to disrupt than the highly localized speech centers in the left hemisphere. Furthermore, data for a possible long-term training effect of MIT on brain plasticity by accessing and reactivating left hemispheric speech centers has been put forward in a neuroimaging study by Belin et al. (1996).

These new neuroanatomical findings create open-ended questions about the neural dynamics that facilitate speech in expressive aphasia through singing. The central question is if there is something special about word production during singing that is not entirely explained by a simple hemispheric shift. Does melodic context facilitate word production? Other facilitating elements worth considering could be the slower production rate in song than in spoken language, the prolonged voicing patterns, the predictability of speech sound encoding based on an external timing plan, the use of a differential pitch system in singing (Natke et al. 2003), and the affective components of music connected to emotional arousal circuitry, which in turn may facilitate speech circuitry activation (Patel 2003).

Research data have also shown successful extensions of MIT techniques to patients with apraxia (Krauss and Galloway 1982; Helfrich-Miller 1984, 1994; Keith and Aronson 1975). Aphasic patients often show dissociations between intact nonpropositional (automatic, reflexlike) speech in the absence of propositional speech. Music and singing as an effective tool to trigger nonpropositional speech—due to overlearning and deep-rooted associations between melodies and song lyrics—has been proposed by Basso et al. (1979) and Lucia (1987).

There is strong physiological evidence that rhythmic sounds can act as sensory timers, entraining brain mechanisms that control the timing, sequencing, and coordination of muscle control systems in speech (A. Smith and Denny 1990). Modulation of speech rates to enhance intelligibility and overcome deficiencies in fluency (stuttering/cluttering) has been shown, using music and rhythm with speakers who are dysarthric due to TBI or PD (Pilon et al. 1998; Caligiuri 1989; Hammen and Yorkston 1996; Hammen et al. 1994; Yorkston and Beukelman 1981; Yorkston et al. 1990; Thaut et al. 2001), apraxic speakers (Shane and Darley 1978; Dworkin and Abkarian 1996; Wambaugh and Martinez 2000; Dworkin et al. 1988), and patients with fluency disorders (Healey et al. 1976; Colcord and Adams 1979; Andrews et al. 1983; Cohen 1988; Glover et al. 1996). Fluency disorders are disorders of timing caused in part by problems of synchronization between phonation and articulation. Similar to auditory rhythm and music being able to regulate timing in gross or fine motor control of movement, the etiology of deficient speech timing may give us a reasonable rationale for speech entrainment mechanisms in music and rhythm (Perkins 2001). It is important to note for differential treatment selection that in several studies, rhythmic speech cuing showed the highest improvement rates with the more severely affected dysarthric speakers (Pilon et al. 1998; Thaut et al. 2001).

The prosodic, acoustical, and physiological similarities in vocal production of speech and singing have given rise to investigations of whether music-based voice training can have a beneficial effect in therapy for voice disorders involving phonation or resonance characterized by, for example, abnormal pitch or pitch ranges, loudness, timbre, respiratory control, excessive breathiness, or hoarseness (Crystal 1980). Voice disorders can have a very wide range of motoric, anatomical, physiological, behavioral, or psychogenic etiologies. Studies have shown that vocal intonation training can, by incorporating musical vocalization techniques, facilitate improvements in voice control (e.g., Bellaire et al. 1986; Darrow and Starmer 1986; Darrow and Cohen 1991; Ramig et al. 1994; Haneishi 2001; De Stewart et al. 2003). An interesting fact that may provide the basis for understanding mechanisms that enhance voice control in music comes from studies showing that the control of fundamental pitch frequencies in singing is more precise than in speech (Natke et al. 2003). Oral motor exercises incorporating musical elements, such as rhythm, for rate control have been shown to enhance articulatory control and speech sound production (Haneishi 2001; Wambaugh and Martinez 2000).

Musical activities are frequently mentioned in the clinical literature as a very effective tools to enhance delayed speech and language development in children. The scientific literature on these claims is not very substantial, although the notion has probably always been well accepted as common sense due to the well-documented natural inclination of children to engage in musical activities throughout their early development. Not until research into musical development had begun to develop significant data was it possible to gain a much broader basis for understanding the nature and mechanisms of musical development in children (cf. Trehub 2003). We now have the beginnings of an exciting database to formulate how music may interact positively with healthy development and may enhance developmental interventions in pediatric therapy. Research suggests positive effects of musical learning and training on language development (Saffran 2003), auditory development (Trainor et al. 2003), dyslexia (Overy 2000; Overy et al. 2003), and communicative development in toddlers with pervasive developmental disorder (Chen et al. 2001). Speech and language development in children with sensory disorders has been shown to improve by using music-facilitated developmental language exercises (Gfeller and Darrow 1987; Gfeller and Baumann 1988; Gfeller and Schum 1994).

One of the more comprehensive reviews of music research in speech and language therapy was compiled by Galloway (1975). The relatively large number of studies and reports included in the review documents impressively how music and speech—due to their obvious correlates and parallels in sensory modality, motoric aspects in vocal production, and functionality as communication systems—have always attracted a good deal of attention in science and therapy. However, as Galloway clearly notes, much of the research up to 1975 lacked rigor and consistency in methodology, leading him to state in conclusion that "the majority of these reports and studies support the concept of music as a medium for speech remediation; however, the use of music with communicative disorders is, at best, in an inchoative, data-gathering stage of development" (p. 47). The recent paradigm shift in the role of music in biomedical applications, based on a much better understanding of speech, language, and music processing in the brain, has helped to improve the status of biomedical research in music and speech/language remediation in terms of scientific rigor, new methodologies, and greater depth. Also, the new developments in neuroscience and music allow us to reinterpret some earlier research data in a more conclusive and productive light, enabling us to view them as early supportive evidence for current research findings. In selected areas of applications, persuasive evidence for music's role in speech and language remediation is emerging. These developments, however, do not diminish the fact that much more research needs to be done.

In appraising the emerging database in clinical and basic science, and analyzing the function of musical stimuli in the therapeutic process, at least four distinct underlying mechanisms emerge:

1. *Differential neurologic processing of music and speech.* The neural circuitry for music and speech, especially in regard to singing, is partially overlapping and partially segregated neuroanatomically. For example, there is evidence that rhythm in speech and singing is controlled by shared left hemispheric functions, with additional bilateral activations depending on task context. Control of pitch and melodic patterns in singing shows predominantly right hemispheric activations. Anatomical centers for reading musical notation and reading written language are in close proximity in temporal-occipital regions, but clearly separated, with notation reading mediated by specific activations in the angular gyrus region. Shared and parallel processes may allow for flexibility to facilitate neuroanatomical reorganization or accessing alternative pathways of function in case of focal brain lesions. Studies have repeatedly shown the somewhat counterintuitive notion that the production of words while singing is unaffected in the presence of disturbed speech. Much of the prevalent rationale for the causative mechanisms of melodic intonation therapy is built on the concept of *differential neurologic processing.*

2. *Rhythm and timing.* The effects of auditory rhythm on speech rhythms, fluency, rate control, intelligibility, articulatory control, and respiratory function are clearly documented for a variety of clinical applications, such as rhythmic speech cuing, vocal intonation therapy, and oral motor and respiratory exercises with a wide range of clinical populations, including those with apraxia, dysarthria, or fluency disorders.

3. *Commonalities between speech production and vocal production in music.* Therapeutic exercises using singing and other forms of vocal intonation, as well as the support of musical accompaniment, have been reported to strengthen the respiratory system, remediate voice disorders, reduce dysfluencies, and improve articulatory deficiencies. The shared modality of aural communication allows for transfer effects of therapeutic exercises using music to enhance therapeutic goals in speech production.

4. *Auditory-based communication systems.* The linguistic components in speech regarding phonology, prosody, syntax, and pragmatics all have counterparts in musical structures. The major difference arises in the referential semantics of language, which is not shared by music. Music can acquire referential meaning—an associative learning process through which music can refer to some nonmusical event, person, or experience—but the sound patterns of musical language initially communicate their meaning through the relationship between the elements of the patterns themselves. For example, notes of a melody have meaning by referring to each other to create a good sound gestalt, such as a well-shaped melody. However, the perception of good musical patterns evokes feelings and thoughts, and consequently those musical patterns can be used to communicate those thoughts and feelings to somebody else, through playing and listening. In that sense, music becomes a symbol-based language allowing the creation of communicative gestures (e.g., in call-and-response or question-and-answer patterns), engaging in dialogues, experiencing and expressing feelings and thoughts, listening to somebody else's communication messages, working together to shape the communication of a common message, or modulating one's own state of feelings and thoughts based on an exchange of messages. Thus, through these shared language processes of the two communication systems, music has been used successfully to enhance and facilitate speech and language development.

4.4 Studies in Cognitive Rehabilitation

Recognizing the importance of temporal organization in cognitive functions, new frontiers in biomedical music research are studying the effect of music and rhythm on critical aspects of timing in learning, attention, executive function, and memory. This aspect of biomedical research was not studied well in the past, possibly because of several problems in conceptualizing the role of music in cognitive functions in a remedial function. The strong reliance in the early and still prevalent understanding of music as a therapeutic tool on fairly global concepts of well-being created an intuitive, exclusive, and often unquestioned emphasis on emotional components in the therapeutic music experience. This reliance led directly to a neglect of other areas of cognition that could be considered important in music therapy. Furthermore, within this model, it is difficult to clearly develop concepts of how music can access and enhance specific cognitive functions unrelated to emotion in a therapeutic setting.

The other factor that had slowed this research was the difficulty of conducting cognitive brain research before the advent of noninvasive research tools to study the human brain in vivo. Brain imaging techniques did not develop fully until approximately between 1985 and 1990, and were slow to become available to musical brain research. Today's wide availability of brain-imaging equipment, together with the considerable refinement in brain-wave measurement techniques via EEG and MEG, has produced a new basis for biomedical research in music cognition.

In recent years, a growing body of research has emerged that sheds new light on intriguing links between music and a variety of cognitive functions, including temporal order learning (Hitch et al. 1996), spatiotemporal reasoning (Sarntheim et al. 1997), and attention (Drake et al. 2000; Large and Jones 1999). The relationship between music and memory is also increasingly well documented (e.g., Deutsch 1982; Glassman 1999; Kilgour et al. 2000).

An examination of music cognition research in the areas of attention and memory illuminates some important points for biomedical theories of how music can access remediation cognitive functions. A large and consistent body of research in musical attention has elucidated the role of rhythm in tuning and modulating attention in music (e.g., Riess Jones et al. 1982; Riess Jones and Ralston 1991; Riess Jones et al. 1992; Klein and Riess Jones 1996; Drake et al. 2000). In this view, rhythmic patterns drive attention focus by interacting with attention oscillators via coupling mechanisms. Bonnel et al. (2001) found evidence for divided attention mechanisms in song between processing of lyrics and processing of music. Deutsch (1982) laid out some of the fundamental organizational processes for memory formation in music, based on the structural principles of phrasing, grouping, and hierarchical abstraction in musical patterns, similar to temporal chunking principles in memory formation.

Much of this basic research points to shared principles for mechanisms in music that drive cognitive process, such as attention and memory, and equivalent processes in nonmusical cognition. One of the most important causative mechanisms underlying these principles refers to rhythm as a temporal structuring and patterning process in perception and learning (Jakobson et al. 2003; Janata et al. 2002). Memory formation in music, as an example, goes beyond mere recognition to include the specific recall of a song's melodic and rhythmic structure, as well as its lyrics (Cook 1999). Through use of such data and models as a starting point, logical hypotheses can be pursued in clinical research transferring learning and perception in music to nonmusical rehabilitative processes. Some of the ensuing research questions were formulated in this way. For example, could musical chunking be used as a carrier to enhance and rehabilitate verbal memory? Could attention training in music enhance auditory attention control in nonmu-sical contexts?

A number of studies have shown that music can serve as an effective mnemonic device to facilitate verbal learning and recall in healthy persons, patients with memory disorders, and children with learning disabilities (e.g., Gfeller 1983; Wolfe and Hom 1993; Wallace 1994; Maeller 1996; Claussen and Thaut 1997). Proposed mechanisms for this effect center on mnemonic models in which music provides a temporal-metrical structure and redundancy that chunk information into more manageable units. Chunking is a helpful mechanism not only in declarative learning and recall, but also in motor learning (Verwey 2001). Indeed, chunking is prob-ably an innate feature across a broad phylogenetic range of nervous systems (Matzel et al. 1988). Thus, researchers believe that the intrinsic structure of sound patterns in music is a highly effective mechanism to facilitate perceptual grouping and chunking (e.g., via metrical organization).

For a simple illustration of the influence of music as a mnemonic device, we may think of the ABC song in which a child learns to sing a song with the letters of the alphabet as the lyrics. The melody and melodic–rhyth-mic phrases serve as the organizing element of chunking, breaking down the string of letters into smaller units coded in identifiable strings by the melodic and rhythmic contour of the song. Chunking or grouping, a critical element in memory coding, is always present in all music as a necessary component to build musical forms through melodic, har-monic, and rhythmic phrasing (Wolfe and Hom 1993). Therefore, music can function as an excellent memory template to organize verbal materi-als during nonmusical declarative or procedural learning (Wallace 1994).

Many clinical reports have emphasized the relative survival of musical memories as part of the cognitive functions in neurologic memory disor-ders (Baur et al. 2000; Haslam and Cook 2002; Halpern and O'Connor, 2000) as well as dementia and Alzheimer's disease (AD) (Crystal et al. 1989; Foster and Valentine 2001; Son et al. 2002). That this function may extend to new auditory-motor memory formation in music was proposed in a recent case study of a violinist diagnosed with AD and profound anterograde and retrograde memory deficits who not only continued to perform familiar music, but also learned to play a new, unfamiliar piece (Cowles et al. 2003).

These studies also report that accessing musical memories provides a gateway for enhanced verbal nonmusical recall and knowledge, thus making musical memory training a tool in enhancing cognitive func-tions in patients (Rainey and Larsen 2002). It is unclear why musical memories often appear to stay more intact or accessible to recall than nonmusical memories in disorders affecting memory functions.

The temporal structure in a highly patterned sensory language may facilitate overlearning. The affective context in which most musical materials are learned may also contribute to more resilient memory functions, since emotional context enhances learning and recall. It is also well known that positive mood states enhance memory function. The access that musical memories provide to triggering nonmusical (e.g., verbal or autobiographical) materials is most likely based on strong associative learning mechanisms, which involve music as a highly salient conditioning stimulus.

In this context, potentially very important findings have recently been provided that show that enhanced short-term memory functioning in patients with Alzheimer's disease activated a network of prefrontal-amygdala connections, while healthy subjects typically activated prefrontal-hippocampal networks (Grady et al. 2001; Rosenbaum et al. 2004). Since amygdala functions are highly implicated in processing emotional stimuli, emotional context and saliency of memory processing may enhance residual memory functions in Alzheimer's disease. This shift in neuroanatomical network activation underlying memory operations in the brain may suggest that presenting information within a musical context—as a highly salient emotional stimulus—may facilitate short-term memory functions in dementia. It may also provide some clues why musical memories in disorders like Alzheimer's disease seem to survive intact for longer periods of time in the face of severe cognitive deterioration (Crystal et al. 1989; Halpern and O'Connor, 2000; Jensen et al. 2004).

Beneficial long-term training effects of music on verbal auditory memory have been reported by Chan et al. (1998) and Ho (2003). More research is needed to determine, based on a larger database, if such long-term transfer of music training on nonmusical functions can be substantiated. This is an intriguing yet open-ended question, in respect not only to memory, but also to other cognitive skills, such as verbal skills and visuospatial reasoning (Schellenberg 2001; Costa-Giomi 2003).

Clinical attention research in music has shown evidence for therapeutic efficacy in selected areas. However, more systematic and in-depth approaches are necessary to develop a more comprehensive database. The models provided by basic science in music cognition offer valuable departure points. Evidence for rhythmical attention control may have strong implications for a better understanding of temporal entrainment of attention function by music and rhythm. Improvement in rhythmic finger tapping exercises to practice sustained attention has been shown to be significantly correlated with other cognitive functions such as memory, executive functions such as reasoning, and psychosocial as well as basic psychomotor skills (Ben Yishay et al. 1980, 1987). Evidence and clinical applications for arousal-based attention training using structured auditory stimulation such as music have been presented and reviewed by Parenté and Herrmann (1996). Techniques in that area focus on stages of basic arousal, orientation, vigilance, attention maintenance, and higher level of attention, integrating discrimination and working memory. Evidence for the efficacy of undifferentiated attention training through music has been provided by Morton et al. (1990) and Gregory (2002).

Preliminary evidence for the temporal entrainment of attention in autistic children has been reported by Thaut and Mahraun (2004). In their study, autistic children performed significantly better on a sustained attention task (card matching) while listening to music or rhythm patterns compared with no music. Interesting correlations emerged in the music and the rhythm conditions between speed of task completion, number of errors, and off-task behaviors such as self-stimulation and eye gaze away from the task. Speed of task and number of errors were inversely correlated: As task speed increased, the number of errors decreased. Such inverse correlation is the opposite of what would be expected on the basis of some psychological theories (e.g., Fitts's Law). In such theories, one predicts a trade-off between speed and accuracy: An increase in speed is usually accompanied by a decrease in task accuracy. During faster task completion, the incidence of inappropriate behavior also decreased. This research may provide some initial and very preliminary clues as to why music and rhythm provided better attention in the autistic children. Because the correlation analysis points to positive changes in task performance being related to change in performance timing, we may hypothesize that music and rhythm—although not directly related to the sustained attention task—may have provided temporal order in the perception process of the autistic children, creating a sensory structure on which they could map their attentional performance rhythm.

Very interesting data was provided by Hommel (1990) on the beneficial effect of musical stimulation for overcoming visual neglect as a result of right hemispheric lesions due to stroke or traumatic brain injury. Music stimuli were superior to other sensory and cognitive cues, such as instructions and speech or tactile cues. The researchers' rationale focused on the well-documented specific arousal effect of music on the right brain hemisphere that is lesioned in visual neglect states. This rationale would also be well supported by the theoretically established link between arousal and neglect in general, which has also been confirmed by research data. Robertson et al. (1998) have shown that unilateral neglect can be dramatically altered by changing the functioning of the brain's arousal system, and have used these findings to develop other arousal-based neglect training techniques (Robertson et al. 1995). Frassinetti et al. (2002a, 2002b) have also shown that auditory stimuli can enhance visual perception in neglect states. However, their data point to multisensory neuronal integration as an explanatory rationale rather than generalized arousal. These examples provide another good illustration of how a neuroscience-guided understanding of auditory and music perception can lead to a profound new understanding of the role of music and sound in neurologic rehabilitation.

A number of studies have researched the evidence for special musical responsiveness and music's role in cognitive and perceptual remediation in autistic children. Evidence that, in autistic children, high musical ability can be present concomitant with low functioning in other cognitive areas has been documented in many studies (e.g., Mottron et al. 2000; Heaton et al. 1988, 2001; Heaton 2003; Hermelin et al. 1997). Evidence for a facilitation effect of musical exercises on executive functions, memory, and affective reasoning as well as psychosocial functions has been provided by Hermelin et al. (1989), Thaut (1988), Wimpory et al. (1995), Heaton et al. (1999), and Ma et al. (2001). The benefit of listening to structured music to enhance a broad range of cognitive measures in autistic children was reported by Bettison (1996). However, the absence of a control group in Bettison's study makes a conclusive interpretation of the data difficult.

4.5 Timing in Music and Timing in the Brain

To extend an understanding of the theoretical underpinnings of music in cognitive rehabilitation further, a brief refocusing on very important components in music perception may be useful. The current scientific model searches for therapeutic mechanisms of music by studying if and how music stimulates and engages parallel or shared nonmusical brain function in cognition, motor control, and emotion (Thaut 2000). For example, rhythmicity is a universal function in the control of movement, and thus can be effectively accessed and regulated through music in patients with neurological movement disorders. Temporal organization and appropriate arousal—universally important functions in perception, attention, memory, and executive function—can be modulated by music in patients with, for example, dementia or traumatic brain injury.

In a second step, by building analogies between neuroscience, acoustics, the elements of music, and aesthetics, we may propose that music, written in the time code of rhythm, which creates meaningful sound patterns in time, simulates or resembles the oscillatory rhythmic synchronization codes of neural information processing in the brain, thus becoming a powerful stimulus to communicate sensory and cognitive-perceptual information to the brain (Merzenich et al. 1993). To put it simply, music may be a language the brain can read with ease because its temporal-based grammar is fundamental to how the brain processes information.

To extend this point further, music is not only sequentially, or horizontally, patterned in time. The spectral nature of sound extends the temporal organization of precise and complex time patterns of sound waves into all aspects of sound production and perception. The simultaneities and sequentialities of pitch, timbre, melody, polyphony, and harmony—based on physical oscillatory vibration patterns transduced into oscillatory electrochemical activation patterns of neurons and neuron ensembles—make music a temporally overstructured and spectrally diverse machinery of rhythms.

Neurophysiological studies have shown that music can arouse and excite the spinal motor neurons mediated by auditory-motor connections at the brain stem and spinal cord levels (Rossignol and Melvill Jones 1976). This priming effect sets the motor system in the brain in a state of readiness, facilitating the execution of movements. However, rhythmic sounds also entrain the timing of the muscle activity, thereby providing a physiological template for cuing the timing of movements. Patients with neurological movement disorders can benefit from this effect of music and rhythm to retrain their motor functions, as many research studies have shown. Thus, music provides a stimulus that substitutes for compromised internal functions, accesses compensatory networks in the brain, and may help build new pathways, thus shaping the plasticity of the brain. The rhythmic patterns of music can help patients with Parkinson's disease overcome extreme slowness and episodes of freezing of movement because the music acts as a sensory sequencer that provides critical neural movement command signals that are not generated reliably in time by brain areas affected by the disease (Hausdorff et al. 2003; Thaut et al. 2001).

Studies involving memory disorders, such as Alzheimer's disease, frequently show patients' retention of musical information longer and out of proportion to their concurrent state of nonmusical memory loss (Cowles et al. 2003). Such data suggest that neuronal memory traces built through music may be deeply ingrained and more resilient to neurodegenerative influences (Foster and Valentine 2001; Haslam and Cook 2002). The organizational basis of music as a temporally overstructured language of sound patterns may play a critical role in such effective memory formation (Deutsch 1982). Recent research has shown that neuronal oscillations, which build rhythmically synchronized firing patterns in network ensembles of neurons, form the neurobiological basis of perception and learning. The precise synchronization of neuronal activation patterns is a crucial element in building the tightly coupled networks that physiologically underlie the process of effective learning (Klimesch et al. 1998). Thus, music's temporality, expressed in its rhythmic nature, may optimize the formation of these rhythmic neuronal networks because music, the learning stimulus that drives the physiological activations in the brain, is already tightly organized within temporal structures.

A brief excursion into the role of temporal information processing in the brain relative to learning may illustrate the parallels in more detail (Merzenich 1993). During learning, cortical networks of neurons generate a progressively more temporally coherent distributed representation of neuronal responses. During performance of an unlearned task, the distributed responses of the neurons that are activated are relatively temporally dispersed. In other words, neurons in a given network that is involved in the learning task fire in a relatively asynchronous, temporally poorly aligned manner. However, with training they quickly align temporally to generate a progressively more coherent distributed response (i.e., firing) pattern in the neuronal ensemble within the network. Several other consequences are associated with this process. The learning process becomes associated with a salient neuronal response signal progressively earlier in time. And, as coherence or synchronization grows in temporal precision through training, the representation of a specific learning input becomes progressively less confusable with other learning stimuli and finer distinctions between sequences of stimuli can be made.

Thinking of the brain as a large orchestra whose individual players are individual neurons and whose different instrumental sections (strings, winds, brass) are networks or subensembles of neurons in the total orchestra, we may compare the learning process to the rehearsal process of an orchestra that tunes itself into finer and finer patterns of coherence and precision through rhythm and synchronization. In this analogy, the conductor who shapes the temporal dynamics of the orchestra represents the training stimulus that drives cortical response networks into temporally synchronized units and subunits. However, the analogy makes it clear that the conductor (the stimulus), in order to create optimal temporal coherence, must operate on an underlying consistent— yet adaptable—beat or clock function.

Without diverging too much into basic perceptual neuroscience, it can be said that the brain has several intrinsic oscillators (e.g., thalamic oscillators) that assume this clock function. However, the progressively faster development of response coherence in synchronized neuronal ensembles is a result of effective learning strategies or learning stimuli, and not the other way around. Furthermore, there is now fascinating evidence that learning drives network formation and reorganization, leading to remodeled or emergent new cell assemblies. New learning inputs can strengthen positive coupling of neurons, resulting in formation of new cell ensembles. This is the process underlying what is frequently called brain plasticity.

Given about 1 trillion neurons in the brain, even within the constraints of its neuroanatomical architecture (e.g., not every neuron can interact directly with any other neuron axonally), the combinatorial possibilities of new network formation appear mathematically almost infinite. Adding a time axis for temporal segmentation of neuronal ensemble responses of course increases the combinatorial possibilities exponentially. Plasticity issues obviously have great relevance for learning and training models in neurologic rehabilitation, providing a model for how function can be recovered through cortical network reorganization.

In this context, the question of the clock or conductor function in stimuli for effective learning and training modalities presents itself in a new light, posing two important questions:

1. Could a well-time-regulated learning process function as temporal conductor template and progressively generate a more coherent neuronal ensemble network in a faster and synaptically stronger manner, resulting in a more stable behavioral learning response? This postulate is derived from Hebb's (1949) groundbreaking work on the effect of learning on changes in synaptic input functions and the shaping of neuronal network formation.

2. Could the temporal structure of rhythm and music effectively operate as an external sensory clock or carrier wave function to enhance internal clock functions in the physiology of the learning process, especially in a system compromised by neurological dysfunction and the presence of lesions? In other words, and considerably oversimplified in expression, can the clock function in a musically rhythmic learning stimulus (e.g., a nonmusical motor task or a cognitive-perceptual task that is embedded in a musical-rhythmic structure) drive a more optimal formation of new coupled neuronal cell assemblies that would be associated with a better learning response?

These theoretical questions apply not just to cognitive learning, but also to motor therapy and speech and language training. The behavioral evidence to suggest a critical role for music and rhythm is quite strong. Some physiological evidence, from electromyography, brain-wave research, and brain imaging, provides at least preliminary support for these ideas. The entrainment of timing and amplitude of muscle activation patterns, the changes in the auditory field potential during the perception of tempo changes in rhythm, and the changes in reorganization of motor cortex representations as a result of intense rhythmic paretic arm keyboard training all point to the strong possibility of these mechanisms underlying music and rhythm's role in learning and training.

We measured short-term plasticity associated with learning verbal information (word lists) via auditory spoken presentation or sung presentation in healthy persons and persons with multiple sclerosis (Thaut and Peterson 2003; Peterson et al. 2004). The behavioral data in the particular design did not show a difference in improvement between spoken and sung modalities. However, topographical maps of brain-wave activations showed very differently distributed neural activation networks in the two conditions, especially in the slow theta frequencies (4–8 Hz), the alpha band frequencies (alpha 1 = 8 Hz; alpha 3 = 12 Hz), and the fast gamma oscillations associated with learning (>30 Hz). A change in learning modality (spoken versus sung) led to a change in neural synchronization strength and in reconfiguring the underlying brain networks that became activated. The same behavioral results were driven by differentially organized networks in the brain, contingent upon the learning modality employed.

These investigations are ongoing and just the beginning of potentially fascinating inquiries into how the rhythmic information processing machinery of the brain interacts with rhythm and music in sound. What makes this research even more intriguing in many ways is the potential for the development of increasingly more effective learning and training strategies and stimuli using music and rhythm. Strong indicators of a new role for and a new model of music and rhythm in therapy and medicine have been shown in clinical research since about 1990.

4.6 A Working Model of Mechanisms

A large number of clinical studies have shown, in great depth and breadth, striking evidence that auditory rhythm and music can be effectively harnessed for specific therapeutic purposes in the rehabilitation of patients with various neuropathologies. These findings further underscore the complex ways in which music engages and communicates to the human brain and in which the brain that engages in music can be—even in states of brain injury—changed through this process.

An analysis of the research literature allows for the development of a preliminary working model that groups into separate clusters or nodes the emerging evidence for specific mechanisms of music as a rehabilitative stimulus. This is not a model that allows for testable mathematical simulations of real data. It is simply a model that summarizes evidence into shared principles and mechanisms as a step toward a clearer understanding of the biomedical properties embedded in music perception. It is also important to remember that in a complex system such as the brain, these putative mechanisms cannot be considered as working linearly in a mutually exclusive manner. They interact, have overlaps and mutual contingencies, and may simply point to other underlying operating mechanisms. However, for heuristic reasons they may present the best available starting point.

A preliminary proposal would suggest that four such mechanisms underlie rationales for biomedical applications of music and rhythm:

1. *Rhythmic stimulation and entrainment.* Much research and clinical evidence shows that rhythmic stimulation has profound effects as coordinative sensory input to entrain timing functions, especially in motor control and speech. Rhythm provides temporal structure through metrical organization, predictability, and patterning. Rhythm regulates physiological and behavioral functions via entrainment mechanisms. Rhythmic entrainment provides immediate time regulation but also can be accessed to enhance long-term training effects. Temporal regulation not only affects timing issues but also provides templates for optimization of spatial and force dynamics.

2. *Patterned information processing.* Timing is a key component in neural information processing in regard to perception and learning (cf. Galaretta et al. 2001). Rhythm and synchronization are critical parameters in this processing, creating temporal structure in neural network activation (cf. Ikegaya et al. 2004; Fries et al. 2001). Time cues in the objects and stimuli of perception and learning themselves may be important facilitators to enhance the underlying physiology of temporal pattern formation, thus enhancing critical aspects of cognitive processes (cf. Lee and Blake 1999). Music is a very complex temporal stimulus. In all dimensions of its temporal architecture—from the spectral patterns of its psychoacoustical foundations to the most complex compositional principles of rhythm and polyphony—we find pattern structures of timing and synchronization embedded as building principles. Research suggests that music can uniquely engage the brain as a language of time, providing temporal structure to enhance learning and perception, especially in the areas of cognition, language, and motor learning.

3. *Differential neurological processing.* The neuroanatomy and neurophysiology of music processing show shared, parallel, and distinct neural processing systems relative to nonmusical functions. For example, speech and singing are mediated by different neural networks. Music regulates attention and arousal in the brain in a complex, bilaterally distributed fashion (Coull et al. 2004). Learning

verbal material through song accesses different neural network configurations than learning through verbal presentation (Thaut and Petersen 2003). Auditory rhythm is a powerful sensory cue that can regulate motor timing and coordination in the presence of a deficient internal timing system in the brain. These are examples of how music can be used as an alternative modality to access functions or provide alternative transmission routes for information processing in the brain.

4. *Affective-aesthetic response: Arousal, motivation, emotion.* Music communicates emotion and meaning through the perception of its intrinsic symbol structure of musical elements as well as through emotional responses that have become connected to it through an associative learning process (Meyer 1956; Berlyne 1971). Many theories of the meaning of music actually see the primary purpose of music as expressing and representing emotions and feelings. Regardless of its precise nature, music is a powerful stimulus that induces emotions. As such, it has a strong influence on affective states. Arousal, motivation, and emotion have important regulatory functions in behavior organization, behavior change, and learning. Attention, perception, memory, executive function, physical response, and learning can all be effectively influenced and enhanced by appropriate affective states.

5

Rhythm-driven Optimization of Motor Control

GARY P. KENYON AND MICHAEL H. THAUT

5.1 Introduction

In this chapter, we will present a mathematical model to show how the temporal structure of auditory rhythm can be used as a physiological template to cue the control of movement. We will present research into mechanisms by which the brain and nervous system might utilize temporally perceived information to regulate the planning and execution of movement. In particular, (1) an optimality criterion is presented that is derived from the constraint that a movement's peak absolute acceleration is minimized, and (2) a mathematical model, based on recursion, is presented that accurately reproduces characteristic features of movement reported in previous research. In each case, it is shown that the *period* of both the stimulus and the movement dominates temporal correction of isochronous, metronome-driven movement, and that the application of a rhythmic driver shapes movement over the entire movement trajectory, rather than merely at movement extremes, where attempted synchronization with the rhythmic stimulus occurs.

This chapter is fairly technical in nature, at times using mathematical nomenclature and requiring basic knowledge of biomechanics and differential equations. However, the interested reader can skip the heavy parts of the text without losing track of the basic concept: how musical rhythm can modulate motor performance and become an effective entrainment stimulus for motor control by accessing auditory-motor integration processes in the brain. These entrainment processes are crucial for motor performance of musicians, as well as for biomedical applications of music and rhythm in sensorimotor rehabilitation. The effect of timing on the brain through rhythm is profound and deeply fascinating. In spite of its technical nature, we have included this chapter in order to present a complete picture of how music and rhythm affect brain and behavior in very complex and previously unknown ways.

5.2 Three Movement Scenarios

5.2.1 Goal-Directed Movement

Our overall objective is to describe how rhythm can be used to regulate human movement and to make that movement more efficient and more precise. But before we can commence, we need to agree on the meanings of the terms that are used to describe human movement. For example, what does it mean to make movement more efficient, or smoother, or more precise? And why might we want to meet any of these objectives?

Suppose, for example, that the physical movement under investigation is throwing a ball. This is by no means an artificial example, since the act of throwing has been studied in great detail (Fleisig et al. 1996; Wilk et al. 2000; Elliott et al.1988; Feltner and Dapena 1986). Furthermore, let us suppose that it is required to get the ball from point A to point B in the least possible time. These two conditions together (throw from A to B, and in minimum time) constitute a *performance objective*. We have defined a problem in human movement: How can you use your body, your human physical apparatus, in such a way as to meet your performance objective, given your physical resources?

Of course, we do not have to limit these tasks to throwing. There are an infinite number of other situations in which a person must interact physically with his or her environment to meet a certain performance objective: playing the three-octave scale in Chopin's A-flat Polonaise on the piano (fast enough to maintain tempo), serving a tennis ball (quite similar to the throwing motion), running a 400 meter race on the track, sweeping a floor, driving a car, paddling a canoe, bowling, skateboarding, drawing and painting, dancing, or eating. Each of these activities can be associated with a performance objective.

An additional complication can result when the person attempting to meet a performance objective has some form of physical limitation, such as damage to the central nervous system resulting from stroke or Parkinson's disease, reduction in muscle strength resulting from disuse, or joint pain from arthritis. However, in all cases the performance objective is most likely to be met through an effective use of the body's available resources.

But what do we mean by the term *effective* as used in this context? Throwing a ball well is the result of a complex sequence of precisely timed muscle contractions. If you already know how to throw a ball, all you have to do to realize the precision required for the successful execution of this sequence is to try to throw with your *other* hand. For a more universal example, consider that walking upright on two feet is a performance objective that took quite an effort to learn and refine.

What is this sequence of muscle contractions that results in a good throw? The interaction with the environment begins where the feet contact the earth. The body weight is primarily on the back foot (the right foot if you are throwing with your right hand), and it shifts to the front foot. This weight shift, resulting from contraction of the big muscles connected to the femur, is the main energy driver for the throwing action. But while this weight shift is taking place, at precisely the right moment a hip rotation is initiated: The right hip rotates in the direction of the target. This hip rotation results in a torsion of the spine (i.e., a twisting about the axis of the spine, a line going roughly through the centers of the vertebrae from tailbone to the back of your neck). Now, given all the muscles attached to the spine, the spine acts as a torsion spring; it gets wound up by the hip rotation, and then unwinds and transfers energy to the shoulders. The shoulders then rotate, with the right shoulder moving toward the intended target. And if the shoulder moves, the right arm also must move. The right pectoralis muscle contracts, driving the upper arm toward the target. Then the right triceps muscle contracts, causing the right elbow joint to extend (straighten out), which moves the right wrist toward the target. Then the flexor muscles of the hand and wrist contract, causing flexion at the wrist joint. Then the fingers release the ball and it is on its way to the intended target.

Notice a few things about this sequence of muscle contractions:

1. At each successive step of the sequence, a less massive body part was involved: legs, hips, shoulders, upper arm, lower arm, and hand.
2. At each successive step of the sequence, the velocity of the ball (held in the hand) increased.
3. For best results, each successive muscle-group contraction must be initiated and forcefully executed at exactly the right point in time. What do we mean by best results? The ball is released from point A at the correct angle, and with the greatest possible velocity, to arrive at point B in the minimum amount of time.

With this example, we have elaborated the basic elements of a rhythm-driven optimization problem: a performance objective is well defined, relative to the external environment; the performance objective is most effectively met by means of a sequence of contractions of specific muscle groups; and each contraction must be precisely timed in terms of its initiation and application of force. And, as we know, precise timing (an exact temporal distribution of events) and rhythm go hand in hand.

5.2.2 Rhythmic Movement

Now that we have a concept of what it means to optimize a goal-directed movement, let's focus on a class of movements with a distinguishing characteristic: They are regularly repeated in time. As an example, we will analyze a movement that most of us engage in from time to time: walking.

Learning to walk skillfully (optimally) required a period of study and practice that extended over many months. The first subskill to be mastered was that of balancing on two feet while maintaining a vertical posture. Then came the first step forward; this involved, quite literally, a leap of faith, because falling forward is involved in making the weight shift necessary to transfer balance from the back foot to the front foot. Over time, the skill required to link several steps together was developed, and this skill was refined over a period of many years as our bodies reached physical maturity. By that point in time, the entire process became more or less automatic, and was unique to every individual. Corresponding to this unique program is its unique expression—the way an individual uses his or her body for locomotion—which, in many cases, may allow us to identify a walking person from a great distance, without any other perceptible cues.

And what makes this skill different from throwing a ball? It's intrinsically cyclically rhythmic! If we examine EMG recordings of activity from the muscle groups involved in walking, we not only find a specific sequence of muscle activations in time, but also that these activations are repeated in time, as successive steps are taken. This is where the rhythm comes in.

Suppose you have a small, credit-card-size metronome hanging from your neck on a small chain, and that the metronome is set at 120 clicks per minute. You begin walking in time with the metronome; every time the metronome clicks, you take a step. More specifically, every time the metronome clicks, you contact the surface you are walking on with your heel—alternating, of course, between your right and left heels. Thus, not only are you regulating your movement, you are also regulating the timing of the sequence of muscle contractions that produce the movement. The clicks from the metronome become input to your auditory system, and then to your motor system, to produce the physiological events that result in a steady gait. The rhythmic output from the metronome results in rhythmic output from the motor system, and a necessary consequence is that the sequence of muscle contractions required for walking is also produced rhythmically. In short, rhythm in equals rhythm out.

5.2.3 Rhythm-Modulated Movement

Within the context of rehabilitation, a major focus in research involving the kinematic analysis of human movement has focused on the lower extremities. In particular, this has been the case at the Center for Biomedical Research in Music, where studies dating back to 1993 have resulted in over thirty publications regarding the use of a rhythmic stimulus as a central nervous system driver to aid in the remediation of movement deficits typically resulting from stroke or Parkinson's disease. The rhythmic stimulus can be presented as a simple metronome click or, as is usual in the rehabilitation context, as music with a dominant beat that drives the movement. Subjects in rehabilitation studies involving gait use portable cassette players and headphones to deliver the taped musical/rhythmic stimulus. The tempo of the music is adjusted to accommodate the subject's baseline gait capabilities and then incrementally increased as gait performance improves.

In recent years, after convincingly establishing the therapeutic benefits of rhythmic facilitation in gait rehabilitation (Prassas et al. 1997; Thaut et al. 1997; Miller et al. 1996; Thaut and McIntosh 1999; Thaut et al. 1999; Thaut et al. 1996; Kenyon and Thaut 2000), the focus of our research has moved toward the application of rhythm to the regulation of upper-extremity movement. This represents a fundamental change in the neurological context of the movement. Gait is thought to be (partially) regulated at the level of the brain stem and spinal cord, in neural circuits called *central pattern generators* (CPGs). This circuitry is inherited, not learned (Marieb 1989). The upper extremities, in contrast, most likely have no such regulation imposed upon their output. Thus the study of rhythm-driven upper extremity movement offers the possibility of providing fresh insight not only into the mechanisms by which movement deficits might be rehabilitated, but also into the basic processes by which the brain and central nervous system (CNS) regulate all movement. In the absence of output constraints of the CPGs, a fundamentally different movement scenario is accessible for study.

In availing ourselves of this opportunity, we have investigated (and are continuing to investigate) two different movement scenarios: (1) alternate tapping of two spatially separated targets, driven by a steady metronome beat, performed by stroke patients using the paretic arm; (2) alternate tapping of two targets, performed by subjects with no movement impairment, in which the metronome stimulus was varied by inserting a step change into an otherwise isochronous stimulus sequence. These two scenarios will be discussed in detail, but it is worthwhile to mention here the general purpose of each study. Study 1 was designed to investigate the short-term (immediate rather than rehabilitative) ability of a rhythmic driver to regulate movement that has been compromised by stroke, at the level of the entire arm. Study 2 was designed to investigate the adaptation of the (uncompromised) response to a steady rhythmic driver that was reset (period changed by 2 percent). This was primarily intended to increase our understanding of the neural control of movement at the level of the brain. The results of these two studies have allowed us to draw specific conclusions regarding the rehabilitative uses of rhythm as applied to upper-extremity movement deficits resulting from stroke, and the ability of the brain and CNS to respond motorically to both a steady rhythm and changes in rhythm.

Elaborations of these two studies follow, along with mathematical models that offer possible explanations for how the brain might use rhythm to optimize or improve motor output, and what parameters inherent in the rhythm-synchronization process might be dominant in achieving synchronization.

5.3 Two Studies of Rhythm-driven Arm Movement

Each of the two investigations involved an upper-extremity reaching task in which the subjects made alternate hand contact with two targets arranged on a table surface in an approximately sagittal plane (not a midsagittal plane, but a sagittal plane passing through the shoulder joint). There are several features common to both studies. Subjects selected their own target positions to accommodate their particular preferred range of motion and anatomical geometry, and also selected their own baseline movement frequency. Subjects were seated at the table surface, and made alternate contact with the near and far targets under two conditions: with and without a rhythmic stimulus supplied by a metronome. A reference coordinate system was set up so that the x-axis was in the midsagittal plane and on the table surface, the y-axis was in a transverse plane and on the table surface, and the z-axis was directed upward and perpendicular to the table surface. In study 1, each trial lasted for 30 seconds. In study 2, each trial lasted for 56 movement cycles. The major differences between the two experiments involved the nature of the subject pool and the temporal characteristics of the stimulus sequence.

5.3.1 Study 1: Upper Extremity Entrainment in Stroke Patients

Ten stroke patients performed the target contact task using their paretic arm (Thaut, Kenyon and Hurt et al. 2002a). The metronome provided a constant-period (isochronous) stimulus that was matched to their self-selected preferred movement frequency. This experiment was designed to answer the following questions:

1. Can a rhythmic driver decrease the spatial variability of the arm movement?
2. Can a rhythmic driver decrease the temporal variability of the arm movement?

The data consisted of the 3-D spatial coordinates of a wrist marker attached to the paretic arm, obtained through software analysis of video-taped movement records. The data were further organized into a consecutive series of trajectories, with each trajectory defined by a movement from one target to the other. One complete movement cycle consisted of two trajectories, one from the near target to the far target, involving elbow joint extension, and the other from the far target back to the near target, requiring elbow joint flexion.

Question 1, regarding spatial variability, was approached by writing software that used the 3-D coordinates of the wrist marker as input. This software calculated the position of a vertical midplane for each subject. This plane bisected, and was perpendicular to, the line segment connecting the two targets. For each trajectory, the point of intersection with the midplane was determined. For a given trial, this resulted in a set of intersection points of the wrist marker with the midplane, one point for each trajectory. Such intersections occurred at the middle of the trajectory, where spatial variability of the trajectory in the y-z plane would be expected to be maximal.

Thus the distribution of points in the midplane was an indicator of the spatial variability of a subject's sequence of trajectories for a given trial. A typical result for one subject is shown in figure 1, where the self-paced trial is on the right and the metronome-driven trial is on the left. The points marked with an "×" were generated by elbow joint extension, and those marked with a "+" were generated by elbow joint flexion. The points that are enclosed in a circle are the corresponding means of the points of intersection of the wrist marker with the midplane.

A visual comparison of the two graphs provides the following conclusions for the metronome-driven trial, compared with the self-paced trial:

- Overall spatial variability decreased.

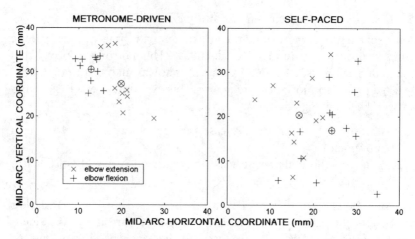

Fig. 5.1 The spatial distribution of the trajectories at mid-arc, in a plane perpendicular to, and bisecting, the line segment connecting the two targets.

- The grouping of extension points and the grouping of flexion points became more distinct from one another.
- The locations of the mean positions for each group (flexion and extension) were reversed, relative to each other.
- The metronome-driven responses tended to be higher (have a larger vertical coordinate) than the self-paced responses.

The groupings for flexion and extension are not surprising because different muscle groups drive the two movements.

A static measure of pattern coherence was also used, by calculating the average distance from the midplane location of the trajectory mean of all the points in the pattern, then averaging over the entire group of subjects. Using this measure, spatial variability decreased by 40.5 percent under the influence of the rhythmic driver.

Variability in movement period was quantified using the coefficient of variation (CV), which is defined as the standard deviation divided by the mean, multiplied by 100, and expressed as a percent. The use of this statistic allowed comparisons of variability for movements occurring at different tempos. Movement *period* is defined as the time interval between successive target contacts. Without the metronome stimulus the CV was 20 percent, and with the metronome stimulus it was 13 percent, a reduction in variability of 35 percent.

This study clearly indicates that under the influence of a rhythmic driver, not only did temporal variability of the responses decrease (as might be expected), but the spatial variability of the trajectories of the entire trial also decreased. The imposition of a temporal constraint upon the movement had the effect of regulating the movement not only in time, but also in space.

5.3.2 Study 2: Adaptation to a Subliminal Period Shift

Ten music students served as subjects (Thaut and Kenyon 2003). The metronome stimulus consisted of a sequence with three distinct sections, but only the second and the third sections, and primarily the transition from the second to the third, are of interest here. The second section consisted of an isochronous metronome signal for 16 cycles. The third section consisted of 24 cycles, with the metronome period shifted by percent, relative to the second section. The 2 percent period shift is considered to be below the threshold of conscious recognition for period/frequency shifts (Killeen and Weiss 1987). The subjects were instructed to make target contact on the *off* beat, that is, midway in time between two audible clicks of the metronome. (In contrast with most other studies of this type, there was no attempt to synchronize the stimulus and the response.) In addition, each subject performed five trials at preferred (baseline) frequency, five trials at 25 percent higher frequency (shorter period), and five trials at 25 percent lower frequency (longer period). The usual relationship between period T and frequency f applies: $T = 1/f$. Also, trials were conducted in which the period was increased by 2 percent, and also decreased by 2 percent, in the transition from the second section to the third. Thus each subject performed $2 \times 3 \times 5 = 30$ trials.

For purposes of analysis, all trials were normalized so that the stimulus period in the second section was 1,000 milliseconds. Thus, the normalized stimulus period in the third section was 1,020 milliseconds following the 2 percent period increase, and 980 milliseconds following the 2 percent period decrease. The data was aggregated (i.e., averaged) so that the underlying features of the movement might be revealed. The aggregation had the effect of canceling out variations in response due to system noise. In this case, the system was the human body, and the noise was the inherent temporal variability in the electrical and chemical processes that drive motor nerve firing (polarization and depolarization), which, in concert, creates the cascade of motor unit contractions that results in the sequence of muscle contractions that drives the movement.

Discussion of pertinent results requires the definition of two terms related to stimulus-driven movement. These definitions presuppose the existence of a monotonically increasing sequence of stimulus times and the corresponding sequence of response times. In this experiment, all such times were measured to the nearest millisecond. In this context, then, the *synchronization error* (*sync error*) is defined as the *response time minus the corresponding stimulus time*. For a given stimulus-response pair, this typically falls into the range of ±50 ms, although the response has a tendency to precede the stimulus by about 20 ms. This has been observed in experiments conducted since the mid-1950s. The *response interval*, also referred to as the *interresponse interval (IRI)*, is the time difference between successive responses. The *stimulus interval*, also referred to as the *inter-stimulus interval* (or *ISI*), is the time difference between successive stimuli. For this experiment, the stimulus interval was equivalent to the metro-nome period. For a stimulus interval of 1,000 ms, the response interval was typically within the range of 1,000 ± 50 ms.

A graph of the sequence of response intervals is presented as the upper part of figure 2. The horizontal lines represent the stimulus inter-vals (1,000 ms before the period change, and 1,020 ms after), and the dashed vertical lines mark the step change in the stimulus period. Of particular interest is the observation that adaptation of the response interval to the step change in stimulus interval is almost immediate. The response interval (period) is relatively stable in following the new stimu-lus interval (period) within two movement cycles (four data points), and significant adaptation has occurred within one cycle. This is not the case

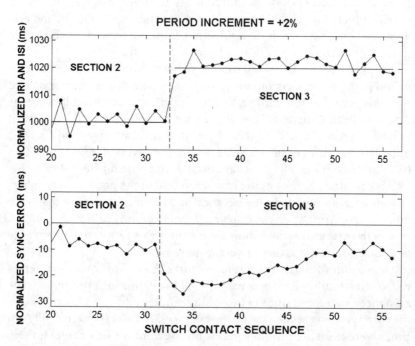

Fig. 5.2 Graphs of normalized IRI/ISI (upper graph) and normalized synchronization error in response to a 2 percent (subliminal) period shift.

for the adaptation of the synchronization error, as shown in the lower part of figure 2.

Keeping in mind that sync error equals response time minus stimulus time, a negative value for sync error indicates that the response occurred *before* the stimulus. Both the magnitude and the direction of the change in sync error at the transition from section 2 to section 3 are consistent with the +20 millisecond step change in the stimulus period. The tendency to reproduce the previous response (based on the expectation that an isochronous stimulus will continue to be isochronous), combined with the stimulus occurring 20 ms later than its expected/anticipated time, results in the shift in the graph immediately following transition from section 2 to section 3. Another significant observation of the graphs in figure 2 is that the sync error only *gradually* returns to its pre-step-change values. This return of sync error is complete within about ten movement cycles (twenty data points).

These adaptation characteristics of response interval/period and sync error are accounted for in a mathematical model that we will offer later in this chapter.

5.4 Background to Movement Optimization

5.4.1 The Link Between Rhythm and Motor Behavior

Why does end-point matching of a cyclic movement to an isochronous (constant period) rhythmic stimulus result in an optimization/modification of the spatial and temporal characteristics of the movement, as was demonstrated in the two studies? As an example, consider a simple arm movement involving the cyclic contact with two targets on the surface of a table. Suppose, first, that the subject is allowed to find his/her preferred (natural) frequency of oscillation between the two targets. This preferred frequency has been identified as the resonant frequency of the muscle-limb system (Hatsopoulos and Warren 1996). We may also assume the existence of a central nervous system timing mechanism that helps to regulate and control motor behavior. Its existence is evident from the fact that humans are able to synchronize movement with external rhythmic sources, as in dancing or clapping to music. Furthermore, after synchrony of tapping to a metronome beat has been attained, the rate of tapping can be maintained after the metronome stimulus has been removed. If we assume this mechanism has a role in controlling cyclic movement that is *not* driven by an external rhythm, we may expect that the consistency/variability of the timing of target contact will be a function of the precision of this internal timing system. It is obvious that the quality or the temporal resolution of this timekeeper varies tremendously by individual. Tests are available to measure rhythmic ability (Shuter-Dyson and Gabriel 1981; Whybrew

1962), and the existence of varying scores on these tests supports the idea of an internal timing system of variable (per individual) precision that is involved in the perception of rhythmic stimuli and the regulation of rhythmic motor behavior. Since the period of movement of a subject varies slightly from cycle to cycle, it can be expected that the *kinematic* parameters of movement (trajectory/position over time, velocity, acceleration) will also vary. This has been observed experimentally.

Now suppose that the subject's average period of movement has been determined, that a metronome has been set at this exact tempo (period, frequency), and that the metronome is used to drive the subject's movement. Assume that the subject has been instructed to make contact with the targets in synchrony with the metronome beat. It can be speculated that the metronome might be acting to refine the precision of the subject's internal timing mechanism. Given such a (proposed) refinement of period, the associated kinematic parameters might be expected to undergo a corresponding refinement.

From a more mathematical viewpoint, the requirement that target contact be synchronous with the metronome beat imposes an additional temporal constraint on the physical/neurological problem of moving between targets. A spatial constraint is a consequence of the position of the two targets, with respect to each other and with respect to the subject. Other physical constraints are a consequence of the mass distribution of each segment of the arm.

Once the time constraint is added, the timing system has been presented with a well-defined optimization problem: how to move from target A to target B while minimizing some objective function that relates to the body's cost in making such a movement (Beale 1988), at the same time matching the time interval provided by the stimulus. It has been proposed that such cost factors include total energy output, total muscle force, total power output, peak acceleration, squared joint torque, smoothness of movement, and the square of the magnitude of the derivative of the acceleration integrated over the period of movement (also known as "jerk cost") (Nagasaki 1989; Uno et al. 1989; Schneck 1990; An and Bejjani 1990).

5.4.2 An Optimization Criterion

In this context, we make a case for optimization of movement in terms of the *minimization of peak absolute acceleration over the entire movement cycle.* Because translational acceleration is proportional to applied force (Newton's Second Law) and angular acceleration is proportional to the joint torque resulting from muscle contraction (the angular-motion variant of Newton's Second Law), there is an immediate link between applied muscle force and the resulting arm segment accelerations required to produce the desired movement. The accelerations we are considering may be viewed from either of two perspectives: (1) the translational acceleration through 3-D space of a joint center, or (2) the angular acceleration of two body segments connected at a joint. Either perspective may be used to describe the movement of a human body. We may specify how all the joint centers are moving (translating) through space, or we may specify how all the joint angles are changing. The method by which movement is specified is secondary to (and derived from) the movement itself.

Using either approach, the minimization of peak absolute acceleration results in a unique acceleration-time curve over the movement cycle. Once the acceleration history is known and combined with the *boundary conditions* (the movement status of the body in terms of position, velocity, and acceleration of the joint centers or joint angles at the point in time when data recording begins), both the velocity-time and position-time curves are known. This is a result of the fundamental mathematical relationships between position, velocity, and acceleration, and follows directly from their definitions. Thus application of this particular optimization criterion implies that the position of some anatomical reference point is known throughout the movement cycle. Therefore, the body's attempt to synchronize its movement to a rhythmic stimulus may be expected to produce more consistent kinematic results.

It is also possible to replace the requirement of end-point matching (touching targets on the metronome beat) with period matching, in which movement period corresponds to stimulus period, but may be out of phase with the stimulus. The time interval between target contacts is still fixed, and so the same analysis applies: Movement is regulated over the entire cycle, with rhythm serving as a continuous time reference for the brain throughout the movement cycle. This is in marked contrast to the much weaker assertion that such period matching results only in time regulation at the geometrical extremes of the movement.

One consequence of the minimization of peak absolute acceleration over the duration of a movement is the concurrent minimization of peak force applied by the effector muscles during the movement. This follows from Newton's laws for translational and rotational motion, stated here for the case of plane motion of a body segment:

$$\sum \vec{F} = m\vec{a} \tag{1}$$

$$\sum M = I\alpha \tag{2}$$

Equation (1) relates the *translational* (vector) acceleration $\vec{a}$ of the center of mass of the body segment that results from the net (vector) force $\Sigma\vec{F}$ applied to the center of mass of the segment of mass m. Equation (2) relates the *rotational* acceleration α that results from the sum of the moments (torques) ΣM applied to the segment, where I is the rotational moment of inertia of the segment about its center of mass.

5.4.3 *Kinematics Governing Movement in One Dimension*

Suppose that the movement under consideration is the cyclic movement involved when alternately touching two targets, A and B, on the surface of a table; target A is closer to the body. The targets are located in a sagittal plane through the (fixed in space) shoulder joint. The arm may be modeled as a three-link system consisting of upper arm, lower arm, and rigid hand, with hinge joints at the shoulder, elbow, and wrist. Assume a coordinate system in this sagittal plane, with the origin at the center of (circular) target A, and the x-axis extending through target B. Also assume the z-axis is perpendicular to the table surface at the origin. For this arrangement, a movement from A to B would involve extension of the elbow joint, and a movement from B to A would involve flexion of the elbow joint.

A discussion of the kinematics of this cyclic movement can be simplified by considering one movement cycle (A to B to A) of the fingertip that will contact the target centers. Assume that a marker on the wrist joint of the moving hand follows a trajectory in the xz-plane. The position of the wrist at any point in time t_i can then be described by an ordered pair of position components (x_i, z_i). In a laboratory/clinical setting, such motion is generally recorded by using 60-Hertz videocameras (which take 60 pictures per second) to follow the movement of markers placed on the joints. Thus one movement cycle of the wrist joint will consist of a finite number of position coordinates (x_i, z_i), each associated with a time value t_i, where the subscript i identifies the order of the data within the sequence. To further simplify the discussion, initially only the x-coordinate of position will be considered; the z-coordinate will be considered subsequently.

If we momentarily consider $x(t)$ to be a continuous (rather than a discrete) function of t, several statements can be made regarding the general nature of this movement. These follow directly from the definitions of position, velocity, and acceleration, and employ calculus concepts of the derivative and the integral:

- The velocity $v(t)$ at any time t is the first time derivative of position $x(t)$ and is equal to the numerical value of the slope of the position curve at time t:

$$v = \frac{dx}{dt} \qquad (3)$$

- The acceleration $a(t)$ at any time t is the second time derivative of position $x(t)$ and the first time derivative of velocity $v(t)$, and is equal to the numerical value of the slope of the velocity curve at time t:

$$a = \frac{dv}{dt} \qquad (4)$$

- The position $x(\tilde{t})$ at any time $\tilde{t}$ is numerically equal to the area under the velocity-time curve between 0 and $\tilde{t}$:

$$x = \int_0^{\tilde{t}} v(t)dt \qquad (5)$$

- The velocity $v(\tilde{t})$ at any time $\tilde{t}$ is numerically equal to the area under the acceleration-time curve between 0 and $\tilde{t}$:

$$v = \int_0^{\tilde{t}} a(t)dt \qquad (6)$$

5.5 Consequences of Temporal Synchronization

Given this background information, it is now possible to show that the minimization of peak absolute acceleration $|a(t)|_{max}$ implies the existence of a unique relationship between $x(t)$ and t.

The concept of peak absolute acceleration may require some elaboration. Acceleration of a point (such as a joint center) in one dimension can be positive or negative, relative to the coordinate system in which it is measured. Furthermore, the selection of a coordinate system is purely arbitrary, and the system is usually chosen so as to make descriptions of motion as simple as possible. What does it mean for acceleration to be positive or negative? For motion in one dimension, positive accelerations result from one of two conditions. Either the object is moving in the positive direction and speeding up, or it is moving in the negative direction and slowing down. Similarly, negative accelerations result when an object is moving in the positive direction and slowing down, or moving in the negative direction and speeding up.

As an example of peak absolute acceleration, suppose we record the movement of a joint center and calculate its translational acceleration at two different points in time to be +32 and –48. The absolute values of these accelerations are +32 and +48, by definition. Taking the absolute value of a negative number makes it positive, and the absolute value of a positive number is positive. Thus the peak absolute acceleration is 48, because 48 > 32. This is the value we want to minimize, according to our stated optimization criterion. It doesn't matter if the acceleration is positive or negative, because the sign of acceleration has significance only relative to the coordinate system in which it is measured. Wherever the absolute peak occurs, that is where the effort (provided by muscle contraction) required to produce the movement is greatest.

So now suppose that target points A and B are a distance d apart, and that one movement cycle (A to B to A) has a period (time duration) of $2T$ seconds. Also suppose that target contact times are synchronized to a metronome, and that target contact occurs as the metronome clicks, once every T seconds. Thus one movement cycle (elbow joint extension followed by flexion) may be regarded as the following sequence:

- Touch target A at time $t = 0$.
- Touch target B at $t = T$.
- Touch target A at $t = 2T$.

Figure 3 contains versions of the acceleration-time (a-t), velocity-time (v-t), and position-time (x-t) graphs. The shape of the a-t curve is a direct consequence of the optimality condition, while the shapes of the v-t and x-t curves are derived from the acceleration constraint and the boundary conditions of the movement.

The first half of the movement cycle (from $t = 0$ to $t = T$) may be analyzed as follows. At time $t = 0$, we know that $x(0) = 0$ and $v(0) = 0$. In other words, the fingertip is touching target A and is motionless. At time $t = T$, we know that $x(T) = d$ and $v(t) = 0$ (since the fingertip has moved to target B and is again momentarily motionless during contact). These four boundary conditions are marked by open circles on the x-t and v-t graphs. Keeping in mind that only the x-coordinate of position, velocity, and acceleration (of the fingertip) is being considered, the movement from A to B consists of an interval of positive acceleration, during which velocity increases from 0 to some maximum value v_{max}, followed by an interval of negative acceleration, during which the velocity decreases from v_{max} back down to 0. Because $v(T) = 0$, the area under the acceleration-time curve between $t = 0$ and $t = T$ must equal 0 (a consequence of equation 6), with areas below the t-axis considered to be negative. In the

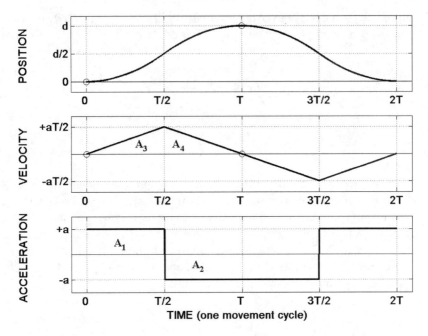

Fig. 5.3 Optimized position, velocity, and acceleration curves over one movement cycle.

acceleration graph of figure 3, the area above the time axis, A_1, must equal the area below the time axis, A_2.

There are two immediate consequences of the optimality criterion that peak absolute acceleration is minimized. The first is that the acceleration is constant when positive and constant when negative. The second is that the acceleration must switch sign precisely at t = T/2. Because we have the requirement that $A_1 = A_2$, any other point in time would require different values for the positive and negative amplitudes, which would increase a = (dv/dt). Until the final steps of the derivation are reached, we will identify this (unknown) acceleration as a. Its value will ultimately be determined by the application of the boundary conditions. Thus the requirement that peak absolute acceleration be minimized constrains the acceleration to constant values of a during the acceleration phase and of –a during the deceleration phase. In each phase the peak absolute acceleration is equal to a. Any deviation from this rectangular configuration would increase peak absolute acceleration.

Once the configuration of the acceleration-time curve is fixed (known), the velocity-time curve can be developed from the boundary conditions and equation (6). It is already known that $v(0) = v(T) = 0$ and that the constant acceleration values of a and –a are the slopes (see equation 4) of the velocity-time curve over the intervals (0, $T/2$) and ($T/2$, T). Thus the velocity-time curve from $t = 0$ to $t = T$ has the triangular shape shown in figure 4, with a peak value of $v = aT/2$ at $t = T/2$. In terms of equations,

$$v(t) = at \quad \text{on} \quad [0, T/2] \tag{7}$$

and

$$v(t) = -at + aT \quad \text{on} \quad [T/2, T] \tag{8}$$

Once the configuration of the velocity-time curve is known, the position-time curve can be constructed. Because $v(0) = v(T) = 0$, the x-t curve has zero slope, or horizontal tangents, at those two times. The symmetry of the v-t and a-t curves implies symmetry of the x-t curve, which requires that $x(T/2) = d/2$. This also follows from the fact that $A_3 = A_4$ in figure 3.

We may now integrate the v-t curve piecewise to obtain the configuration of the x-t curve. On the interval [0, $T/2$]:

$$x(t) = \int v(t)dt = \int atdt = \frac{1}{2}at^2 + c_1$$

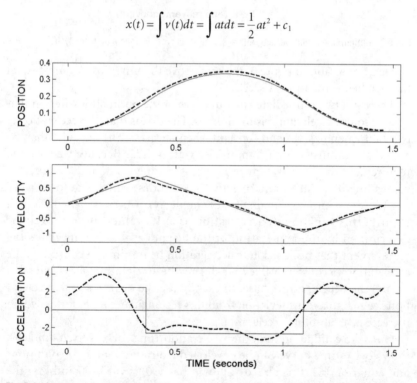

Fig. 5.4 Case study results (dashed line) plotted over optimal results (solid line) predicted by equations (12) through (17).

Applying the boundary condition $x(0) = 0$ gives $c_1 = 0$, resulting in

$$x(t) = \frac{1}{2}at^2 \quad \text{on} \quad [0, T/2] \tag{9}$$

Now, on the interval $[T/2, T]$,

$$x(t) = \int v(t)dt = \int (-at + aT)dt = -\frac{1}{2}at^2 + aTt + c_2$$

Applying the boundary condition $x(T) = d$ gives $c_2 = d-(1/2)aT^2$, resulting in

$$x(t) = -\frac{1}{2}at^2 + aTt + (d - \frac{1}{2}aT^2) \quad \text{on} \quad [T/2, T] \tag{10}$$

To this point, the value of a has not been specified or determined. However, we may now apply the boundary condition $x(T/2) = d/2$ in equation (9) to evaluate a in terms of d and T, resulting in

$$a = \frac{4d}{T^2} \tag{11}$$

The previously unspecified constant acceleration a has now been expressed in terms of physical parameters of the experiment. Furthermore, the equations for position and velocity may now also be specified in terms of the same parameters:

$$x(t) = \frac{2d}{T^2}t^2 \quad \text{on} \quad [0, T/2] \tag{12}$$

$$x(t) = \frac{-2d}{T^2}t^2 + \frac{4d}{T}t - d \quad \text{on} \quad [T/2, T] \tag{13}$$

$$v(t) = \frac{4d}{T^2}t \quad \text{on} \quad [0, T/2] \tag{14}$$

$$v(t) = \frac{-4d}{T^2}t + \frac{4d}{T} \quad \text{on} \quad [T/2, T] \tag{15}$$

And for the sake of completeness,

$$a = \frac{4d}{T^2} \quad \text{on} \quad [0, T/2] \tag{16}$$

$$a = \frac{-4d}{T^2} \quad \text{on} \quad [T/2, T] \tag{17}$$

Equations (12) through (17) thus completely specify the x-coordinate of the motion of the wrist marker.

If the targets are not located precisely in a sagittal plane, the analysis can be duplicated exactly as above for motion in the y (transverse) direction; only the value of parameter d is different. The same analysis can also be carried out for the z (vertical) direction, although in this case the distance traversed is not linked to target positions, as was the case for movement in the x and y directions. However, in our experiment, the target positions were determined by observing each subject's natural/preferred range of motion. Thus, in each case the distance to be traversed was established by the subject. The function of the targets was to keep the movement consistent over the entire trial (23 full cycles) and to provide an electrical contact surface used to determine contact times by sending an electrical signal to external equipment.

Furthermore, the analysis for the second half of the movement cycle, from the far target to the near target, is exactly the same as for the first half. Thus the path as a function of time in 3-D space is uniquely determined as a consequence of the optimality condition, which implies that *the entire movement cycle, not just the end points, is fixed in time.* This means that (provided the optimality condition is adhered to) at any point in time t, the position and velocity of the fingertip can be determined simply by substituting the value of t into equations (12) through (15). Keep in mind that the variables d and T have numerical values that are specific to each person participating in such an experiment.

Figure 4 presents a visual comparison of a particular subject's movement cycle curves with the optimized predictions, based on the computed results of equations (12) through (17) for the target positions and metronome setting used by the subject. Very good agreement is seen in the position and velocity curves. The subject's acceleration curve roughly follows the optimized values. The acceleration, as a second derivative of position (actually a second-order divided difference for discrete data), is much more sensitive to variations in position than is the velocity. Examination of several consecutive cycles, however, showed that the subject's acceleration curve tended to agree on average (i.e., after smoothing) with the optimal values. Furthermore, examination of the acceleration curves for the slow, normal, and fast trial conditions described in study 2 revealed a progressive reduction in the variance from the optimized acceleration values as the stimulus period decreased. This can be at least partially accounted for by the need to reduce dwell time on the target as the time available to complete the movement cycle was decreased. As the demands of the time constraint were increased, time spent in contact with the target was decreased, and the subject's acceleration tended to be less variable.

5.6 Modeling Rhythmic Stimulus Perception and the Corresponding Production of Motor Events

In this section, a mathematical model will be developed that will yield some insight into the perceptual information that the brain and nervous system might use to synchronize a motor response to an audible stimulus. This model is based partially on the feedback of information from the previous movement cycle. This information includes (1) the perceived error in making target contact in synchrony with the stimulus, and (2) the perceived error in matching the movement interval (or period) to the stimulus interval (or period).

But first, it is necessary to present some general definitions and notation pertaining to the time sequences that constitute the data in any experiment involving motor responses to rhythmic stimuli:

$st(i)$ = the time that stimulus i occurred
$rt(i)$ = the time that response i occurred
$sp(i)$ = the time duration of stimulus period i
$rp(i)$ = the time duration of response period i
$se(i)$ = the error (synchronization error) in matching response time i to stimulus time i
$pe(i)$ = the error (period error) in matching response period i to stimulus period i

In these definitions, the letter i is an interger variable that indicates the order of a data value within a sequence of such values. Given this notation, the following equations follow from the structure of the data-collection protocol, and also from the previous definitions:

$$sp(i) = st(i) - st(i-1) \tag{18}$$

$$rp(i) = rt(i) - rt(i-1) \tag{19}$$

$$se(i) = rt(i) - st(i) \tag{20}$$

$$pe(i) = rp(i) - sp(i) \tag{21}$$

In creating any recursive model (i.e., one in which the value of a variable depends on prior values of variables), initial values of model variables must be defined:

$st(1) = 0$	the clock starts when the first stimulus occurs
$rt(1) = 0$	the first response occurs at the same time as the first stimulus
$sp(1) = T$	T is the metronome period
$rp(1) = T$	set $rp(1) = sp(1)$
$se(1) = 0$	a consequence of $st(1) = rt(1)$
$pe(1) = 0$	a consequence of $sp(1) = rp(1)$

Some of these initial values follow from previous definitions, and some are rather arbitrary, but based on reasonable assumptions employed to provide seed values for particular variables that allow the process of recursion to commence. In any recursive model, the data set consists of a sequence of values for the set of variables. The elements of the sequence (i.e., the data values) are associated with an integer i that indicates an element's order/position within the sequence.

For example, suppose we collect 5 seconds of position data using a 60-Hertz videocamera, which takes 60 pictures per second. The sequence of values for the x-coordinate of the wrist marker is represented symbolically by

$$x(1), x(2), x(3), \ldots x(i-1), x(i), x(i+1), \ldots x(299), x(300)$$

Here the i in parentheses represents some arbitrary element in the sequence. If, for example, i represents the 48th value for the x-coordinate of the wrist marker, then $i-1$ represents the 47th value and $i+1$ represents the 49th value. The essence of a recursive model is that any value of a variable depends on previous values of that variable or other variables. In other words, the value of $x(255)$ depends on the value of $x(254)$. But isn't this precisely what we might expect for the experiment under consideration? If we are perceptibly late in matching tap 254 to metronome click 254, we will attempt to adjust response 255 to try to make a correction that will produce an on-time response. Thus, any response depends on the previous response (relative, of course, to their corresponding stimuli).

Given the definitions, relations (18) through (21), and the initial conditions, the recursive model for computing response period $rp(i)$ is given by

$$rp(i) = w_{sp} \cdot sp(i-1) + w_{rp} \cdot rp(i-1) - w_{se} \cdot se(i-1) - w_{pe} \cdot pe(i-1) \quad \text{for} \quad i = 2,3,...N \tag{22}$$

where w_{sp}, w_{rp}, w_{se}, w_{pe} are weight values, and N is the total number of stimulus/response pairs. Notice that a given response period $rp(i)$ is computed from the *previous* values of the stimulus period, response period, synchronization error, and period error, which are indicated by using i-1. These four values are precisely the pieces of information that could be useful in producing the next response.

The four terms on the right-hand side of (22) may be interpreted as follows. The $sp(i-1)$ term drives the next response (i.e., it *is* the stimulus period). The response period $rp(i-1)$, together with its corresponding weight, quantifies the inertia, both physical and neurological, of the responding system. The upper extremity has both translational and rotational inertia, due to its mass distribution. It may be hypothesized that the neurological system has its own form of inertia; if the (isochronous) stimulus stops, the neurological system can continue to drive the physical system at the same rate for extended periods of time. Thus, the previous response has a tendency to replicate itself. Note that $w_{sp} + w_{rp} = 1$ is a required mathematical condition for the continued relative synchrony of stimulus and response. The term $pe(i-1)$ is the dominant correction factor. It has been observed experimentally (see figure 2) that response period corrections due to a step change in stimulus period tend to occur almost immediately. The $se(i-1)$ term tends to maintain or restore synchrony of stimulus and response. Without this term, the response *times* can drift away from the stimulus *times*, while maintaining relative equality of stimulus and response *periods*. This return to synchrony of response and stimulus, after a step change in the stimulus period, has been observed experimentally (see figure 2) to occur over many more movement cycles than the corresponding period adjustment. Thus the value of w_{se} is significantly less than that of w_{pe}.

Figure 5 presents a graph of the output of this model, from equation (22), for weight values of $w_{sp} = 0.6$, $w_{rp} = 0.4$, $w_{se} = 0.1$, $w_{pe} = 0.5$, these weight values evolved over many simulations that were intended to reproduce the response characteristics illustrated in figure 2. The input for this simulation was a step change of +20 ms in the stimulus period, followed by a step change of –20 ms. In the upper graph of figure 5, the curves have been offset by 0.4 millisecond (so the solid line does not obscure the dashed line) to illustrate the equality of stimulus and response periods over the first ten stimulus/response pairs in the sequence.

It is clear from figure 5 that this model reproduces the salient features of the response characteristics shown in figure 2 for the stimulus period step

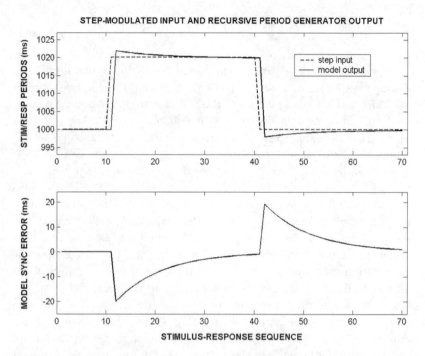

Fig. 5.5 Recursive model output for a step change in stimulus period, as computed using equation (22).

It is clear from figure 5 that this model reproduces the salient features of the response characteristics shown in figure 2 for the stimulus period step change occurring in the transition from section 2 to section 3. The response period makes a rapid adjustment to the step change in the stimulus period. Figure 5 illustrates this for both an increase and a decrease in the stimulus period. Also, the return of the sync error to its pre-period-shift levels is much more gradual. These two factors characterize the response to a step change in stimulus period.

Figure 6 shows the model output superimposed on the data of figure 2.

5.7 Summary

5.7.1 The Primacy of Period

The periods of rhythmic stimuli and their corresponding responses play a dominant role in the planning and execution of motor events. Evidence for this comes from several sources. The fact that a constraint on the response period (as provided by the stimulus period) results in a well-defined optimization problem allows for a mathematical analysis that

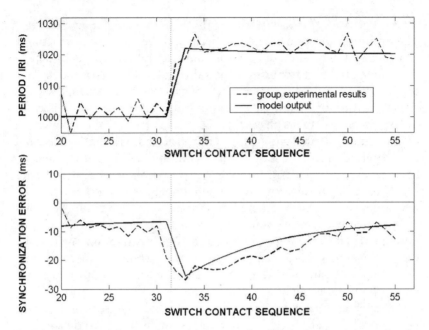

Fig. 5.6 The output of the recursive model, from equation (22), is shown superimposed on the data from study 2, previously shown in figure 2. The dotted vertical lines indicate the step change in stimulus period.

results in the complete specification of the three-dimensional coordinates of an upper-extremity movement trajectory. Thus, the result of study 1, in which mid-arc position variability is decreased, is a natural outcome of the response period constraint provided by the metronome.

Also, the data of study 2 (see figure 2) shows unequivocally that a step change in stimulus period is followed almost immediately (within two cycles) by complete adaptation of the response period. The return to relative synchrony of response and stimulus, however, occurs much more gradually (after about 10 cycles). This empirical observation has a mathematical correlate in the recursive period model described by equation (22), namely, that the weight value associated with the correction for period error is five times greater than the weight value associated with the correction for synchronization error. The fact that the model accurately reproduces the underlying (i.e., independent of system noise) behavior further supports the claim that stimulus and response periods have a more crucial role in determining adaptive behavior than stimulus and response phase relationships, as quantified by synchronization error.

5.7.2 Timing-Based Optimization of Movement

The optimization model, while appearing to be based on a kinematic constraint (minimization of peak absolute acceleration), is equally dependent on spatial and temporal constraints. Spatial constraints can be derived from the objectives of a variety of goal-based movements, but it is the imposition of a timing constraint, based on the period of a cyclic movement and *not* on its phase, that allows for the well-defined expression of any additional kinematic optimization criterion. Without a constraint on the period of a cyclic movement, the minimization of any kinematic (or kinetic, or metabolic, or neurological) parameter may be satisfied simply by extending the movement over an infinitely long time period. If you have as much time as you want to move your hand from point A to point B, of course you can minimize the acceleration required to make the movement. Thus, the imposition of a timing constraint on any realistic cyclic human movement seems to be a necessary condition for movement optimization, regardless of the specific criterion (i.e., objective function) on which the optimization is based.

The apparent agreement of the optimization model predictions for the position, velocity, and acceleration profiles with the measured outcomes of the case study (see figure 4) lends support to the assertion that minimization of peak absolute acceleration might be *one* method by which the nervous system regulates movement. It is also possible that there are multiple methods that operate, some of which might depend on the movement frequency, the anatomical components involved in the movement, and the effector muscles involved, and some of which might be in concurrent operation. Indeed, it has been proposed that stable movement patterns are the result of the interaction between components of the central nervous system and the physical dynamics of the musculoskeletal system (Kelso and Tuller 1984; Kugler and Turvey 1987). Furthermore, it has been suggested that a movement outcome may be the result of multiple constraints that minimize the "costs" to the system (Sparrow 1983), and that these costs may be prioritized by their relevance to the desired movement (Fetters and Holt 1990). In the case of walking by nondisabled adults, these costs have included physiological energy consumption (measured by heart rate or oxygen consumption), mechanical energy expenditure, asymmetry of lower limb movements, and intralimb coordination (Jeng et al. 1996). Thus, given the apparently unlimited number of factors upon which movement optimization might be based, it is not unreasonable to look beyond the perhaps simplified idealization that movement control is the outcome of the regulation of some single specific physiological attribute, and seek to identify some more fundamental process that is common to all movement, in all contexts.

Timing is fundamental to any movement event. In many cases, there may be no external timing constraint, so the timing of a movement sequence may be determined by multiple internal factors, such as mood, energy level, and mental focus, as well as by various physical factors, such as distribution of the mass of relevant body segments, spatial relationships with target objects, balance, and relative motion between body center of mass and target objects. This was the situation during the first part of the experiment in study 1, when the subjects were moving between two targets at their own self-selected rate. Other examples are reaching for an item on a shelf, turning on a light switch, combing or brushing hair, and eating with a fork.

In other cases, external conditions may generate some nonspecific timing constraint, such as hurrying to catch a bus or running down a fly ball in center field. In these situations, the number of factors that influence the movement outcome may be reduced (and made more specific) relative to the more general case, but absolutely precise movement is still not a necessity. However, when the timing constraint becomes precise, the movement must follow. Examples of this include playing a musical instrument in an orchestra and following the rhythm set by the conductor, and moving between two targets to the beat of a metronome, as in study 1. Thus, the ubiquitous influence of time on the organization of precision movement makes the control of the rhythm of a movement a possible criterion for the optimization of the movement.

In actual practice, we do not really know what optimization criterion (if any) the central nervous system applies to control movement. It has even been suggested that many of the proposed optimization criteria give equivalent results when applied to gait characteristics (Collins 1995). It has also been suggested that in arm movements, the function being optimized (in this case minimized) is the variance of the spatial accuracy of the final position of the hand, relative to the target, for a specified movement duration (Harris and Wolpert 1998). An equivalent formulation of this criterion would be the minimization of the variance of the temporal accuracy (relative to an audible stimulus) for a specified target position because the two outcomes (temporal and spatial) are tightly coupled in certain movement contexts, such as those described in this chapter. The extent of such coupling is determined primarily by the timing constraint, as it relates to physiological, anatomical, and neurological factors. If the period specified for a cyclic movement is too long or too short, there is no coupling between temporal and spatial outcomes. If the period is too long, it is possible to produce a wide variety of trajectories and still meet the time constraints for target contact. If the period is too short, it becomes physically impossible to maintain temporal synchrony of stimulus and response. But within the time range typical of goal-directed movement, these two equivalent criteria are independent of any specific kinematic or kinetic characteristic of the movement, and are not directly related to any anatomical, physiological, or neurological parameter.

It is important to note that the one common element in all of the proposed optimization paradigms is the existence of a time constraint on the duration of the movement. As was seen in the derivation of equations (12) through (17), such a time constraint can result in the complete specification of the dynamics of the movement over the entire movement cycle, thereby functioning as a continuous time reference. This seeming universality of a time constraint may be viewed as an opportunity to develop and better understand therapeutic modalities using sensory stimuli whose temporal pattern structures function to plan and execute movement in learning and training paradigms. The clinical research base in rhythmic facilitation in gait rehabilitation—which has been critically reviewed for stroke patients (Hummelsheim 1999; Jeffery and Good 1995) and for patients with Parkinson's disease (de Goede et al. 2001)—has produced an array of significant data strongly suggesting the efficacy of rhythmic time cuing. Recent upper-extremity research (Thaut, Schicks, McIntosh et al. 2002; Georgiou et al. 1993; Thaut, Kenyon, Hurt et al. 2002) has shown similar effects for movements whose neural control circuitry is not based on intrinsic biological rhythmic constraints.

This chapter has provided experimental and mathematical evidence for a model of motor control mechanisms that underlie the effects of temporally structured sensory cues, such as auditory rhythm, and result in the improvement of motor function.

6
Music in Therapy and Medicine: From Social Science to Neuroscience

6.1 Historic Paradigm Shift

The history of modern music therapy—often considered starting around the middle of the twentieth century—has been philosophically rooted mostly in social science concepts: The therapeutic value of music is derived from the various emotional and social roles it plays in a person's life and a society's culture, based on the accepted uses, norms, and functions for the arts. Music has been given the age-old roles of emotional expression; of creating and facilitating group association, integration, and social organization; of symbolically representing beliefs and ideas; and of supporting educational purposes.

From research in music anthropology, we know that in all societies throughout human history music has been used to express emotions, ideas, and feelings not revealed through ordinary discourse. Similarly, music has always been widely used to bring people together and structure their interactions: in listening to music performances, in singing or playing together, in dancing and moving to music, or in sharing rituals and experiences accompanied and enhanced by music. There is strong anthropological and sociological evidence that music has always played a critical role—in historical and contemporary societies, literate and nonliterate cultures—in expressing and supporting societal values, in marking special events in the life cycle, and in communicating and enforcing religious beliefs, social rituals, or political ideas. And finally, the role of music for educational purposes has been widely described in all cultures in a variety of applications, such as to enhance social learning, to guide and motivate physical learning, to help support cognitive learning tasks (e.g., to remember facts, events, names, or rules), or to support a child's physical, emotional, and cognitive development by engaging in age-appropriate music activities.

The professional role of music in therapy has been shaped since the mid-1950s by an extension of these concepts and applications of the cultural value of music in society. At the core of traditional music therapy practice and philosophy, we most frequently find as a premise and primary goal some general concept of well-being, promoted through the emotional and motivational qualities of music. Connected to and derived from this central theme are the other functions of music that are considered therapeutic in the areas of social, physical, and general cognitive functions. The clinical practice that has been based on the premise of well-being has created a diffuse, more ancillary, and complementary role for music therapy, as opposed to a central role defined by a focus on diagnosis-specific, functional therapeutic goals.

The notion of music as therapy is based on ancient cross-cultural beliefs that music has a therapeutic effect on the mind and body. Historical interpretations of the mechanisms of music in therapy have almost always emphasized cultural- and social science-based causalities within educational, emotional-motivational (cathartic), or spiritual and religious models of explanation and application. However, in its most intrinsic definition, music is an art form, a perceptual language of rule-based forms and patterns in the acoustical sensory domain. As such, music communicates initially and primarily itself, that is, its own shapes, patterns, and structures. These patterns of musical events are meaningful and pleasurable to the listener through the perception and comprehension of the embedded syntax, the skillful manipulation and modulation of rules of different musical languages formed in different cultures. Beyond this intrinsic communication process, musical communication takes on very complex extramusical meanings through learned associations and through the specific uses and functions of music in different societies and persons' lives.

As far as recorded history is capable of ascertaining, music as an art form has existed in all known cultures throughout human history. That fact gives rise to thought. Obviously, music is not connected to direct material and biological necessities of survival of the human organism as far as we can understand; it is not on the same level as food, water, air, or shelter. The capability of human beings to create music, the great pleasure we derive from music, and the pervasiveness of music in human culture may suggest to us that there is a biological and neurological basis of music in the human brain that plays a role in shaping brain and behavior function considerably beyond general concepts of musically induced well-being.

The study of art forms—empirically, theoretically, and philosophically—is the domain of the discipline of aesthetics. Aesthetics is often misunderstood as the study of beauty in art. However, the word "aesthetics" is based on the Greek word *aisthesis*, meaning "sensory-related." Aesthetics as a term thus was originally related to the process of perceiving, the study of perception. A realization of this etymological history gives us some interesting clues about the recent radical shift in understanding of the role and function of music in therapy. Furthermore, with the advent of modern research techniques in cognitive neuroscience, such as brain imaging and brain-wave recordings, that are enabling us to study humans' higher cognitive brain functions in vivo, a highly complex picture of brain processes involved in the creation and perception of music has emerged. Brain research involving music has shown that music has a distinct influence on the brain by stimulating physiologically complex cognitive, affective, and sensorimotor processes (see chapters 2, 3, and 4). The fascinating consequence of this research for music therapy has been a new body of neuroscientific research that shows effective uses of music with therapeutic outcomes that are considerably stronger and more specific than those produced within the general concept of well-being. Thus, this research has put traditional applications and theories in serious question by showing that music works best in very different areas of therapeutic applications than previously imagined and tried.

By progressing from the social-science framework for music in therapy, we find underneath the cultural uses and functions of music physiologically complex brain processes that can shape and modulate brain and behavior function. This is a very critical step in the historical understanding of music in therapy and medicine. Rather than being viewed as an ancillary and complementary discipline that can enhance other forms of therapy, or that claims primary ownership of providing good culture in the therapeutic environment, music-based therapeutic techniques—applied within a neuroscientific framework—can be focused specifically on areas such as motor therapy, speech rehabilitation, and memory and attention training. For example, studies have shown that the rhythmic entrainment of motor function can actively facilitate the recovery of movement in patients afflicted with stroke, Parkinson's disease, or traumatic brain injury (see chapters 3 and 4). The rhythmic sounds are believed to act as sensory timers, entraining regulating brain mechanisms that control the timing, sequencing, and coordination of movement. Recovery of speech functions can be facilitated with music by employing its strong timing mechanisms to access and entrain oscillatory speech circuits in the brain. Recent research is showing that music can influence perception and organization of behavior in autistic children. New frontiers in music research include the effect of music and rhythm on critical aspects of timing in learning, attention, and memory.

By shifting one's notion of music in therapy from functioning as a carrier of sociocultural values in the therapeutic process to a stimulus that influences the neurophysiological basis of cognition and sensorimotor functions, a historical paradigm shift has emerged, driven by scientific data and insight into music and brain function. We can now postulate that music can access control processes in the brain related to control of movement, attention, speech production, learning, and memory, which can help retrain and recover functions in the injured or diseased brain.

6.2 The Rational Scientific Mediating Model

The study of the neurobiological basis of music ability is inherently linked to the study of music's influence on brain function. In other words, we need to recognize a reciprocal relationship in musical behavior: The brain that engages in music is also changed by engaging in music. Although much has been learned since the early 1990s about the effect of music on brain structure and function, a transformational framework, a theoretical model, is needed to explain how musical responses can be generalized and transferred into nonmusical therapeutic responses. This new scientific model searches for the therapeutic effect of music by studying if and how music stimulates and engages parallel or shared brain function in cognition, speech and language, motor control, and emotion, based on the psychological and physiological processes in music perception. Therefore, one can also describe the paradigm shift as a shift from an interpretive social science model to a perceptual neuroscience model.

However, we must still keep in mind for a moment that—within the context of understanding music as an art form—the aesthetic perception of music as a cultural art object or as sensory experience of an acoustical language does not initially contain any direct and obvious therapeutic attributes. Therefore, the therapeutic application of music necessitates a rational translation of a musical experience into a therapeutic experience that is able to answer this core question: What is the mechanism through which music psychologically and physiologically influences human behavior in a therapeutically meaningful and predictable way? Interestingly, concepts from experimental aesthetics help us a great deal to build a meaningful and coherent framework for understanding these translational mechanisms.

Experimental aesthetics is generally interested in a scientific-empirical and theoretical understanding of the physiological and psychological foundations of music perception and production, and their influence on human behavior. One of the key concepts suggested in understanding the role of artworks in perceptual processes is their function as mediating responses, as described in Berlyne (1971). Berlyne contends that aesthetic stimuli can have a facilitating, clarifying, and amplifying function in the perception and analysis of nonaesthetic objects and behavior experiences. Furthermore, they can facilitate the development of adequate and adaptive responses to these objects and experiences. For example, while one is listening to music, the emotional reactions to the music can function as a mediating response by arousing psychophysiological reactions, which may enhance and facilitate the experience of emotions and mood states. A theatrical play can facilitate the translation of a feeling into a prototypical experience of human emotional conflict. A visual or musical artwork can organize and focus attention by encouraging approaching behavior, by stimulating curiosity, exploration, or change in perceptual focus (e.g., heightened concentration, silence, shift in attention, observation, or sensitization).

The concept of music as a mediating stimulus is a useful one for music therapy because it gives us a new starting point in conceptualizing how music can engage behavior and mediate change in behavior. Adapted to music therapy, the music response would mediate between current behavior or brain function, the goals of therapy, and the desired therapeutic response. In experimental aesthetics, the mediating response in music is caused by a meaningful perception of the intrinsic pattern in the music itself, as well as by other symbolic, iconic, or behavioral meanings that have become linked to the music through some associative learning process.

This is an important point for music therapy because it means that its theoretical models have to be based on understanding the processes involved in musical behavior before translational therapeutic concepts can be developed. Consequently, models of the influence of music on nonmusical behavior, in order to be foundational therapeutic models, have to be based on (a) music cognition, (b) music and affective response, and (c) music and sensorimotor processes. The advantage of using this approach is that models in these three areas and their multifaceted interactions can be driven by scientific data, and can then be analyzed for possible parallels and similarities with nonmusical behavior. There are suggestions in the literature that such a scientific anchoring of music therapy in psychological and physiological models of musical behavior was originally envisioned by Gaston (1968) and Sears (1968) in their pioneering thinking about the future foundations of music therapy. However, the development of scientific theory in this direction has not been systematically pursued since the 1960s.

Adopting the concept of music as a mediating stimulus for nonmusical behavior allows us to develop an epistemological theoretical model of music in therapy based on the psychology and physiology of musical responses. The mediating concept helps to explain important attributes of music to generate a foundation for our model. As a mediating stimulus or response, music, based on its unique ordering of sensory patterns in aesthetic forms, initially engages human behavior meaningfully by arousing, guiding, organizing, and focusing attention, perception, and behavior in the affective, cognitive, and sensorimotor domains. Behavioral learning and change become ordered and structured within the perceptual demands of music. From this concept as a beginning, a stepwise, simple model can be developed on four levels that provide the transformational framework for music, nonmusical behavior, and therapeutic applications. This is the Rational-Scientific Mediating Model (R-SMM) of music in therapy and medicine (Thaut 2000).

The R-SMM functions as an epistemological model, that is, a model to show ways of generating knowledge concerning the linkage between music and therapy. In the epistemological application, the R-SMM helps us to know how to know (or to learn how to learn). It does not speak to the specific content of the mechanisms in music that produce therapeutic effects; it shows how to find them in a logical, systematic structure by linking the proper bodies of knowledge and showing what information is needed to logically support the next steps of inquiry and thus build a coherent theory. However, in one sense the R-SMM also speaks to and biases the content of the theoretical foundations by making an argument that (a) therapeutic responses in music can be derived only from an understanding of the psychology, physiology, and neurology of musical behavior; and (b) the application of rational, scientific principles is necessary to create a convincing foundation for music in therapy and medicine. In addition, the R-SMM helps researchers and clinicians to systematically survey and appraise the existing research literature base. There are parts of a potentially useful research base in music and the behavioral and neurosciences that are pertinent to this model, but they have not been sufficiently examined.

The R-SMM is based on the premise that the scientific basis of music therapy is found in the neurological, physiological, and psychological foundations of music perception and production. On this basis, the logical structure of the R-SMM proceeds in the following steps of investigation:

1. Musical response models: neurological, physiological, and psychological foundations of musical behavior
2. Nonmusical parallel models: processes in nonmusical brain and behavior function

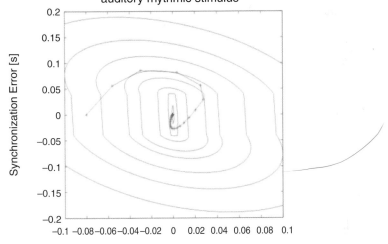

Trajectory of return of a motor response to steady-state synchronization after an 80 msec tempo change, mapped onto the equipotential contours of the attractor field of an auditory rhythmic stimulus

Synchronization Error [s]

Difference between Stimulus and Response Interval [s]

Color Figure 1 This schematic diagram illustrates the strong entrainment function of auditory rhythm on the motor system. A rhythmic motor response that is synchronized to a metronome in phase and period is re-attracted to the metronome rhythm after the metronome tempo is changed. The x-axis shows the time difference between the metronome interval and the response interval; the y-axis shows the synchronization error (the time difference between the occurrence of the metronome beat and motor response). For more details on research and analysis, see Chapter 3.2, "Processes in Rhythmic Synchronization."

Different synchronization strategies as
a result of the nonlinear controller

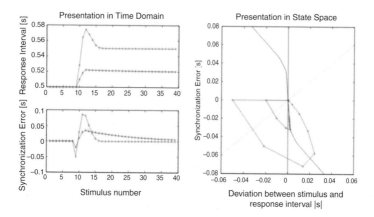

Color Figure 2 This diagram illustrates the existence of two different synchronization strategies found in rhythmic entrainment research. The red lines represent synchronization responses during small tempo changes in the rhythmic stimulus (5 percent or less of base interval). The period of the motor response (e.g., finger taps) immediately adjusts to the new rhythmic stimulus period at response number 10, changing from 500 msec to 520 msec (top graph). This period adjustment leads to a change (increase) in synchronization error. The enlarged synchronization error is slowly readjusted to the original time difference. The green lines show synchronization strategies during large tempo changes (5 percent or more of base interval). The period of the response period is immediately over-corrected at the moment of tempo change to bring the synchronization error quickly back to its original position. The right diagram shows the left time patterns in three-dimensional state space. For more details on research and analysis, see Chapter 3.2, "Processes in Rhythmic Synchronization."

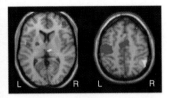

Rhythmic Tapping

right hemisphere   left hemisphere

left hemisphere   right hemisphere

L   R   L   R

■ isochronous tapping versus listening to tones
■ 20percent tapping vs. isochronous tapping
☐ random tapping versus isochronous tapping

Color Figure 3 This PET brain image* shows the brain networks mediating rhythmic motor synchronization to auditory rhythms. The red areas are associated with isochronous (i.e., equidistant beats) rhythms. The green areas are additionally activated during a rhythmic pattern that has a continuous tempo change modulated at a rate of 20 percent of base interval (e.g., 1000 msec, 1200 msec, 1000 msec, 800 msec, 1000 msec, 1200 msec...). The yellow areas are activated during tracking of random rhythms. For detailed description of the neuroanatomical regions depicted, see Chapter 3.3, "Neurophysiological and Neuroanatomical Evidence."

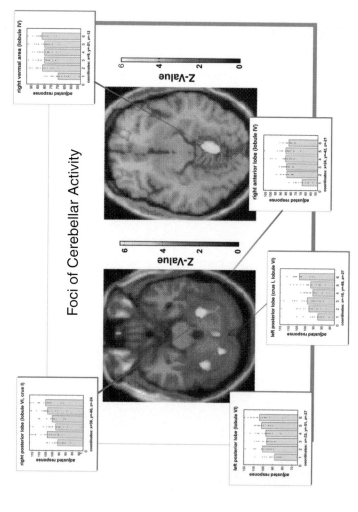

Color Figure 4 Specific activation areas, as measured by PET*, in the cerebellum are associated with different aspects of rhythmic synchronization tasks. The bar graphs show activation strengths in the respective areas. The experimental conditions in each bar graph are (left to right) 1=listening to isochronous rhythm; 2=tapping to random rhythm; 3=tapping to steady isochronous rhythm; 4=tapping to small tempo changes modulated at 3 percent of base interval; 5=tapping to medium tempo changes modulated at 7% of base interval; 6=tapping to large tempo changes modulated at 20 percent of base interval. Right vermal area and right anterior lobe show same activations across all tapping conditions. Right and left posterior lobes show activation strengths that scale with the magnitude of the tempo changes. Activation strength in a separate area in the left posterior lobe scales only with tracking the large tempo changes. For detailed description and interpretation of the data, see Chapter 3.3, "Neurophysiological and Neuroanatomical Evidence."

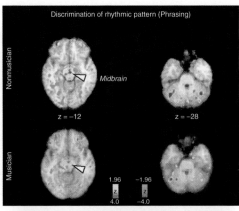

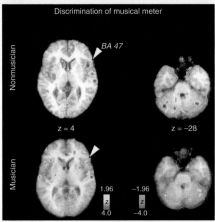

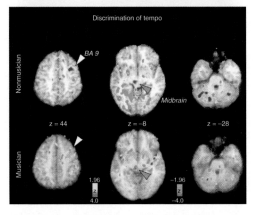

Color Figure 5 The PET brain images* show the distinct neural brain networks associated with different tasks in rhythm perception regarding discriminating differences in pairs of rhythmic patterns, meter, and tempi. Also clearly visible are the differences in brain activation between musicians and non-musicians in performing the tasks. For detailed description, see Chapter 3.3, "Neurophysiological and Neuroanatomical Evidence."

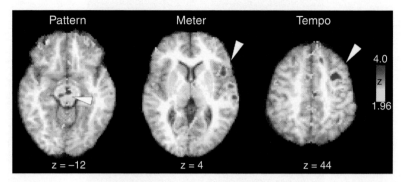

Color Figure 6 The PET brain images* summarize the results for nonmusicians from the same study as Plates 5a, b, and c showing the different neural brain networks associated with different tasks in rhythm perception regarding discriminating differences in pairs of monotonic rhythmic patterns, meters, and tempi. Specifically shown is activity in the midbrain for monotonic pattern discrimination, in right inferior frontal cortex (Brodman area 47) for meter, and right frontal medial cortex (Brodman area 9) for tempo. For detailed description, see Chapter 3.3, "Neurophysiological and Neuroanatomical Evidence."

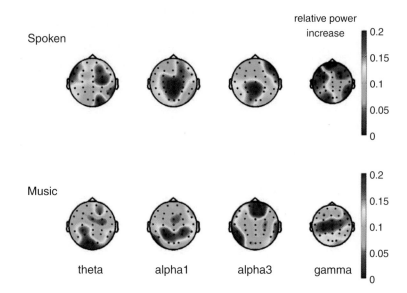

Color Figure 7 The brain images show the topographical distribution of brain wave activity (EEG) associated with learning to remember a list of 15 unrelated words. The list is presented either spoken or as words in a song, using music as a mnemonic device to organize verbal material in metrical groups or 'chunks'. The memory recall performance in the two groups was similar, but the brain networks 'driving' the cognitive performance show different topographical organization in verbal and music-facilitated learning (red=higher activation; blue=lesser activation). Four frequency bands of brain rhythms are depicted: slow theta waves (4–8 Hz); faster alpha waves (8–12 Hz); very fast gamma waves (30 Hz and above). For detailed description, see Chapter 3.4, "Brain Rhythms and Musical Rhythms in Musical Cognition."

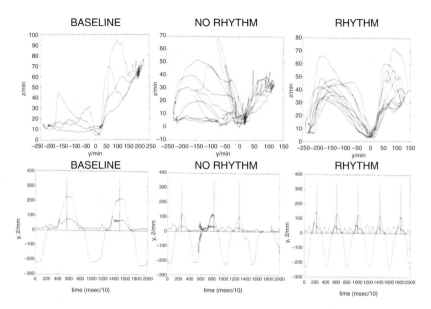

Color Figure 8 The top figures show movement paths (trajectories) of the wrists of stroke patients moving their paretic arm across a table surface and touching three target sensors on the tabletop. In the top diagram, the x-axis shows the distance on the tabletop, the y-axis the height of the movement. The farthest touch point to the left (between −200 and 250 mm) is the starting target, the second target is at 0, and the third target is elevated on a small ramp between 100 and 200 mm. Baseline shows data before training, the no rhythm condition shows data after repetitive exercise of the motion for 30 sec, and the rhythm condition shows data after 30 sec of repetitive exercise with a rhythmic cue (metronome). Clearly visible is the strong smoothing of the movement with rhythmic cuing. The movements were recorded in the sagittal plane with a digital camera and sensors attached to the wrist. The bottom diagram shows the same data of height and distance combined (y-axis) over time (x-axis). For more detail and data on rhythmic stimulation in motor therapy, see Chapters 4, 5, and 6.

*All PET images are group means for each task (compared with passive auditory listening) overlaid on anatomical MRI scans.

3. Mediating models: influence of music on nonmusical brain and behavior function
4. Clinical research models: therapeutic effects of music

6.2.1 Musical Response Models

In this step, the R-SMM requires investigations into the basic psychological and physiological mechanisms of music perception and performance in the areas of affective behavior, cognition, and sensorimotor processes. In the affective domain, topics of special interest are mostly concerned with models of mood and emotion in music, such as cognitive models (Meyer 1956) and gestalt models (Berlyne 1971). Relevant questions include how music communicates emotional meaning, the nature of communication signs in music pertinent to the mood response, psychophysiological responses in music, and affective neuroscience and the neurology of emotion in music.

In the cognitive domain, topics of special interest are models of music cognition regarding—for example—memory, attention, executive function, cognitive information processing, neural network distribution, multimodal sensory integration, learning in music, auditory imagery/scene analysis, time perception, and recall. Relevant questions are concerned with memory formation in music, the effect of stimulus patterns on information processing, hemispheric and other cerebral distribution of music functions, and auditory pattern processing, among others (see Bregman 1990, Deutsch 1982, Halpern 1992, Serafine 1988).

In the area of music and sensorimotor function, topics of special interest include aspects of motor control in music related to motor learning and physiology, distributed neural sensorimotor networks, rhythm formation and control of rhythmicity, timekeeper function, rhythmic auditory-motor synchronization and entrainment, and auditory-motor arousal. Relevant questions are concerned with motor control issues in music performance, connections between the auditory and motor systems, tempo and time control in music performance, the effect of sound on the motor system, rhythmic motor control, rhythmic entrainment models, and so on.

6.2.2 Nonmusical Parallel Models

This step is concerned with establishing meaningful links between musical behavior and nonmusical behavior processes by way of a comparative analysis. Investigations focus on identifying parallels and/or similarities between nonmusical and musical models of perception and behavior. The major question is whether there are similar or parallel cognitive, affective, and sensorimotor processes between musical and nonmusical behavior and perception in areas of therapeutic interest, which would allow us to postulate an enhancing or facilitating influence of music on nonmusical behavior.

Topics of nonmusical parallel models in affective behavior are concerned with the nature and mechanisms of mood and emotional states, as well as the interaction between mood/emotional states and cognitive and psychomotor behavior. Models of interest include the associative network theory of mood and memory, affect-cognition models, theories of nonverbal behavior and nonverbal communication, communication of feeling experiences and mood states, emotional information processing, and theories of arousal and affect. Relevant questions address the nature of mood and emotional behavior; how feeling and mood states are experienced, identified, and communicated; how affective states contribute to the organization and control of behavior in general; and what role mood and emotion play in shaping cognitive responses and in memory access and recall. These processes need to be compared for parallels and similarities with affective responses in music. Questions of essential interest concern the differential contributions of affective and cognitive processes, and the difference between mood experiences in music and in nonmusical context; whether musical mood response generalizes to nonmusical mood states; and the nature and function of communication signs in music versus spoken language regarding communication of feeling states and experiences.

Investigations into nonmusical parallel models in cognition are concerned with models of memory organization, attention processing, and speech/language function. Relevant questions concern mechanisms and principles of efficient memory strategies, perceptual mechanisms in different types of attention behavior, and basic mechanisms in speech/language function. Nonmusical models in memory, attention, and speech/language can be contrasted for similar or parallel mechanisms in music. For example, how are the principles of effective nonmusical memory strategies different from or similar to musical memory formation, and are they potentially accessible through musical memory training? What are the differences between auditory and visual memory decay times? By subsuming the multifaceted area of speech and language under the cognitive domain (although motor and affective systems are also involved), questions can be asked as to what extent neural networks of speech and language are different from or overlap with networks in music. What are attention-enhancing variables in nonmusical perception, and to what extent are there parallels in musical elements facilitating attention?

Investigations into nonmusical parallel models in sensorimotor function are concerned with the role of rhythmicity and timing in motor control, mechanisms in motor memory and motor imagery, principles of motor learning, sensorimotor synchronization, and the role of motor programs in movement planning and execution. Concepts and mechanisms of motor control in music should be compared for parallels and similarities with principles and mechanisms of motor control and learning outside of music. For example, what is the neural basis of rhythmic behavior (e.g., gait)? What roles do different sensory systems play in controlling movement in musical and nonmusical motor performance? What are the mechanisms of rhythm production, developing motor programs, and time control in music performance or dance compared with functional movement or motor skills outside of music?

6.2.3 Mediating Models: The Influence of Music on Behavior

This step entails the development of mediating models that are designed to systematically study the linkage between musical and nonmusical behavior. These models are based on the parallels and/or similarities identified in step 2 between affective, cognitive, and sensorimotor processes within and outside of music. The goal is to provide good theory and rationales for building future research hypotheses in order to be able to study the therapeutically meaningful influence of music on behavior and brain function. If no parallel or similar processes in analyzing behavior and brain function are found in the two previous steps, no further reasonable hypothesis building for inquiries in step 3 and subsequent clinical research in step 4 is possible. To illustrate this point, let us assume that our analysis of the affective response in music (step 1) and outside of music (step 2) shows that they are distinct and unrelated, without the possibility of any mutual influence. This would be the case, for example, if emotional experiences in music are confined to the musical experience, and emotion evoked by music could not influence emotional states and other behavior outside of music. Then no reasonable therapeutic use of the affective response in music would be possible (for example, in psychotherapy applications) because there would be no generalizing transfer effect of the musical response to nonmusical behavior learning and change.

Similar examples can easily be constructed in the cognitive and sensorimotor areas to show the absolute relevance of a comparative analysis of steps 1 and 2 before proceeding to meaningful investigations and theory building in steps 3 and 4. For example, if musical rhythm has relevance only in influencing a musician's motor control in performance, and does not access general rhythmic functions of motor behavior, then no therapeutic use of musical rhythm is possible. If memory formation in music follows principles that are entirely different from other forms of memory training, then the use of music to stimulate nonmusical memory and facilitate retention and recall of nonmusical cognitive information is meaningless.

Based on analyses of step 1 and step 2, step 3 models can be developed to study the influence of music on human behavior. Research in this step does not entail the study of long-term clinical treatment effects. It emphasizes studying the effect of the psychology and physiology of music on healthy and dysfunctional brain and behavior processes based on, as already mentioned, the parallel models of music and nonmusical behavior function identified in step 2. However, the findings in step 3 are essential for clinical research, because they lay the groundwork of data for scientifically founded connections and mechanisms that link music to behavior learning and change. It cannot be overemphasized that the first two steps are necessary to make scientific inquiries in step 3 reasonable. Without understanding the musical response (step 1), the inquiry into parallel processes (step 2) would be impossible, and the input determination in scientific models about music in therapy (step 3)—that is, the role of music in behavior change—would lack objective and reasonable foundations.

Examples of mediating models in the affective domain are studies that pursue questions regarding affect modification through musical mood induction/vectoring and its role in controlling behavior. As an example, the associative network theory of mood and memory (Bower 1981) provides an interesting framework for determining how mood states can determine access to thoughts, memories, and behavior evaluation. Bower's research has shown that changing mood states can facilitate cognitive reorientation. Research in step 3 investigates whether musical mood responses are stable and generalizable enough to shape and select access to specific nonmusical thoughts, memories, and behavior choices. Preliminary evidence shows that music is an efficient mood induction stimulus and that musical mood induction can influence cognitive reorientation, thus facilitating access to desired thoughts and/or memories outside the musical context (Sutherland et al. 1982). If this finding holds true with normal patients, as well as with those with mental disorders, then it could provide a rationale for researching music as a primer and catalyst, as well as a potential training tool in psychotherapy to access healthy cognitions and to influence emotional states. This would be the next logical step in our inquiry toward a theory of musical therapy in step 4.

Another important inquiry in step 3 concerns whether changes in affective content and structural coherence of musical expressions (e.g., in musical improvisation) can be related to an ability to experience, identify, and express feeling states. This research builds on models paralleling and contrasting the structure and content of spoken language and nonverbal musical language. The outcome of this research could be a communication model in music improvisation that assesses coherence in musical expression as a reference to nonmusical affective expression and cognitive organization of thought. This research model provides a reasonable rationale for studying music improvisation as a training tool to improve cognitive and affective behavior coherence, for example, with psychiatric patients. Research studies would then investigate whether an improvement in musical coherence during clinical improvisation is correlated with improvement in coherence of nonmusical behavior (e.g., reality orientation, clarity of thought and comprehension, emotional stability, or a reduction in delusional thinking).

Cognitive mediating models in music therapy research mainly focus on the areas of music's effect on memory, attention, and speech/language function. Since rapid progress in the cognitive neurosciences is currently occurring, new mediating models will be added to future theory building in this domain. A useful paradigm in memory research is music's effect as a pattern organizer (e.g., the chunking principle) on enhancing memory function for nonmusical materials (Deutsch 1982).

Another line of inquiry is the study of the principles of overlearning in music and how they are applied to nonmusical learning. New developments in understanding mechanisms and neurological correlates of working memory may allow us to study music as a training tool to enhance working memory functions (Parenté and Herrmann 1996). In regard to attention research, mediating research models are concerned with identifying attention-organizing elements in music and their application to nonmusical perceptual contexts. In regard to speech and language facilitation research, interesting models include study of the extent to which neurological networks in music and speech/language are separated or share overlapping neuronal circuitry, and whether there is a physiological basis for musical training to enhance speech and language function (Pilon et al. 1998).

Mediating models in sensorimotor processes are focused on the effect of motor control mechanisms in music on motor function outside of music. General topics for research in this area deal with interactions of the auditory and motor systems in regard to physiological responses, as well as motor learning. Several research models have recently been explored, and show promising results for clinical applications. One useful model is concerned with motor learning and facilitation through rhythmic synchronization and entrainment. Important fundamental research questions include whether auditory rhythm can facilitate movement patterns such as in gait or the functional use of arms, hands, or fingers. Rhythmic stimuli are studied as timekeepers, as well as pattern organizers, to enhance the control of motor function. Auditory-motor arousal circuitry is studied, for example, in regard to audiospinal projections via reticulospinal pathways.

In regard to motor learning, principles of learning strategies facilitated by musical stimulus attributes are being transferred and studied in regard to nonmusical movement. For example, motor learning and motor memory in music are based, to an important extent, on pattern organization of movement sequences, especially of the arms, hands, and fingers. Patterned, rhythmically cued repetitions of functional movements have been shown to be very useful in physical rehabilitation, suggesting that the implementation of a musical motor learning model can be of great benefit to the recovery of motor function. Many of these research questions require prior study with normal subjects in order to establish good reference data before applying them to people with motor deficits. Important evidence for the facilitating effect of rhythm and music on motor control in people with movement disorders has accumulated (McIntosh et al. 1997; Miller et al. 1996; Thaut et al. 1993; Thaut et al. 1996).

6.2.4 Clinical Research Models

The research agenda of step 3 in the affective, cognitive, and sensorimotor domains provides the necessary data to build valid models for clinical outcome research. In areas where mediating effects of music on normal behavior and behavior dysfunction have been found, systematic treatment research can be pursued. In step 4 of the model, the research focus in music therapy and music medicine is on therapeutic change, that is, lasting functional behavior change and carry over after treatment. A few examples may illustrate important research topics.

In the affective domain, affect modification techniques in music need to be assessed in conjunction with enhancement of counseling and psychotherapy techniques (Unkefer and Thaut 2002). Another topic is the effect of musical coherence training through improvisation on nonmusical cognitive and emotional coherence and social competence (for example, in psychiatric patients). The effect of musical mood induction, the isoprinciple, and mood vectoring techniques on facilitating affect modification and accessing positive cognitive networks in the treatment of mental disorders (e.g., depression) are other research topics.

In the cognitive domain, several clinical research models have emerged in the areas of memory, attention, and speech/ language training, including music's effect as a mnemonic device in memory training with cognitive disorders; attention training with syndromes, attention deficit disorders, and other deficits of cognitive organization; speech and language facilitation with various pathologies; speech facilitation for aphasia based on neuroanatomical models; and pacing and patterning in fluency disorders, apraxia, and/or dysarthria and vocal training in voice disorder, although the latter techniques could also be subsumed under the sensorimotor domain.

In the cognitive domain, the research application of the scientific model has already produced the development of standardized, research-based treatment techniques, such as musical mnemonics training, musical attention control training, melodic intonation therapy, rhythmic speech cuing, vocal intonation training, and oral motor training.

Music to facilitate and retrain sensorimotor function needs to be researched by assessing the efficiency of musical rhythmic models in the treatment of movement disorders. The effect of rhythmic facilitation in gait training with stroke, traumatically brain injured, or Parkinsonian patients has recently emerged as an important clinical research model, as has the effect of rehabilitative motor learning through therapeutic instrumental music performance (for example, using percussion and keyboard technique for rehabilitating dexterity and arm and hand function). Musical cuing to pattern and retrain functional movements of daily living is another area of considerable interest for clinical research in music and sensorimotor function. Research, guided by the scientific model, has produced three standardized sensorimotor rehabilitation techniques in music therapy: rhythmic auditory stimulation (RAS), patterned sensory enhancement (PSE), and therapeutic instrumental music performance (TIMP).

6.2.5 Summary

The R-SMM provides an effective epistemological model integrating the perception of music and rhythm into a framework that allows us to extract and transfer its influence on general, nonmusical brain and behavior function into a rehabilitative context. The R-SMM is a dynamic and open-ended model connecting the emergence of research data into an algorithm of deductive reasoning to continuously build new rationales and evidence for the effect of music and rhythm in therapy. It integrates the physiological and psychological bases of music perception and production into a wider framework of the neuroscience of perception, cognition, motor learning, and other areas of brain function. Most important for the history of music therapy, not only is it the first scientific model of music in therapy, but it anchors the understanding of music's therapeutic function in music perception per se and not in some borrowed interpretation of music's role in therapy from nonmusical fields.

6.3 The Emergence of Neurologic Music Therapy

The years since about 1990 have seen an unprecedented development of research in the biomedical sciences of music. This research—by enabling a new understanding of the biological basis of music—has led to the development of clusters of scientific evidence for the effectiveness of specific biomedical interventions of music within therapy, rehabilitation, and medicine. In a comprehensive analytical effort by researchers and clinicians in music therapy, neurology, and the brain sciences, these evidence clusters were codified into a system of therapeutic techniques of what was subsequently termed neurologic music therapy (NMT). This codification— which was started in the late 1990s—has resulted in the unprecedented development of clinical techniques that are standardized in applications and terminology, as well as supported by evidence through scientific research. Because the system of techniques is research-based, it is dynamically open-ended in terms of future development and knowledge.

Five basic definitions articulate the most important principles of neurologic music therapy:

- NMT is defined as the therapeutic application of music to cognitive, sensory, and motor dysfunctions due to neurologic disease of the human nervous system.
- NMT is based on a neuroscience model of music perception and production, and the influence of music on functional changes in nonmusical brain and behavior functions (R-SMM).
- Treatment techniques are evidence-based: They are based on data from scientific and clinical research and are directed toward functional nonmusical therapeutic goals.
- Treatment techniques are standardized in terminology and application and are applied to therapy as therapeutic music interventions (TMI), which are adaptable to the patient's functional needs.
- In addition to training in music and NMT, practitioners are educated in the areas of neuroanatomy and physiology, brain pathologies, medical terminology, and rehabilitation of cognitive, motor, speech, and language functions.

Clinical applications of NMT are subdivided into three domains of rehabilitation: (a) sensorimotor rehabilitation, (b) speech and language rehabilitation, and (c) cognitive rehabilitation. In each domain, NMT can be applied to patient treatment within different clinical fields and disciplines, such as inpatient and outpatient neurologic rehabilitation, neurogeriatrics, neuropedioatrics, and neurodevelopmental therapies. Depending on the patients' needs, the therapeutic goals are directed toward functional rehabilitative, developmental, or adaptive goals. Within this framework, the only major area of therapeutic rehabilitation not covered is psychiatric rehabilitation. However, as the understanding of the nature and the mechanisms of mental illness progresses, our understanding of effective rehabilitation strategies will improve. Within an emerging framework of neuropsychiatric models it will possible to design effective treatment techniques in NMT, most likely within the domain of cognitive rehabilitation (Unkefer and Thaut 2002).

Within the comprehensive clinical and scientific focus of this book, many detailed clinical issues have to be omitted or can be mentioned only in brief overview. These two brief comments are specifically mentioned in our selective treatment of clinical issues due to their particular significance for music in rehabilitation:

1. Technique standardization—although frequently mentioned as an important goal—has eluded music therapy for its entire history. Techniques were sometimes defined by aesthetic adjectives, such as creative music therapy, or by reference to music elements, such as improvisational music therapy. Other attempts at definitions have used activity-based descriptors, such as reminiscing or song lyric analysis or music and movement. At times, technique definitions were introduced as terms borrowed from other fields, such as psychoanalytic music therapy or group music therapy.

   In NMT, two parameters of technique definition were introduced to allow for the development of standardized descriptions and applications. The first parameter is based on the functional goals of the therapeutic music exercise—for example, to improve range of motion of arms, enhance declarative memory, train selective attention, or facilitate speech encoding in a patient with expressive aphasia. The second parameter is based on the mechanism in music that facilitates the therapeutic change: rhythm as a sensory timer for motor control, musical pattern perception as a mnemonic device to enhance learning and recall through metrical organization of verbal materials, or singing to access alternative neural pathways to encode verbal output. Within those normative parameters, techniques can be uniquely and consistently defined in a way that separates them from each other by therapeutic mechanism in the music and functional therapeutic goals. The actual design of the therapeutic exercise, on the other hand—within its standardized structure—draws on an unlimited number of musical resources and experiences to be translated creatively, yet logically, into a functional therapeutic experience for the client.

2. Assessment is an essential component for implementing best practice standards embraced internationally by many rehabilitation professions to ensure quality care for patients. Assessment is a process with which music therapy has wrestled for decades without conclusive solutions. Part of the dilemma can be summarized in a simple question: What do music therapists assess that is unique to

their professional role in facilitating best treatment options for the patient? In order to understand the full extent of the dilemma, however, we may take the argument a step further. Best practice standards assign to assessment the critical role of collecting data about the patient's status of functioning to allow the best choice of treatment with the highest degree of confidence in positive outcome. In other words, assessment plays the critical role in helping to decide which treatment is the right one for the patient's diagnostic status and which treatment option has the greatest likelihood of success. This process, however, can be meaningfully applied only when standardized treatment techniques exist and when something is known about treatment success rates. This knowledge can be obtained only by clinical research investigating standardized techniques and elements of their mechanisms. Without standardized treatment techniques and a comprehensive evidence basis that is grounded in scientific mechanism and outcome research, a therapy profession faces a paradoxical situation that prevents the meaningful development of assessment procedures. As we have outlined above, in NMT, assessment can be applied in a meaningful way because standardization has been achieved and outcome data is available on an increasing level, contingent upon the growth in clinical research that will allow for a logical implementation of the assessment process.

6.4 Principles of Neurologic Rehabilitation

A brief outline of current principles of neurologic rehabilitation may help the reader to link the mechanisms of NMT even more strongly with an understanding of how music functions effectively as a therapeutic modality within a neuroscience paradigm. Excellent textbooks and papers on the theory and practice of neurologic rehabilitation are widely available. Therefore, we will provide only key concepts in this section as an introduction to the subject.

First, a brief remark about the use of the word "rehabilitation." In the strictest semantic sense, rehabilitation applies only to illnesses and disorders that allow for actual restoration of function. However, this strict definition creates problems in usage (e.g., when applied to degenerative diseases such as Alzheimer's or Parkinson's disease). Therefore, for other forms of therapy, terms such as "habilitation" or "adaptation" have been used. However, in common use, the term rehabilitation is probably used much more flexibly than the technically correct semantic meaning implies. Throughout this book, the term is used in such a broader sense.

Table 6.1 summarizes the four essential paradigms and principles for state-of-the art treatment in neurologic rehabilitation to which NMT adheres.

The principle of neuroscience-guided rehabilitation refers to the necessity to build treatment techniques around known principles of brain function based on the best available evidence from brain research. This requires a close working relationship on many levels between the community of neuroscientists and rehabilitation specialists. Furthermore, this principle requires the implementation of models of best practice in rehabilitation built on the best available research data for the effectiveness of therapeutic techniques. This evidence-based therapy requires two components in treatment applications; treatment is selected on the basis of (1) the best available assessment data, and (2) the best available outcome data for a specific technique in the clinical research literature.

The overwhelming evidence in the research literature is that the only effective forms of therapy in neurologic rehabilitation are based on learning and training paradigms (Whitall et al. 2000, Hummelsheim 1999, Robertson 1999). Effective rehabilitative exercises should be task-oriented, highly structured (timing, repetition), attention demanding, and rewarding. Learning and training paradigms also imply long-term commitments to therapeutic training to improve and sustain motor, cognitive, and speech

TABLE 6.1 Four Essential Paradigms for Neurologic Music Therapy Techniques

1. Neuroscience-guided rehabilitation	Treatment based on data and concepts from brain research and clinical studies
2. Learning and training models	Rhythmic motor learning and training
	Temporal structure and organization of therapeutic interventions and stimuli to enhance cognitive, speech, and language training
3. Cortical plasticity models	Music as complex, rhythmically organized, and spectrally diverse language to drive neural network patterns through temporal modulation of sensory input
4. Neurological facilitation models	Patterned multimodal sensory input (e.g., via auditory rhythmicity, musical patterns) to enhance motor, speech/language, and cognitive functions

function. Therapy within such a paradigm is not a closed process. The patient is viewed as a lifelong learner, in a way similar to the continued practice an athlete or musician needs in order to reach and maintain optimal skills. To maximize the effect of learning and training for therapeutic gains, different modalities of delivery have to be developed and implemented: from acute and rehabilitative inpatient units to outpatient therapy, home care, community support groups, therapeutic fitness centers, and educational approaches for patients and caregivers in the community. Efforts also have to be expended to find and implement the most effective learning and training strategies.

The brain has considerable plasticity that can be shaped and modulated by experience, learning, and activities. Training and learning drive neuroplasticity (cf. Nudo et al. 1996; Pizzamiglio et al. 1998; Rossini et al. 1998). The context of neuroplasticity also informs the critical issues of restitutive versus compensatory approaches in rehabilitation. The evidence of neuroplasticity suggests that through appropriate learning and training stimuli, restitution of function is possible, mediated by actual changes in neural circuits that underpin normal function. Much still needs to be learned about the extent of possible plasticity through targeted therapeutic techniques on specific lesions. Also, no sufficient quantitative models of neural connectivity and lesion impact exist to help choose between compensatory and restitutive approaches based on reliable neurological information. Much of current assessment and treatment selection is based on the existence of residual behavioral functions. However, restitutive recovery of function through rehabilitation based on neuroplastic processes is an important new and promising paradigm that is generating a continued research emphasis in neurologic rehabilitation.

Within the context of these principles and paradigms, the importance of proper therapeutic facilitation of rehabilitative techniques is of critical importance. It is crucial to develop and implement therapeutic strategies that optimize learning, training, and processes of neuroplasticity in order to access optimal channels of recovery. Strategies and facilitative stimuli for efficient motor learning, cognitive learning, and speech training must be carefully evaluated in terms of their effect on recovery of functions.

A neuroscience-based understanding of the perception and production of music and rhythm underpins the concepts of neurologic music therapy. Therefore, NMT offers critical contributions to all four paradigms. Its techniques and rationales are based on insights and data from neuroscience in regard to brain function, music, and rhythm. The effectiveness of NMT techniques has been widely demonstrated by clinical research, thus building a substantial evidence base. Therapeutic exercises, stimuli, and experiences involving learning and training involving musical-rhythmic materials are easily constructed. NMT can offer a wide range of perceptual-receptive and active performance exercises in music and rhythm that are goal-oriented, build appropriate arousal and attention, are affectively intrinsically rewarding, and have a high degree of temporal structure. The intrinsic rhythmicity and temporality of music create a framework to postulate that musical-rhythmic stimulation, by temporally structuring learning and training, is a highly effective driver to facilitate and shape neuroplasticity through synchronization and entrainment. In summary, the principles and paradigms of neurologic rehabilitation are integrated in NMT, making it a valid and effective contributor to rehabilitation.

6.5 A Transformational Design Model (TDM) for Neurologic Music Therapy Practice

The application of the four steps of the R-SMM will result in a research process that will generate a large, scientifically validated database as the foundation for clinical techniques and rational treatment applications in neurologic music therapy. However, an additional model is needed to direct the clinical translation of research findings from the R-SMM into functional music therapy practice. For this purpose, we developed a model that teaches neurologic music therapists the basic mechanisms for designing functional therapeutic music applications whose validity is based on the R-SMM.

The transformational design model (TDM) provides a system for the therapist to immediately translate the scientific model into functional clinical practice. The TDM, we believe, also helps students and therapists avoid two potential weaknesses of therapeutic music interventions: (1) an activity-based approach in which generic musical activities are adapted to therapeutic goals, and (2) the use of therapeutic music techniques that address therapeutic goals very broadly and generally, and are only weakly related to functional therapeutic outcomes. The basic five steps of the TDM are the following:

1. Diagnostic and functional assessment of the patient
2. Development of therapeutic goals/objectives
3. Design of functional, nonmusical therapeutic exercises and stimuli
4. Translation of step 3 into functional therapeutic music experiences
5. Transfer of therapeutic learning to functional, nonmusical real-world applications

The first three steps and the fifth step in the TDM are basic processes common to all therapy disciplines: step 1 entails diagnostic and etiological assessment of the client; step 2 consists of the development of appropriate therapy goals and of measurable objectives as criteria to assess their achievement; and step 3 consists of the design of therapeutic exercises and activities (or the application of therapeutic stimuli) to implement and accomplish the clinical goals and objectives. This design process is based upon functional behaviors of the patient and does not yet include musical considerations. The planning of these therapeutic experiences is similar to, or at times even based on, therapeutic plans utilized across rehabilitation disciplines. This approach also ensures patient-centered, rather than discipline-centered, therapy programs. In patient-centered approaches, all disciplines work together to support the same therapeutic goals from different angles, using as many collaborative and interdisciplinary techniques as possible. In discipline-centered therapy, patients move from one therapy session to the next through their daily schedule, being treated for different aspects of rehabilitation with little consideration given to collaborative planning and treatment.

The crucial clinical process for neurologic music therapists occurs in step 4. Here, their unique role emerges: translating functional and therapeutic exercises and stimuli into functional therapeutic music exercises and stimuli that are isomorphic (i.e., they have the same functional structure) to the nonmusical therapeutic exercises. For example, social interaction exercises are translated into musical group improvisation structures that simulate the content of the specifically intended interaction and communication exercises; emotional communication exercises are translated into musical, possibly nonverbal, group dynamic improvisation exercises to express emotions; and access to positive cognitive networks in psychotherapy and counseling is facilitated by mood vectoring through guided music listening, putting the client into the desired mood state to be able to access positive cognitive networks. Speech pacing in dysarthria rehabilitation may be accomplished through rhythmic cues in musical structures. Attention training may be accomplished through different types of musical perception training. Memory training may be facilitated by mnemonic devices embedded in musical structures. Exercises to improve range of motion and limb coordination are translated into structures of therapeutic instrument-playing exercises. Functional reaching and grasping exercises are facilitated by rhythmic patterning in musical structures. Gait training exercises are facilitated by rhythmic entrainment and audiospinal stimulation. It is important to remember that it is not the goals or objectives that are translated into music applications but the structure, process, and elements of functional exercises and therapeutic stimuli.

In step 4 of the TDM, the rules of a good isomorphic (identically shaped) transformational process in neurologic music therapy are determined by three principles:

1. The therapeutic validity or scientific logic of the translation of functional behavior into music therapy. This translation process must be congruent with the scientific information developed in the R-SMM, especially in its step 4. For example, appropriately researched models of memory training allow for the development of logical and valid techniques using music for cognitive retraining in neurologic rehabilitation. If music is used for memory training without considering the basic and clinical research knowledge about musical memory and its parallels to nonmusical memory processes, nonfunctional and only spuriously effective techniques are likely to evolve.

2. The musical experience in therapy has to conform, even on the most basic level, to the aesthetic and artistic principles of good musical forms. In other words, the musical experience has to be aesthetically well composed and performed, whether active or receptive music techniques are applied (e.g., listening exercises, improvisation, rehearsed performance, or movement to music). The beneficial influence of music on structuring, organizing, and enhancing perception, learning, and training in the therapeutic process can unfold only within optimal musical patterns, regardless of the level of complexity. However, we must remember that the application of a certain musical technique, such as improvisation, does not create, in itself, a theoretical model of music therapy practice.

3. The therapeutic music experience has to be isomorphic in therapeutic structure and function to the general therapy experience. The group dynamic structure of a psychotherapy exercise has to be captured and simulated in the structure of the musical experience in order to truly facilitate and enhance the intended therapeutic process. For example, exercises designed to improve the range of arm motion through playing musical instruments must entail the functional motions of the nonmusical therapy goals in order to accomplish useful training for the patient. Thus, a well-trained neurologic music therapist needs to learn how to create appropriate musical analogues for nonmusical behavior and stimuli. Here the logic and creativity of functional musicianship and translational nonmusical to musical thinking and reasoning form a necessary third prerequisite to isomorphically molding functional therapy into functional music therapy.

The TDM in neurologic music therapy is a practical guide for the therapist to compose goal-oriented therapeutic music experiences based on a functional reasoning process that links assessments, goals, and learning and training experiences. The TDM is the clinical complement or practical extension of the scientific theory model, the R-SMM. The validity of the isomorphic transformation of a therapeutic experience into a therapeutic music experience is measured against the scientific evidence in step 4 of the R-SMM. For example, the musical and transformational logic of a certain therapeutic music exercise may be fulfilled (e.g., a well-structured, musically creative, and motivating exercise using reading and playing musical notation in order to help reading letters), but the scientific logic is missing because no evidence for the therapeutic value of music exists in a certain area of application (reading musical symbols does not transfer to enhanced reading of letters). Thus, the R-SMM functions as a check on the validity of NMT techniques developed within the TDM system. On the other hand, the use of the TDM allows the music therapist to examine the research evidence of the R-SMM for applicable information to optimize treatment variables. The use of the R-SMM may also help to identify weak areas in bodies of knowledge and may stimulate the ongoing and dynamic development of new research agendas in neurologic music therapy. Through this exchange, the clinician shares in the three basic principles of research-based therapies: (1) skepticism, (2) determinism, and (3) empiricism. The scientific evidence available regarding the R-SMM allows us to understand why step 4—the translation of functional therapy into functional music therapy—is not an unnecessary detour of the treatment process rather than a facilitating and optimizing process to provide best practice interventions.

The clinical music therapist may enter the process of validating functional music interventions by using the TDM. At the critical juncture of step 4—the stage of isomorphic translations of therapy into music therapy—the TDM will lead the therapist to the scientific theory model, the R-SMM, for information crucial to a therapy informed by best practice standards. The researcher and scientist, on the other hand, will more likely enter the process through the scientific theory model, which sets the structural stage for a coherent inquiry into music's role in therapy and medicine. At the continuation of step 4 of the scientific model, the researcher will look to the clinician to translate research evidence into effective therapeutic practices. Furthermore, as a scientific theory, the R-SMM opens links to other bodies of scientific knowledge and lines of research in neuroscience, psychology, and music, because many of the inquiries in its first two steps are also germane to those fields. Thus, the R-SMM helps ground neurologic music therapy in scientific discipline. Finally, rather than beginning with clinical research models (step 4), research agendas can be structured so that the four steps are followed in proper order.

In summary, the R-SMM provides a method for redesigning and refocusing future research that allows building the foundations of music in therapy in a logical and scientific sequence. This effort is crucial for the future quality of music therapy as a health profession. Second, it provides for the growth of validated clinical practice in music therapy by anchoring the transformation process, inherent in the TDM-based functional application of music to therapy, to objective, data-based evidence in therapeutic assessments and outcomes. This is an effort we unequivocally owe to patients and clients.

6.6 Summary

In this chapter, we have discussed several important historical, theoretical, and clinical developments in music in therapy and medicine. On the basis of new directions in brain research, a historical paradigm shift has occurred, moving music therapy from an interpretive social-science paradigm to a neuroscience paradigm based on music perception. Research allows us to investigate and determine the influence of music on brain and behavior function. As a translational framework to transfer and generalize musical brain functions to nonmusical behavior learning and change, we introduced the rational-scientific mediating model (R-SMM). The R-SMM provides a theoretical framework to study the influence of music on nonmusical behavior within a scientific research model. By definition this model does not predetermine outcomes, but within the principles of scientific inquiry, provides an open-ended and dynamic system for the development of new knowledge and change in state-of-the art clinical practice. Based on the scientific paradigm shift, neurologic music therapy (NMT) has emerged as a rehabilitation discipline based on basic and clinical research and evidence-based developments in understanding the foundations of music in the brain sciences. For a conceptualization of how to design functional therapeutic exercises and stimuli in NMT, we introduced the transformational design model (TDM). We explained the mechanisms and principles of translation, how nonmusical therapeutic goals and therapeutic stimuli are functionally shaped into therapeutic music exercises.

7

Neurologic Music Therapy in Sensorimotor Rehabilitation

7.1 Introduction

One of the most intriguing aspects of the effect of music on the brain that has come into new focus in recent research has been the effect of music on movement. Using music to elicit motor response and enhance motor behavior has been a part of all documented societal functions of music, as well as of many healing rituals throughout history in many cultures (Merriam 1964). In particular, rhythmical accompaniment of motor activities, such as dancing, has been a common part of therapeutic practice. More recently, however, the impact of music and rhythm on motor processes has become the focus of scientific study and clinical practice in neurologic rehabilitation.

An extensive body of research has shown a relationship between the neural processing of auditory stimuli and arousal (priming) and timing functions of the motor system (Rossignol and Melvill Jones 1976). Motor neuroscience has demonstrated that auditory rhythmic stimuli can enhance or promote motor responses and, even more directly, elicit movement. The timing aspects of music, through its rhythmic components, have a strong influence on temporal regulation of movement. Rhythm may be best described as a sensory timer that utilizes the physiologically very sensitive connections between the auditory and motor systems in the brain to influence time control in movement. Interestingly, as we discussed in chapter 5, comprehensive regulation of movement dimensions of space and position, as well as of force, can be accessed through the regulation of time. Furthermore, sound has a strong impact on arousal and priming of the motor system to set it into states of readiness through reticulospinal pathways on the brain stem and spinal cord level.

Three less-researched aspects of music and rhythm in motor control need to be mentioned as potentially contributing factors. Memory formation in music is primarily driven through its strong pattern and phrasing structure, which creates temporal metrical organization (see chapter 4). The effect of music on motor memory has not been well researched, but similar mechanisms may be potential facilitators of remembering functional movement sequences as exercised in rehabilitation. Second, music has considerable saliency as a conditioning stimulus in associative memory formation. Music can bring back memories associated with certain experiences (the "honey, they're playing our song" phenomenon). This associative learning mechanism in music, well recognized in aesthetic theory, accounts for a good deal of our experiences of emotional meaning in music. For certain patient groups who suffer from restrictions and limitations on their movement capacities (e.g., due to dementia or other neurologic illness), music may provide a strong associative trigger to engage in movement through memory recall.

Even without specific associations between a musical piece and a movement experience, the motivational character of music to elicit physical response may provide a powerful stimulus in therapy to facilitate at least initial movement responses, which can then be further developed toward more functional goals in rehabilitation. The rehabilitative qualities of music are—as we now know—based on specific physiological auditory-motor mechanisms. However, within a full compositional musical context of rhythm, form, harmony, and melody, musical patterns apparently translate with ease into motor images via mechanisms of gestalt perception.

7.2 Neurologic Music Therapy Techniques in Sensorimotor Rehabilitation

In this chapter, three techniques in neurologic music therapy (NMT) for sensorimotor rehabilitation will be defined and their specific applications to therapy explained and illustrated:

1. Rhythmic auditory stimulation (RAS). A technique of rhythmic motor cuing to facilitate training of movements that is intrinsically and biologically rhythmical. In humans, the most important type of these movements is gait. Therefore, RAS is used almost exclusively

for gait rehabilitation. It uses rhythmic cues in 2/4 or 4/4 meter, presented either as pure metronome beats or as strongly accentuated beats in complete musical patterns, to cue gait parameters such as step cadence, stride length, velocity, symmetry of stride length and stride duration, and double and single support time of leg stance.

2. Patterned sensory enhancement (PSE). PSE uses the rhythmic, melodic, harmonic, and dynamic-acoustical patterns of music to provide temporal, spatial, and force cues to structure and regulate functional movements. The auditory-musical patterns or kinematic compositions are derived from translating all components of the kinematic patterns of the movement in space, time, and force into sound patterns. For example, the rhythmic patterns simulate the timing patterns of the movement, pitch patterns simulate changing spatial positions, and harmonic and dynamic patterns simulate applications of force and muscle tone. PSE has its equivalent in sports training in the concept of sonification. PSE can be used to structure, in time, space and force, any functional movement patterns and sequences, regardless of whether they are intrinsically rhythmic or discrete of the upper trunk, arms, hands, or whole body (e.g., reaching, grasping, lifting motions; sit-to-stand transfers; etc.).

3. Therapeutic instrumental music performance (TIMP). TIMP uses playing of musical instruments to exercise and simulate functional movement patterns in motor therapy. Musical instruments and spatial configuration of instruments and motor patterns for playing are selected on the basis of functional considerations to train appropriate ranges of motion, endurance, strength, limb coordination, and functional movements entailing finger dexterity, grasp, flexion/extension, adduction/abduction, rotation, supination/pronation, and so on.

7.3 Rhythmic Auditory Stimulation

Rhythmic auditory stimulation (RAS) is a neurologic technique using the physiological effects of auditory rhythm on the motor system to improve the control of movement in rehabilitation and therapy. RAS is mostly used in gait therapy to aid in the recovery of functional, stable, and adaptive walking patterns in patients with significant gait deficits due to stroke, Parkinson's disease, traumatic brain injury, effects of aging, or other causes. The basic neurological enhancement of gait through RAS is mediated by a rhythmic entrainment effect in which the rhythm, as an external timekeeper, entrains desired movement frequencies and retrains motor programs through anticipatory cuing of functional movement patterns.

Through frequency entrainment of motor patterns, rhythm stabilizes the timing, kinematic control, and force applications in movement.

RAS can be used in two different ways:

1. As an immediate entrainment stimulus providing rhythmic cues during the movement. For example, individuals may listen to a metronome or rhythmic music tape while walking to enhance their walking tempo, balance, and control of muscles and limbs.
2. As a facilitating stimulus for training; patients train with RAS for a certain period of time in order to achieve more functional gait patterns, which they then transfer to walking without rhythmic facilitation.

A body of research has recently shown that both applications work quite effectively for patients with a variety of gait disorders. RAS has been demonstrated to significantly improve the gait ability of stroke patients in immediate applications (Thaut et. al. 1993, reviewed in Jeffery and Good 1995; Prassas et al. 1997) and as a therapeutic training technique (Mandel et al. 1990; Thaut et al. 1997; Schauer et al. 1996; Mauritz 2002; Schauer and Mauritz 2002; Hummelsheim 1999). RAS training for patients with Parkinson's disease has been researched, e.g., by Morris et al. (2004), Fernandez del Olmo and Cudeiro (2003), Freedland et al. (2002), Howe et al. (2003), Thaut et al. (1996), and Miller et al. (1996). Immediate RAS effects on Parkinsonian gait have been demonstrated by McIntosh et al. (1997) and Richards et al. (1992). Long-term carryover effects of RAS on gait ability of Parkinsonian patients have been shown by McIntosh et al. (1998). The effect of RAS on gait in other patient groups has been shown for Huntington's disease patients by Thaut, Miltner, and Lange et al. (1999), for patients with traumatic brain injury by Hurt et al. (1998) and Kenyon and Thaut (2000), and for children with cerebral palsy by Thaut, Hurt, and Drogan et al. (1998).

7.3.1 How Therapeutic Techniques Influence Brain and Behavior Function

This may be a good place to briefly review basic mechanisms underlying auditory-motor interactions in regard to therapeutic applications. For the specific discussion of research studies, the reader may want to review chapter 4.

Since about 1990, a considerable research effort has been made to identify probable physiological mechanisms underlying the profound effect of auditory rhythm on motor control, and especially gait performance. Taking together the best available evidence, the neurological basis for the effect of auditory rhythm on the motor system may be best described in four areas:

- Rhythmic entrainment
- Priming of the auditory-motor pathway
- Cuing of the movement period
- Stepwise limit cycle entrainment

7.3.1.1 Rhythmic Entrainment   Many studies have documented the basic physiological attractor function of auditory rhythm to entrain motor responses with immediacy and strong time stability. The physical basis for the perception of rhythm is the detection of periodicity patterns in amplitude modulations of the sound spectrum. The auditory system is superbly equipped to detect these patterns because of its sensitivity to changes in sound intensity. The numerical range between the physical sound pressure measure at the threshold of hearing (one decibel) and the threshold of pain (120 decibels) is one to 1 trillion. Thus, it should come as no surprise how quickly and accurately the auditory system can detect amplitude fluctuations and extract any regular pattern in them. Evidence for rhythmic auditory entrainment comes from mathematical and statistical analysis of rhythmic motor responses, as well as from physiological recordings of electromyography (EMG), electroencephalography (EEG), and magneto-encephalography (MEG) data. The magnet effect of auditory rhythm to synchronize and entrain movement patterns can be simulated most effectively in one-way, weakly coupled oscillator models. The attractor strength of auditory rhythm on the motor system has recently been further substantiated by the observation that motor responses can be entrained by auditory rhythmic patterns even at levels below conscious perception. Therefore, the basic mechanisms of rhythmic entrainment appear to be strongly based on direct, dynamic, sensorimotor coupling, which can take place without major contributions from cognitive learning efforts.

7.3.1.2 Priming of the Auditory-Motor Pathway   Early landmark studies by Paltsev and Elner (1967) and Rossignol and Melvill Jones (1976) have shown that physiological entrainment of muscle activation patterns through auditory rhythm takes place via reticulospinal pathways, and that this effect is utilized in functional locomotor tasks. Evidence for audio-spinal motor facilitation has been reported in many subsequent studies, such as a study by Miller et al. (1996), which showed physiological entrainment of EMG patterns in the legs after RAS training in Parkinsonian patients. EMG amplitude variability became more consistent, showing more efficient motor unit recruitment patterns, whereas variability of EMG timing actually increased, providing evidence that a higher degree of adaptive flexibility for gait pattern modulation had been established.

Recent brain imaging research with positron-emission tomography (PET) technology and MEG revealed a neural network for rhythmic entrainment with an emphasis on right lateralization in thalamo-parieto-temporal loops with contributions from basal ganglia and hemispheric bilateral cerebellar structures. Limited prefrontal activation during rhythmic motor synchronization supports the concepts of direct sensorimotor coupling and immediacy of rhythmic auditory-motor entrainment. Support for these concepts is also provided by the observation that many components of the neural synchronization network were already activated and entrained during simply listening to the rhythm (Stephan et al. 2002a, 2000b).

7.3.1.3 Cuing of the Movement Period The analysis of rhythmic synchronization strategies has shown that both period information (the adaptation of the movement duration to the rhythmic stimulus duration) and phase information (the coincidence of the response event to the occurrence of the rhythmic beat) play a role in keeping oneself synchronized. Actually, mathematical analysis has shown that frequency information and period adaptations (i.e., the matching of the movement period to the stimulus period) may be more essential for tracking a rhythm pattern (Thaut and Kenyon 2003). Therefore, when synchronizing our movement to an auditory rhythm, we can assume that the rhythm not only entrains the phase dynamics (i.e., cues the end point of the movement to the beat event), but actually entrains the entire duration of the movement to the rhythmic interval. As a consequence, frequency entrainment, as can be shown in oscillator models, entrains time stability across the entire movement period. The rhythmic cue provides a continuous time reference during the planning and execution of the movement. Kinematic optimization models show that period or frequency entrainment has to result in enhanced kinematic stability via trajectory modulation by scaling kinematic parameters (acceleration, velocity, position across time) and periodic force input in the absence of an intact internal timekeeper. Therefore, rhythmic entrainment via RAS will enhance that total kinematic pattern of movement by cuing period and trajectory dynamics.

7.3.1.4 Stepwise Limit Cycle Entrainment In application to rehabilitation and therapy, RAS needs to conform to a treatment protocol that enhances the intrinsic control functions of movement. First, because RAS is based on the metronome or pulse function of rhythm (also applicable to these functions in music, i.e., the perception of the basic beat), RAS is best used to cue movement that is intrinsically pulse-rhythmic, such as gait. More complex functional movement patterns (e.g., in sequential arm, hand, or finger movements) can be more effectively cued by more complex rhythmic patterns, which can be adapted to express more complex metric, rhythmic, and dynamic space-force patterns (see the concept of sonification and gestalt perception in music as a basis for the therapy technique of patterned sensory enhancement).

Second, in order to enhance kinematic stability through frequency entrainment, RAS frequencies need to be set initially at the current natural or intrinsic frequency of the person's movement. This process of resonant frequency entrainment is based on the concept of limit cycles in movement. Limit cycles are frequencies at which any moving system performs optimally. RAS should be adapted to the patient's current limit cycle (i.e., the current step cadence when applied to gait). The initial purpose of RAS is to stabilize and optimize the movement parameters at that limit cycle. Once stability has been achieved at that level, new limit cycles can be gradually entrained through a stepwise entrainment process that will increasingly approximate the patient's premorbid optimal movement frequencies. Biological constraints due to injury may result in optimal limit cycles that are different from the preinjury ones.

It is important to note that the concept of limit cycle entrainment implies optimization of the entire movement kinematics. For example, when RAS is used to entrain higher step rates in Parkinsonian patients, stride lengths will increase, too, due to the mechanical properties of the gait-generating system, as long as the limit cycle frequencies stay in the optimal range (which is implied in the term itself). This effect has been demonstrated in several clinical studies. In the case of a nearly normal cadence with shortened stride length, RAS will be used to entrain the current cadence or a slightly lower one in order to increase stride length through the added kinematic stability emerging in the rhythmic entrainment process.

Natural movement frequencies can be determined by assessing a patient's current cadence. There are also mathematical models to compute optimal resonant step frequencies. Stepwise limit cycle entrainment (SLICE) is currently the most frequently applied RAS treatment protocol in gait therapy and rehabilitation. SLICE has been shown to be effective for RAS applications to improve gait performance online through the immediate entrainment effects. The SLICE protocol has also been shown to be effective as a long-term training procedure in which the patient learns to transfer the entrainment effects in order to maintain improved walking ability without the facilitating stimulus being present.

7.3.2 The Clinical Protocol of RAS

7.3.2.1 Assessment The start of each training session should include a warm-up that is used to assess gait parameters, measuring the following:

(a) Cadence, by counting heel strikes for 60 seconds.

7.3.2 The Clinical Protocol of RAS

7.3.2.1 Assessment The start of each training session should include a warm-up that is used to assess gait parameters, measuring the following:

(a) Cadence, by counting heel strikes for 60 seconds.
(b) Velocity, by measuring on the floor how many meters (feet) the patient walked in 60 seconds (tape marks on the floor every meter or foot).
(c) Stride length, by dividing velocity by (cadence / 2). For example, (30 meters per minute) divided by (100 steps per minute / 2 minutes per stride) = 0.6 m or 60 cm or 2 feet or 24 inches. Normal values are cadence=105–120 steps per minute, velocity = 60–80 meters per minute (age dependant).

One of the most important factors to determine the length of the training session is the patient's endurance. Inpatient therapy sessions may typically last from 10 to 30 minutes, once or twice daily.

7.3.2.2 Resonant Frequency Entrainment The goal of the first part of the session is to match the RAS frequency to the patient's gait cadence and walk. Also, for patients who are not ready for sustained walking, specific pregait exercises may be trained during this step with matched RAS prior to the initiation of gait. Some pregait exercises, such as stationary weight shifting, are better performed with a 6/8 meter. RAS may be played via headphones/personal stereo or via speakers from an audio system. Hand-held assistance supporting the arm or holding a gait belt may be necessary. Initial verbal cuing, such as counting or talking through the movement by saying "left, right" or "step, step" may be helpful to track the rhythm. The therapist should give as little feedback as possible. However, basic cues to maintain good gait mechanics, such as regarding stride length, arm swing, posture, or toe clearance, may be needed and appropriate.

7.3.2.3 Frequency Modulation At this stage of the session, an increase in RAS frequency should begin. Frequency increases should be based on a percentage of the baseline cadence that is noticeable (no less than 5 percent) and attainable for the patient without compromising good gait mechanics. There should be room for verbal corrections of gait pattern (e.g., use heel strike, don't shorten strides), but feedback should be minimal in order to avoid interrupting normal goal-driven programming tendencies of the brain. In some cases it is necessary to enhance the RAS perception by verbal cues (e.g., counting, rhythmic speech: "left-right") to strengthen the signal-to-noise ratio in the patient's ability to extract the perception of the rhythmic cue. Some patients who have attention/orientation problems due resonant with the preinjury, normal pattern-generator frequency (see the concept of stepwise limit cycle entrainment, SLICE). Trunk control, balance, and arm swing are most affected by the natural normalization tendency. Also, leg swing and stride length symmetry can be practiced better at higher frequencies (symmetry is one of the most treatment-resistant gait features in stroke). Instead of accelerations, decelerating gait cadence is meaningful with patient groups who have a tendency to hasty and unsafe walking patterns.

7.3.2.4 Advanced Adaptive Gait   In this therapy unit, free tempo modulations can be practiced (change between slow, fast, and normal) with the help of RAS. Also, stop/go exercises with RAS may be indicated here, such as walking on different surfaces, inclines, and other advanced gait exercises including stairs, turns, and reversal of direction.

7.3.2.5 Fading   In the last part of the session, RAS should be faded systematically to practice transfer. Fading should be gradually increased to train independence or mental practice (rhythm imagery).

7.3.2.6 Reassessment   The therapist should reassess the patient, using another baseline walk without cuing to determine whether gait performance was improved through RAS. The basic gait parameters should be reassessed and recorded to provide documentation for data-driven therapy and being able to quantify improvement.

7.3.2.7 Additional Points   The basic steps outlined above would be used in a long-term training application over the duration of therapy to enhance kinematic stability in gait patterns and gradually entrain higher gait cadences if appropriate (SLICE). In inpatient therapy, daily applications of SLICE are most common. In outpatient therapy, gait training may be spaced out several times a week or may involve the use of various types of retraining schedules. For example, intense training periods once a month, including closely spaced sessions, may be implemented.

RAS can facilitate pregait exercises as long as those exercises are organized rhythmically.

The concept of RAS is based on pulse-type rhythms that facilitate intrinsically rhythmic pulse-timed movements such as gait. Upper extremity (arm, hand, and finger) movements range from simple, symmetric pulse-type movements (e.g., repetitive flexion-extension or adduction-abduction patterns) to more complex movements. However, the respective movement components for the upper extremities and other movement patterns (trunk rotations, sit-to-stand, etc.) always need to be organized into sequences following metric or complex rhythmic patterns that simulate or actually perform functional movements. The use of metric or complex rhythm patterns and other dynamic musical elements (pitch, loudness, timbre, register, rate of change) to translate and entrain movement patterns that are externally structured into rhythmic patterns is called patterned sensory enhancement (PSE).

7.3.3 Practical Considerations for the Use of RAS in the Clinic

- The therapist should have good rhythmic-musical skills. Gait patterns are best supported by even rhythmic pulses, such as those produced by metronomes or rhythmically accentuated music. RAS is organized in 2/4 or 4/4 meter with strong ON (on beat 1 or beats 1 and 3) versus OFF beat patterns.
- A basic understanding of the concept of rhythm is useful. Rhythm can be understood on four levels of time organization:
  1. Rhythm as symmetric, even pulse (e.g., as found in a metronome beat).
  2. Metered rhythm, in which even pulses are grouped by accent into repeated groups of two, three, four, and so on.
  3. Periodic rhythm patterns consisting of a repeated rhythmic phrase whose beats have different numerical ratios (e.g., a long beat followed by a short beat half as long as the previous one, followed by two even shorter beats twice as short as the previous one, etc.). Such rhythmic patterns are often found in music as recurring rhythmic motifs or in dance music as repeated basic beat and step pattern.
  4. Nonperiodic rhythmic patterns that are similar to periodic patterns except that they do not repeat themselves at all or only occasionally during the musical piece. They function as the organizing thread for the timing of all musical events by, for instance, creating the particular rhythmic structure of a melody.

For RAS metric (2) and pulse rhythms (1) are most applicable, whereas cuing of more complex movement sequences may require metric (2) and/ or patterned rhythms (3, 4).

- The emotional-motivational quality of rhythm and music is a desirable secondary effect if (a) the musical elements enhance rhythm perception; (b) the music is familiar and preferred by the patient; and (c) the patient can perceive complex acoustical stimuli and does not get confused by complex sound patterns. Well-composed music can enhance rhythmic perception and movement rhythmicity.
- Studies have shown that in healthy individuals, accuracy of rhythmic synchronization is similar for music and metronome cuing. Therefore,

stimulus selection depends on the best perceptual response of the patient, as well as on the tempo of the rhythm. The perception of the timing of cues in very slow beat patterns may be enhanced by complete musical patterns with regularly occurring beat events between the beat cues.

- An essential technological feature of RAS therapy is that the rhythmic timekeeper frequency is adjustable. The metronome is the simplest device. For more complex rhythmical-musical stimuli, MIDI-audio technology provides an excellent option via programmable sequencers and synthesizers. The only other way to provide different stimulus frequencies is to make audiotapes with different metronome markings from digitally available sound sources; commercial prerecorded audiotapes are usually not accurate rhythmically and the tempo cannot be changed. Live music for RAS cuing has trade-offs in advantages and disadvantages. An advantage is that live music provides for flexibility and quick adjusting of music selection, enhanced musical interaction with the patient, and the ability for quick tempo adjustment. Among the disadvantages, live cuing is applicable only in cooperative therapy because one needs a therapist for guiding the walk and a performing therapist; rhythmicity can be very inaccurate; modulation rates to speed or slow down are inaccurate; and there may be a subconscious tendency of the music therapist to entrain to the movement tempo of the patient, rather than to maintain a steady rhythm to entrain movement. Skillful applications in cooperative therapy can, however, be very effective.
- Live music is not desirable during research projects because of the lack of control and accuracy of the rhythmic stimulus.
- Musical preferences or the musical background or talents of the patients are not essential for the efficiency of RAS. RAS enhances and facilitates physiologically intrinsic biological movement rhythms. In RAS therapy, the patient is not taught new step patterns or dance movements.
- Hemispheric site of lesion appears not to significantly affect the perception and transduction of rhythm into motor patterns during gait. The neural networks for rhythmic synchronization appear to be independent of laterality and characterized by parallel processing on multiple levels of brain function.

7.3.4 Practical Summary of the Therapeutic Mechanisms of RAS

It is very important for the RAS clinician and researcher to understand the brain strategies underlying rhythmic synchronization. The rhythmic adaptation of the motor response in rhythmic synchronization is driven primarily by internal time matching of the response interval (in gait, heel strike to heel strike) to the stimulus period of the rhythm, and not by event synchronization (matching the response event to the beat event). The event matching errors (technically speaking, the synchronization or phase errors) are quite different for different people, and corrections from beat to beat are quite sluggish. Interval corrections are much more immediate and seem to be the primary temporal tracking mechanism.

Therefore, we propose the following strategic hierarchy in rhythmic motor synchronization:

- From psychophysical research in rhythmic synchronization, we know that steady-state interval templates of the rhythmic periods are established rapidly by the listener, allowing for a steady-state tapping response almost instantaneously. Steady-state response has also been shown by stroke patients when moving their paretic arm to a metronome cue (Thaut et al. 2002a). Therefore, clinicians can expect that the patient, after hearing two or three rhythmic beats, will immediately construct a stable interval template as a time reference in the brain. These templates or reference intervals emerge fast, are very stable, and have a strong and immediate magnet or entrainment effect on the performance of movement (i.e., the movement timing is physiologically attracted to follow the time patterns of the rhythm). This effect can also be demonstrated on levels below the perceptual threshold of the moving person. The motor response interval is embedded into the click sequence by establishing a preferred synchronization error at either end of the interval between the motor event (tap or heel strike, for example) and the click event. These preferred phase positions are very different for different people, and seem to reflect rather subjective perceptions of time coincidence.
- The synchronization sequence is maintained and corrected by matching the click interval to the response interval (i.e., frequency coupling drives the synchronization rather than phase coupling).
- For movement cuing in patients, this means:
  - Phase errors (i.e., event coincidence between beat and motor response) may fluctuate. The patient appears not always to be exactly on the beat, although he/she still successfully tracks the frequency of the rhythmic cue. This is important to realize when trying to help patients stay with the rhythm. It is not necessary to see the patient march stiffly in exact time to the beat.
  - Because interval matching seems to be the dominant strategy of the brain to synchronize, time stability is enhanced throughout the

entire duration and trajectory of the movement. The clinically relevant end result is that during RAS, a deficient movement is not performed deficiently yet synchronized to the beat at the movement end points; rather, the entire movement is synchronized to the stimulus interval and stabilized across time.

º Rhythm, by fixating the time interval for the execution of a certain movement, enables the brain to scale the time parameters of movement (i.e., acceleration and velocity) smoothly across the duration of the movement. Once acceleration and velocity are set, however, the spatial position-time curves of movement are also determined. Thus, by smoothing acceleration and velocity of movement, rhythm forces an optimization of movement paths or trajectories. This can be shown mathematically as an optimization problem, and has been empirically well documented by kinematic data during RAS versus non-RAS trials. (For a review of this fascinating process, see chapter 5.)

In conclusion, rhythm will improve not only timing or speed of movement, but also spatial aspects such as stride length, knee-joint stability, range of motion, smoothing trajectories, and the associated muscle-activation patterns. For therapeutic purposes, rhythmic entrainment modulates the total pattern of movement in a time-space-force matrix.

7.4 Patterned Sensory Enhancement

The underlying neurologic mechanisms that we have discussed for RAS extend to the technique of patterned sensory enhancement (PSE). As research has shown impressively, music provides a sensory cue that temporally structures and regulates movement patterns, thus facilitating the efficient (re)learning and execution of functional movement exercises in motor rehabilitation (Brown et al. 1993; Georgiou et al. 1993; Williams 1993; Buetefish et al. 1995; Pacchetti et al. 1998; Effenberg and Mechling 1998; Whitall et al. 2000; Thaut, Kenyon, Hurt et al. 2002; Luft et al. 2004).

However, there are distinct differences between RAS and PSE. One of the major differences is found when studying the auditory-kinematic translations embedded in PSE. PSE utilizes all musical elements in a multidimensional framework to use sound patterns to cue movement patterns, whereas RAS operates exclusively on rhythmic time cuing. PSE operates in two distinct processes within a consistent feedback-feedforward loop. The first process is a translational process in which all kinematic aspects of the movement serve as feedback patterns to be translated into sound patterns. This translation unfolds in a three-dimensional matrix of spatial, temporal, and force cuing related to the three dimensions in which motor performance occurs: The spatial, temporal, and dynamic parameters of a movement are translated into musical elements and patterns signifying the time aspects of tempo and rhythm, the space aspects of position and trajectory, and the dynamic aspects of force applications of the movement. During this process, we may speak of a kinematically based composition process in music. Once the movement pattern has been translated into an appropriate sound pattern, a kinematic melody, the sound pattern is then used in a feedforward fashion to cue the execution of the movement pattern for the patient in order to provide a stable, continuous, and anticipatory time reference that also integrates meaningful references to the spatial and dynamic force aspects of the movement pattern. Using terminology from psychology and aesthetics, we may succinctly summarize the process of PSE as translating movement gestalts into sound gestalts and using the latter to regulate—and thus enhance—the performance of the movement gestalts.

This understanding demonstrates that PSE accesses additional and more complex sensorimotor integration processes in the brain than RAS does. The highly patterned structure of music in regard to all spectral, dynamic, and temporal components (i.e., pitch, harmony, intensity, timbre, rhythm, etc.) is used perceptually to stimulate and facilitate patterned information processing to build templates for the regulation of enhanced motor performance. The intrinsic structure and the underlying perceptual mechanisms of PSE therefore make it a highly specialized and highly effective technique to cue complex movements beyond the range of biologically wired rhythms, such as those found in gait. Most functional movements involving upper extremities, upper and lower trunk, and coordination of full body movements have complex positional patterns unfolding in time, space, and force. PSE gives the therapist a sensory template in the auditory modality to build functional movement sequences and use PSE as a complex cue system to entrain motor planning, programming, and execution.

In the following sections, we will describe how music can be used to represent these motor performance dimensions, and thus guide or elicit motor behavior in a therapeutic context.

7.4.1 Clinical Principles of PSE

PSE's clinical goal is the practice of functional movements of daily life activity or the fundamental motor patterns underlying these movements. Functional movement organized in repetitive patterns facilitates active training and learning, a common and effective strategy of motor rehabilitation. In applying PSE, the clinician must establish isomorphic analogies of music and movement structure. Essentially, the music has to fit the movement pattern to be practiced. Finding the parallels between musical and movement gestalts is both a research objective and necessary for effective neurologic music therapy practice.

PSE poses a considerable challenge to the therapist because it requires the application and integration of several skill and knowledge bases. First, the therapist must conceptualize the desired movement pattern by kinematic analysis. Second, by expressing or illustrating essential movement parameters with music, the music therapist translates the desired movement pattern into a neurologic music-therapy exercise. The translation requires two skills in integration: First, the therapist needs to be able to create logical isomorphic analogies between movement and musical elements. Second, she needs to possess a considerable skill base in musical techniques, such as improvisation, in order to execute the musical translations.

7.4.1.1 Spatial Cuing   Due to their motor impairments, patients are often unable to perform a required movement in an effective, adaptive way. To address this deficit, clinicians can use music in a variety of kinematic translations. Musical patterns can be used, for example, to cue range of motion in the horizontal and vertical (saggital and frontal) planes. Spatial cues in the music accompaniment can designate turning points in movement sequences, indicate directions, and provide a reference for the spatial dimensions of the movement task. Musical patterns may create feedback for the attainment of specific positions in space to enhance visual or proprioceptive feedback.

Some musical elements and examples of the spatial movement properties they represent include the following:

Pitch   Low and high notes can represent target points in the vertical plane. The pitch variation found in melodic lines or arpeggios can also indicate directions and cue movement trajectory. For example, ascending melodic lines can cue upward movement and descending lines, downward movement. A broad register can be used to cue movements with a large range of motion, such as stretching arms overhead or bending toward the floor.

Loudness   Increasing loudness can illustrate a gradual movement expansion (i.e., larger movements away from midline, or abduction). Decreasing loudness can cue a limb back toward the body in adductive movements.

Sound duration   Long sound duration can illustrate an extended and even movement trajectory, such as sliding feet or reaching slowly with the arms.

Harmony   Tone clusters or chords played in open or closed position can refer to the spatial dimension or size of a movement. A cluster or closed chord can represent a small movement, and an open spacing can suggest a more expansive movement. Polyphonic patterns (simultaneous melodies and rhythms in different tone spaces) can cue the coordination in space of different movements.

7.4.1.2 Temporal Cuing   Motor function impairments, diagnosis-related malfunctioning, or unhealthy compensation strategies require rehabilitation of the timing of movement performance. Musical elements that can cue the temporal dimension of an exercise are tempo, meter, rhythmic patterning and form:

Tempo   The tempo of a musical piece is usually measured in beats per minute (bpm). This number should match the desired frequency of the movements to be performed. If the speed of movement performance is part of the therapeutic focus, acceleration and deceleration of tempo are to be stressed.

Meter   Meter, expressed in fractions (4/4, 6/8, etc.), indicates the grouping of the underlying beats, and can be used to reflect the inherent temporal structure of a movement. Metric beat perception allows for harmonic entrainment by cuing movement at different integer ratios in relationship to the basic metric structure (e.g., moving only on the first beat or on beats 1 and 3 of a 4/4 measure instead of on every beat). Harmonic entrainment can be particularly important when cuing groups of patients at different levels of functioning that require different movement frequencies simultaneously for each patient. Using music with strong accentuation of the first and third beats provides a metrical structure, important for the repetitive performance of many movement patterns. For example, music in a 2/4 meter can refer to the steady pulse of two legs walking (gait).

Rhythmic Patterning   Rhythmic patterning addresses movement patterns that are more differentiated and that require additional cues beyond the metrical beat. Essentially, the musical elements provide an auditory translation of the rhythmic structure of the more complex movements. Patterned cuing is especially effective for facilitating movement initiation. For example, pickup notes prior to the first bar can help the client to anticipate the movement onset. Accents on notes prior to strong beats can facilitate hopping on the beat by supporting movement anticipation. Rhythmic polyphony can cue coordination in time between different movements.

Form   The form of a musical piece can play an essential role when a therapeutic task consists of a sequence of movement patterns. One example is a sit-to-stand transfer exercise. Patients can sit during verses and stand during the chorus of a song. The musical form includes cues for initiation and termination of the particular task and indicates the duration of each position.

7.4.1.3 Force Cuing   To stimulate muscle activity, the musical elements of loudness, harmony, timbre, and tempo can be used effectively.

Loudness   Changes in loudness can cue changes in strength of muscle activation.

Harmony   The musical tension and resolution patterns found in harmonic progressions across musical phrases can represent sequential muscle contraction and relaxation.

Timbre   Changes in timbre (for example, soft to harsh) can cue changes in muscle activation from relaxed to more contracted.

Tempo   Tempo can influence two muscle activation responses, readiness (activation) and relaxation. Faster tempi can induce stronger muscle activation patterns. Rhythmic patterns set at slower tempi can induce slower movements associated with muscle relaxation. Anticipatory rhythmic patterns can cause a priming effect so that appropriate force is generated to create readiness for movement.

7.4.2 Practical Considerations in Applying PSE

In musical PSE compositions it is very important to consider essential principles of musical forms. In clinical reality, the development of PSE stimuli is—from a musical skill view—very much based on strong improvisational and compositional qualities. In therapy, the patient processes music as a total gestalt pattern no different from that in music appreciation. The basic principles of music perception are not changed. Therefore, complex PSE patterns must be clearly constructed around musical forms—resemble good music—in order to be easily comprehensible to the patient in a meaningful way.

PSE exercises have a wide range of applications. Simple flexion-extension exercise of the arm can be cued, as well as more basic exercise-type movements such as arm reaching, upper and lower extremity stretching, and trunk rotations. Complex large body actions such as sit-to-stand transfers or dressing can be cued. PSE also allows the therapist to sequence discrete movement actions into larger units that can then be exercised in a regular, cyclical, repeated, and coordinated fashion in order to maximize learning and training effects for the patient. These units could consist of, for example, a sequence of arm movements involving reaching, grasping, and lifting objects of different shapes in different locations.

One of the common mistakes when considering PSE is to conceptualize it as movement accompaniment. As we have already discussed, PSE regulates movement as a complex sensory cuing system based on very precise translational processes between sound and kinematics. Furthermore, PSE can serve effectively as a substitute sensory feedback system for reduced visual and proprioceptive feedback.

7.5 Therapeutic Instrumental Music Performance

Playing musical instruments involves a large number of complex kinesiologic processes. Appropriate instrumental performance optimizes gross, as well as fine, motor skills, and can require the use of repetitive movement patterns. In addition, playing an instrument requires attentional skills, processing of sensory information, and complex levels of sensorimotor integration. Research has shown that fundamental movement patterns underlying functional motor tasks can be simulated quite effectively through therapeutically structured playing of musical instruments. This is the therapeutic goal of therapeutic instrumental music performance (TIMP): to design physical exercises that involve playing of musical instruments that simulate functional nonmusical movement patterns (Clark and Chadwick 1980; Cross et al. 1984; Elliott, 1982; Sutton 1984; Pascual-Leone et al. 1993; Hund-Georgiadis and von Cramon 1999).

The therapeutic design of the TIMP exercise is based on three elements:

1. The musical structure facilitating the organization of movement in time, space, and force dynamics
2. The choice of instruments and the mechanics for playing the instruments to enhance therapeutically meaningful movements
3. The spatial arrangement and location of the instruments to facilitate desired motion paths of the limbs and positions of the body

One of the most accessible families of musical instruments is the percussion family. All percussion instruments require a similar motion of flexion-extension movements of the arm. Therefore, they are relatively easy for nonmusicians to access in regard to basic sound production. Furthermore, the percussion family includes instruments that are nonpitched, as well as instruments that have indefinite or definite pitch. Consequently, during TIMP the patient can engage in a large variety of active, creative musical playing experiences, improvisatory or predesigned, while functionally exercising motor tasks. However, other instruments can also be of considerable value for TIMP exercises, such as keyboards for finger dexterity and arm control, or autoharps or dulcimers for wrist and arm control via strumming motions. The therapeutic appropriateness of instrument selection is based on a thorough assessment of the physical abilities and motoric restrictions of the patients, as well as a kinematic analysis of motor functions required to play different instruments (Elliott 1982).

All TIMP exercises involve the coordinated effort of stability and mobility of the body and body parts. Within stability and mobility, different instruments require different muscle groups to produce flexion, abduction, rotation, pronation, and supination in different limbs. Motions require different muscle coordination patterns, such as reciprocal or synergetic activations. TIMP exercises address muscle strength, as well as movement speed and dexterity in alternating or simultaneous, bilateral or unilateral patterns. Sensation and perception in the visual, auditory, tactile, and proprioceptive modalities are engaged. Furthermore, all TIMP exercises require certain amounts of respiratory and cardiac exertion, which can be tailored to the rehabilitative needs of the patient.

In summary, TIMP applications for motor rehabilitation can contribute to the process of relearning functional movement skills, overcoming unhealthy compensation strategies, and increasing strength, endurance, and motor control in therapy.

Several of the neurologic mechanisms that contribute to the therapeutic efficiency of replicating functional movement through instrument playing have already been discussed for RAS and PSE. Arousal mechanisms via audiospinal facilitation that result in auditory priming and timing effects on the motor system are certainly shared by RAS, PSE, and TIMP. Rhythmic entrainment effects, discussed in detail under RAS, are also active in TIMP, regulating motor timing and anticipatory motor programming, which enhances the temporal, spatial, and dynamic aspects of motor control. Furthermore, PSE mechanisms related to comprehensive kinematic cuing through the translation of movement elements into sound elements could easily be integrated into TIMP structures. The spatial cuing is considerably enhanced in TIMP through the flexible possibilities of various configurations of instruments and playing motions in space, based on the patient's needs. TIMP adds an even higher degree of complex patterned temporal information processing to PSE and RAS because the patient is not just moving in synchrony to a sensory timer but is now part of the actual musical pattern production. A second active component in therapeutic mechanisms produced by TIMP refers to the auditory feedback process through playing of an instrument. The patient receives knowledge of results at every step of his movement patterns.

There are two other important considerations in discussing the role of TIMP in motor therapy:

1. The nature of musical group play reflected in TIMP allows the therapist to design musical exercise structures that can facilitate group activities for patient groups within which patients can train

their specific functional therapy exercises while also contributing meaningfully to the musical group's product. Harmonic entrainment can help to cue different movement frequencies for individual patients within the same metrical structure of a musical piece. This unique adaptability of TIMP has several key advantages for the therapeutic process: It creates motivation for the patient to engage in therapy through the social context of the therapy session; it helps to strengthen social interactions between patients and medical staff; it can facilitate cost-effective yet highly treatment-effective programming of rehabilitation efforts.

2. Due to the attentional focus on music and the enjoyable nature of the performance, the patient's motivation for the therapeutic training regimen may be greatly enhanced.

7.5.1 Clinical Principles of TIMP

TIMP involves the playing of musical instruments to stimulate and practice functional movement patterns. The therapeutic application of instruments can enhance range of motion, endurance, functional hand movements, finger dexterity, and limb coordination. For example, instruments can be used as targets that delimit the range of motion in an exercise.

Several clinical considerations should be taken into account when applying TIMP exercises to motor therapy.

7.5.1.1 Traditional Versus Nontraditional Playing The application of TIMP in therapy may require both traditional and nontraditional playing and positioning of instruments. Traditional music instrument playing addresses many movements of everyday life. For example, the tripod grip (holding with thumb, index, and middle finger) can be used to hold a guitar pick. This skill is similar to the kind of motion used when writing with a pen. In many cases, simply enhancing the range of the traditional playing motion might serve the therapeutic purpose. For example, increasing the movement range (i.e., moving the arm up and down) of a mallet when playing a drum enhances flexion and extension of the arm.

Sometimes, in order to create motions that exactly meet the patient's needs and goals in rehabilitation, the instrument may need to be played in a modified or nontraditional way. The playing and positioning of the instrument can be varied. A tambourine, for example, can be placed knee, high in front of a seated patient, who will be instructed to make it sound by kicking it with his foot. By lifting his leg, he thus practices repetitive knee flexion and extension. In addition to modifying how to play and position instruments to facilitate motions, the musical equipment itself may need to be adapted.

7.5.1.2 Adaptation of Musical Equipment Traditional use of instruments, picks, mallets, and bows sometimes requires a high level of fine motor skills that are beyond the patient's capacities. For individuals with involuntary neurological impulses, missing limbs, or restricted motor abilities, adaptive equipment or assistance is often necessary (Clark and Chadwick 1980). Examples of adaptation include the use of Velcro bands to secure mallets to the palm of a weakened hand, adapting handles of beaters, using large individual tone bars instead of tone bar instruments, and using pick holders that can be strapped onto the palm of the hand.

7.5.1.3 Musical Considerations in Applying TIMP Techniques As in our discussion on PSE, the presence of discernible and well-constructed musical forms is essential to utilize the cue function of music to facilitate motor and attentional functions. Furthermore, the utmost facilitation of musical performance quality through adaptive techniques is a key component of successful TIMP. While much research has investigated the impact of isolated auditory musical components on human behavior, the therapeutic value of music as a complex sensorimotor stimulus depends greatly on its holistic gestalt patterns. The patients must be able to perceive the music as an organized and meaningful whole in order for it to have a regulating effect on their perceptual-motor functions. This consideration requires clinicians to carefully design and select musical materials while keeping in mind the client's needs and functioning level. Therapists must take into account not only the physical and motor needs of the client, but also cognitive deficits, as well as cultural context of the patient's musical familiarity and preference. A client with lower cognitive functioning, for instance, may find simple auditory stimuli far more appealing than complex musical structure.

TIMP stimuli may be created by a specific compositional or improvisational process the therapist uses to accommodate the specific needs of the patients. At times, the therapist may use familiar songs with appropriate musical structures to support the ease with which patients can follow the music with their own playing. TIMP exercises can be purely instrumental as well, such as in keyboard exercises for finger, hand, arm, and postural control, or in tone bar exercises to practice shoulder adduction and abduction or elbow flexion and extension exercises.

7.5.1.4 Meter With the exception of gait, most movements are not biologically rhythmic. The temporal structure of a movement pattern, however, has analogues in musical structures, such as meter. Musical meter in movement accompaniment should match the inherent temporal structure of the movement to facilitate repetitive motor performance. Some movements are traditionally linked to and commonly associated with a specific meter. In western European culture, marching is typically accompanied by a 2/4 meter and many lullabies are sung in 6/8 or 3/4 meter. For the rhythmical cuing of motor exercises, the clinician must match the meter to the movement while taking into account the patient's limited ability to perform the movement in a therapeutically desired way.

7.5.1.5 Accentuation   The musical accompaniment should accentuate the beats on which motor responses are expected. Accents should be strong and well distinguished from softer instrument attacks. Most motor exercises consist of at least two motions (e.g., elbow flexion/extension). Consequently, the accents ought to be placed at both points of motion, and especially at the onset of each motion, to facilitate movement initiation. In order to help patients anticipate the movement onset, weak beats, such as pickup notes or offbeats, should have minor accents as well. For slower movement patterns (e.g., neck turns), it is useful either to sustain the sound of the instrument or to fill in softer accents to smoothly guide the movement.

7.5.1.6 Tempo   Choosing an appropriate tempo for the musical accompaniment of motor patterns requires considerations similar to those for the choice of meter. The desired speed of a movement pattern suggests a particular tempo for the musical accompaniment. Tempo can vary depending on the physical condition of the individual. For example, the load to be moved will partially determine the tempo. Tempo also depends on the joints that are involved, because healthy joints with strong muscles perform faster than fragile joints. The speed of normal or healthy movement performance can be measured and then serve as a goal for an individual or set the pace for an entire group.

In the individual setting, musical accompaniment should match the temporal structure of the performed movement. The patient's individual movement structure is the measure for musical synchronization. The group setting is, of course, different. Because one piece of music cannot match the individual tempo of many patients, a compromise must be made. In such cases, the therapist utilizes the technique of harmonic entrainment, whereby slower or faster subdivisions of a basic rhythmic frequency allow for individual entrainment across groups of patients with very different optimal movement frequencies. In harmonic entrainment, any of the subdivisions (8/8, 4/4, 2/2, or even 1/1) of basic meter can function as a beat that synchronizes movement and music.

7.5.1.7 Harmony   Harmonic changes can function as cues for changes in motion. They can also cue different movement qualities dynamically in TIMP playing, such as tension and release, sustained versus short and abrupt, or soft versus hard contact with the instrument to change sound production. Shoulder abduction and adduction (raising and lowering arms), for instance, can be accompanied by a dominant seven chord (tension) for the abductive and a tonic (resolution) chord for the adductive movement when playing several drums sequentially in different spatial locations.

7.5.1.8 Pitch   Pitch variations, as found in melodic lines or arpeggios, function to illustrate the spatial direction of a movement pattern and may guide full movement sequences. As such, melodic patterns can reinforce the spatial patterns of playing given by the spatial configuration of the musical instruments. For example, a low-pitched tone bar may be placed on the floor in front of the patient while a higher-pitched tone bar may be placed on an elevated surface. The instruments would have to be played following the melodic lines of the song.

7.5.1.9 Singing   If songs are used during TIMP, patients may be encouraged to sing along with the therapist while exercising. In addition to the emotional benefits, singing provides an additional internal pacesetter, helps the patient to maintain better upright posture, serves as a memory cue for the movement patterns, and may help the patient to breathe more efficiently.

7.6 Guide to Clinical Applications

Competence in the application of therapeutic techniques can be developed only through extensive professional training and practice. The following examples illustrate how NMT techniques are planned and applied in relation to clinical goals and diagnostic needs. They cannot be applied by individuals who do not have appropriate training and certification as rehabilitation professionals in NMT.

7.6.1 Domain: Sensorimotor Training

7.6.1.1 Application: Pregait Training

7.6.1.1.1 Clinical Goals

- Increase tolerance of standing in preparation for gait training
- Improve posture and postural stability
- Improve functioning of muscle groups involved in gait
- Improve blood circulation in legs (after long periods of lying down)
- Improve ability to clear feet for swing phase

Examples of Therapeutic Music Interventions (TMI): RAS Technique

Nonmusical Exercise 1: Weight shifting (mediolateral). Performed standing in parallel bars or holding on to other aiding device. Patient shifts weight while standing in stationary position.
TMI: Therapist uses RAS to cue the exercise:

- Music (rhythm) in 6/8 meter
- Slow–to-moderate tempo
- Accentuation on beats 1 and 4
- Gradual increase of duration of time spent standing

Nonmusical Exercise 2: Weight shifting (anterior/posterior). Performed in parallel bars or holding on to other aiding device. Patient swings forward/backward over lower extremity.
TMI: Therapist uses RAS to cue the exercise (See Weight shifting [mediolateral]).

Nonmusical Exercise 3: Lateral stepping. Patient (holding on to walker, etc.) steps sideways out/in.
TMI: Therapists uses RAS to cue the exercise:

- Music (rhythm) in 3/4 meter
- Slow tempo
- Accentuation of beat 1 (stepping out)
- One bar per side
- Technique: TIMP

Nonmusical Exercise 4: Weight shift (mediolateral). Physically supported by physical therapist (PT) or aide, patient sways from side to side.
TMI: Patient shifts weight by playing high and low bars of a marimba or xylophone.
Instrument: Marimba or xylophone with color-coded bars on both ends, two mallets.
Procedure:

1. Prepared instrument is set up waist-high in front of the patient.
2. Shifting weight from side to side, patient reaches out to hit bar.
3. Therapist matches music to the color-coded bars (e.g., I, IV, V blues progression) and indicates weight shifts by changing the chord.
4. Verbal cuing (counting, etc.) facilitates changes.
5. If the exercise is meant to be performed rhythmically, the music should be in 6/8 meter.

Nonmusical Exercise 5: Dorsiplantar flexion. Sitting patient taps his toes/ lifts his heels.

TMI: Patient practices dorsiplantar flexion by playing disco taps or ankle bells.

Instruments: Disco taps (on stone, PVC, or wooden surface) or ankle bells (on carpet).

Procedure: Divide exercise into three sequences:

1. Tap toes
2. Lift heels
3. Rock back and forth

   - One foot at a time or both feet alternating
   - Therapist uses RAS to cue exercise
   - Musical properties of rhythmic cue
   - Music (rhythm) in 4/4 meter
   - Lively, fast tempo
   - Form matches sequences of exercise
   - Therapist matches music to the color-coded bars (e.g., I, IV, V blues progression) and indicates weight shifts by changing the chord
   - Verbal cuing (counting, etc.) facilitates changes
   - If the exercise is meant to be performed rhythmically, the music should be in 6/8 meter

Non-musical Exercise 6: Dorsiplantar flexion: Sitting patient taps his toes/ lifts his heels.

TMI: Patient practices dorsiplantar flexion by playing disco taps or ankle bells.

Instruments: Disco taps (on stone, PVC, or wooden surface) or ankle bells (on carpet).

Procedure: Divide exercise into three sequences:

1. Tap toes
2. Lift heels
3. Rock back and forth

   - One foot at a time or both feet alternating
   - Therapist uses RAS to cue exercise
   - Musical properties of rhythmic cue
   - Music (rhythm) in 4/4 meter
   - Lively, fast tempo
   - Form matches sequences of exercise
   - Accentuation of every beat

7.6.2 Domain: Sensorimotor Training

7.6.2.1 Application: Gait Training

7.6.2.1.1 Clinical Goals

- Improve stride symmetry
- Increase stride length
- Increase gait velocity
- Increase step rate (cadence)
- Reduce double support
- Normalize swing/stance ratio
- Improve walking endurance
- Prevent unsafe gait patterns and falls

Examples of Therapeutic Music Interventions (TMI): RAS Technique
Steps in RAS for Gait Training:

1. Assessment of gait parameters
   (a) Cadence, by counting heel strikes for sixty seconds
   (b) Velocity, by measuring how many meters the patient walked in sixty seconds
   (c) Stride length, by dividing velocity by (cadence x 2)
2. Match RAS tempo to gait cadence
3. Changes in tempo
   (a) Increasing
   (b) Decreasing
4. Gradually fade out RAS to practice transfer

Reassess gait parameters without cuing in order to show progress.

7.6.3 Domain: Sensorimotor Training

7.6.3.1 Application: Advanced Gait Training

7.6.3.1.1 Clinical Goals

- Improve balance during advanced gait exercises
- Improve gait endurance
- Improve stride length, cadence, and symmetry during advanced gait exercises
- Improve functional gait ability during advanced gait exercises
  ◦ Walking with change in direction
  ◦ Walking on different surfaces
    - Stair stepping

- Step variations
- Train functional mobility, using devices such as walker or cane if necessary
- Train combining ambulation and transfers

Examples of Therapeutic Music Interventions (TMI): RAS Technique

Nonmusical Exercise 1: Turning while walking. Patient walks, turns 180 degrees after several steps, walks back, and turns again.
TMI: Therapist uses RAS to cue the exercise

- Music (rhythm) in 2/4 meter
- Eventually decreasing tempo during turns
- Accentuation of every beat
- Verbal cuing during turns if necessary

Nonmusical Exercise 2: Walking on uneven surfaces. Patient walks on uneven surfaces such as ramp, lawn, or carpet.
TMI: Therapist uses RAS to cue the exercise

- Music (rhythm) in 2/4 meter
- Tempo increasing toward normal gait velocity of patient
- Accentuation of every beat

Nonmusical Exercise 3: Initiation/termination of gait (stop and go). Patient alternately starts and stops walking.
TMI: Therapist uses RAS to cue the exercise

- Music (rhythm) in 2/4 meter
- Tempo increasing toward normal velocity
- Interruptions (such as musical chairs)
- Accentuation of every beat

Nonmusical Exercise 4: Anterior/posterior reversal. Patient walks forward, stops, walks backward.
TMI: Therapist uses RAS to cue the exercise

- Music (rhythm) in 2/4 meter
- Tempo slower than with normal gait
- Accentuation of onbeat
- Musical form according to two exercise structures (number of stairs, time needed for turning, etc.)

Nonmusical Exercise 5: Stair stepping. Patient steps up/down one step, starting with the unimpaired or stronger leg.
TMI: Therapist uses RAS to cue the exercise

- Music (rhythm) in 2/4 meter
- Tempo slower than with normal gait
- Accentuation of every beat
- Steps up on the first two beats, steps down on beats three and four

8

Neurologic Music Therapy in Speech and Language Rehabilitation

8.1 Introduction

There is anecdotal evidence—stretching back over many hundreds of years—for the connection between speech and music. For example, observers have noted—often with awe and wonder—the phenomenon that people who are struck by the sudden loss of speech and, sometimes, movement often can still sing. Similarly, it was commonly believed that stuttering or stammering in speech was remediable by singing, and pronunciation and quality of voice improved by singing. The great English Renaissance composer William Byrd actually prefaced his 1588 edition of *Psalms, Sonnets, and Songs* with a strong statement advocating—in modern terminology—the use of music to strengthen the respiratory system, reduce fluency and voice disorders, and improve articulation.

Since the mid-1950s, a more organized and systematic music-speech nexus has emerged in the clinical and research literature. Both music and speech are aural forms of communication. Music and speech share the same acoustical and auditory parameters: frequency, intensity, waveform and timbre, duration, rate, contour, rhythm, and cadential factors, to name a few. Music and speech have long been thought to have common roots in human evolution, with music usually being thought of as an offspring of speech. One can also speculate that music and speech arose in parallel, serving different functions in aural communication and expression as embedded in the biology of the human brain: one being more functional and concrete, the other being more aesthetic and abstract. Whether music came into being as an offspring, in parallel, or as a precursor probably can never be fully ascertained. However, that the human brain had the capacity and propensity (and, consequently, the need) to create aesthetic objects of expression at a very early stage in human history is impressively documented by recent anthropological discoveries that have unearthed sculpted artworks of great elegance and sophisticated form such as ornaments, nature objects such as flying birds, animal cave paintings, and jewelry, dating back 35,000 to 70,000 years.

Speech and music, especially song, have of course interacted strongly throughout human artistic history, creating intertwined art forms and means of aesthetic expression, such as song, opera, drama, and musical theater. With the many similarities between music and speech, it has often been assumed that music, and especially singing, is a valuable tool for the treatment of speech disorders. The clinical and research literature in music and speech therapy is quite extensive, although many papers, especially earlier ones, frequently were not data-based or did not employ the most stringent research methodologies. However, recent developments are showing considerable improvements in rigorous standards of research. In neurologic music therapy (NMT), techniques for speech and language therapy were developed on the basis of diagnostic functions and music variables employed. The research base for all techniques was discussed in detail in chapter 4. In the following sections, we will present the individual techniques in a concise and descriptive manner.

8.2 Melodic Intonation Therapy (MIT)

Melodic intonation therapy (MIT) is a treatment technique for the rehabilitation of expressive (Broca's) aphasia; there is also some evidence for its use with apraxia conditions. Good candidates for MIT are patients with left-side stroke lesions in Broca's area (which is responsible for encoding speech production) or with lesions interrupting the nervous connections between Wernicke's and Broca's areas. MIT utilizes a patient's unimpaired ability to sing to facilitate speech production. The rationale is based on a hemispheric transfer of speech functions from the left- hemisphere Wernicke's area to its right-hemisphere homologue during encoding of speech into singing (see Sparks et al. 1974; Albert et al. 1973; Sparks and Holland 1976; Helfrich-Miller 1984; Belin et al. 1996; Keith and Aronson 1975; Naeser and Helm-Estabrooks 1985; Popovici 1995; Overy et al. 2004).

In MIT, functional sentences or brief statements/utterances are translated into song by translating the speech inflection patterns into musical prosody. Therefore, it is technically more accurate to refer to the sung utterances not as songs, but as melodic intonations. In later stages of the therapy, singing is reduced to *Sprechgesang* (speech singing) and finally to normal speech prosody. The rhythmic and melodic elements are the important characteristics of the therapeutic stimulus.

In order to create a melodic intonation, it is useful to graph out the inflection patterns of the utterance, indicating pitch, accents, and rhythm. It is not important, when plotting the patterns, to relate the speech pitch patterns to absolute musical pitches. It is more important to indicate the difference in pitches in relative pitch space. If an utterance has three distinct pitches, a pitch plot would simply indicate the pitch distribution across the utterance as high, middle, and low. During the transposition of the speech prosody into musical prosody, the pitch patterns are turned into musical intervals, most likely never larger than the span of a fifth. During *Sprechgesang*, the interval range is continually compressed until the pitch prosody resembles normal speech prosody more and more.

The therapy begins with a presentation of the utterance via humming the melody and tapping the client's hand. After that, the stages of MIT basically progress through a variety of exercises of singing alone by the therapist, the therapist and client singing in unison, and singing dialogue between therapist and client. After the humming and tapping stage, the melodic intonations by the therapist are followed by joint singing of the therapist and the client, and finally a fading stage in which the therapist fades out while the client continues. That stage is followed by the therapist and client alternating in singing the utterance, to help the client initiate verbal output and produce the utterance independently. The last stage consists of exercises involving questions by the therapist in reference to the practiced utterance, which the client answers in song and finally verbally, without music.

The MIT process can be implemented by a therapist without musical accompaniment, in a cappella fashion. However, if staffing is available, a speech therapist and a neurologic music therapist can collaborate effectively, using an autoharp or keyboard to accompany and support the singing exercises. It is important to note that the client does not need to have musical skills to engage in and benefit from MIT. The quality of singing is not important in MIT as long as the musical transformation facilitates speech production via accessing alternate intact pathways in the brain. Second, the client does not have to learn new songs. The client intones the pitches, stress points, and rhythms of normal speech, translated into the same, yet amplified or magnified, pitch, accent, and rhythm patterns in music. It is often observed that the rhythm and accent patterns are uttered correctly before the proper word articulation is achieved.

The continued use of the rhythmic tapping is also often seen as having an impellant trigger function to initiate the utterance because the tapping often precedes the initiation of the first word sounds.

Poor candidates for MIT are patients with Wernicke's aphasia and transcortical, global, and conduction aphasia. Although MIT is directed at language, and not at speech production aspects per se, some clinicians have used MIT to improve slurred articulation and phoneme errors in aphasic speech. However, the functionality of language production is the main goal and dominating focus of MIT.

When MIT was developed, all rehabilitation interventions had longer durations because of longer inpatient treatment phases. Modern rehabilitation in structured inpatient units, as well as outpatient settings, has been shortened considerably. Therefore, the applications of MIT must find ways to fit into shorter and more intense treatment protocols. MIT is a highly structured and hierarchical system allowing for gradual progression of difficulty. Scoring instructions to quantify success are very precise and explicit. MIT must experiment with structures that allow compression of treatment steps into shorter units, possibly with higher intensity, without losing its basic structure of regulated progression of difficulty, in order to adapt to modern time constraints in therapy duration. A critical issue in this regard is the involvement of the caregivers in long-term care institutions or the family in the home environment. Community-based educational resources must be directed to these caregiver groups to help them facilitate the continued use of rehabilitation exercises adapted to the daily living environment of the client in order to reach the maximum benefit of MIT and other rehabilitation techniques.

MIT is a powerful technique to facilitate language production when applied properly to the diagnostically appropriate client groups, such as expressive aphasia and, to a smaller extent, developmental apraxia. Although the artistic requirements may appear somewhat daunting to the uninitiated observer or therapist, the design and implementation of the actual musical patterns involved are very straightforward and require minimal musical talent. However, the artistry surrounding it may cause MIT to be underutilized in the rehabilitation of communication disorders. Neurologic music therapists may therefore find an important opportunity to make an essential contribution to the implementation of this technique.

8.3 Musical Speech Stimulation (MUSTIM)

Musical speech stimulation (MUSTIM) is a technique used in aphasia therapy that utilizes musical and music-related materials, such as songs, rhymes, chants, or musical phrases (e.g., short melodic-rhythmic motifs played on a musical instrument), simulating prosodic speech gestures (inflection patterns for questions, answers, exclamations, etc.), in order to stimulate nonpropositional speech in aphasics. It is frequently observed that nonpropositional reflexlike speech, presumably mediated by more subcortical thalamic speech circuitry, is preserved in aphasic clients. In MUSTIM, the therapeutic music exercises are directed to trigger nonpropositional speech through, for example, completion or initiation of overlearned familiar song lyrics during singing, spontaneous production of words via their association with familiar song tunes, or using musical phrases to elicit and shape functional speech responses (Basso et al. 1979).

The therapist may start singing a familiar song, with the goal of triggering a reflexive joining in by the client. The same goal could be addressed by the therapist playing familiar tunes on an instrument without singing. The goal would be to elicit a spontaneous response of singing the lyrics triggered by deeply ingrained associations and overlearned memory. Furthermore, once the patient is involved in an active verbal response to the music, the therapist may fade singing at certain times during the verse, most likely at the end of a phrase, to trigger an automatic verbal fill-in or completion of the words by the client. Verbal associations resulting in spontaneous speech may also be triggered by the strong associative value in music created by its strong emotional saliency. These associations can result in very powerful memories, to which music can then facilitate access. In MUSTIM one would try to elicit some automatic speech output through the recall of memory. In response to playing a well-known wedding march, the client may spontaneously utter "my wedding," for instance.

In a different type of application, speech gestures may be modeled by playing musical patterns (for example, by using upward scales or arpeggios on the piano to support a question statement, or by accenting the dynamics of a brief chord progression to simulate an exclamation). Accompanying these musical patterns with the appropriate verbal statements may trigger an automatic fill-in or statement completion by the client. Rhythmic chanting may be used (e.g., in question/answer format) to evoke an overlearned verbal response.

Music is one of a number of tools that can be used successfully to trigger nonpropositional speech in aphasia. In MUSTIM, music's effectiveness is most likely based on three elements: (1) its deeply ingrained and overlearned associations between music and words to familiar songs; (2) its anticipatory character that provides time triggers to fill in, initiate, or complete words and sentences; and (3) its affective arousal character connecting to deep-layered speech circuitry and mediating more reflexlike speech. One issue of importance in any speech stimulation approach is the question of transfer from automatic reflexlike speech, triggered by an effective environmental stimulus, to propositional speech under complete volitional control. MUSTIM tries to trigger a response first in a more automatic, stimulus-contingent way, and later in gradual increments in a more voluntary, intentional way by removing the facilitating stimulus more and more. However, there is no guarantee—borne out by research data—that speech stimulation will always result in rapid transfer to propositional speech. Nevertheless, by triggering even nonpropositional speech, these techniques access and activate parts of the total neural speech circuitry, with the goals of involving and reactivating more and more parts of the brain systems underlying speech. Within this context, MUSTIM can be one of the more effective techniques to elicit verbal output in aphasia.

8.4 Rhythmic Speech Cuing (RSC)

Rhythmic speech cuing (RSC) is a rate-control technique that uses auditory rhythm—in metronome form or embedded in music—to cue speech (see, Pilon et al. 1998; Thaut et al. 2001; Bellaire et al. 1986; Caligiuri 1989; Hammen et al. 1994; Yorkston and Beukelman 1981; Yorkston et al. 1990). A somewhat different form of RSC would be to use singing rather than speaking to an auditory rhythmic cue. The impelling and anticipatory action of a rhythmic stimulus sequence can also help to initiate speech. RSC has been shown to be effective in fluency disorder rehabilitation for stuttering and cluttering, in rate control to enhance intelligibility in dysarthric patients, and in facilitating rhythmic sequencing in apraxia.

RSC can be divided into two categories: metric and patterned cuing. In metric cuing, rhythmic beats are matched to syllables, resulting in a speech inflection in which each syllable is of equal duration across an utterance. Metric cuing does not create normal time patterns of speech inflection, but can result in better sequencing and timing, overcoming interruption in speech flow due to stuttering or jumbling of phoneme sequences in words in apraxia. In cluttering or dysarthria, the time patterns of the rhythm help to control rate in order to enhance speech intelligibility. Dysarthric speakers can frequently increase intelligibility by slowing speech rates via RSC, a counterintuitive notion because dysarthric speech is often already exceedingly labored and slow. However, further slowing can break up slurring and telegraphing of words into each other. By creating pauses between words, the phoneme articulation, especially at the beginning of the words, can become clearer and the speaker has a preset time interval to prepare for the initiation and enunciation of the next word. Research data have shown that synchronization and entrainment between speech rates and rhythmic stimuli is possible, in a way similar to rhythmic motor entrainment in gait or arm movements.

Patterned cuing uses beat patterns that simulate stress patterns of normal speech inflection. In patterned cuing, durations between beats within an utterance are not equidistant, but asymmetrical, depending on the rhythmic patterns of normal speech. The rhythm of speech synchronized to patterned cues is much closer to normal speech prosody than in metric cuing. Needless to say, patterned cuing is more effective with mildly affected dysarthric speakers than metric cuing. However, in dysarthria rehabilitation, research has shown that RSC is most successful in improving intelligibility with severely affected speakers.

Asymmetric fluency cues that do not necessarily simulate normal speech prosody can be created by singing. Fluency disorders can benefit from singing exercises in therapy. However, two words of caution must be inserted. First, not all stutterers who attain fluency in singing can translate it to speech. Second, depending on the site of the brain lesion, a full musical stimulus can be more confusing than helpful. A patient with a right-hemisphere brain lesion may not be able to benefit from a full musical stimulus—or may even do worse—but will respond well to a simple metronome cue, because many complex melodic and harmonic components in music seem to be mediated by right-hemisphere or bilateral activations.

8.5 Vocal Intonation Therapy (VIT)

Techniques in vocal intonation therapy (VIT) address issues in the rehabilitation of voice disorders. Musical vocalization, through singing, breathing, and other vocal control exercises, is directed at training all aspects of voice control, including pitch, breath support, timbre, loudness, phonation, resonance, and intonation. Therapeutic applications may include relaxation exercises of the head, neck, and upper trunk, which may be followed by vocal warm-ups that include diaphragmatic breathing exercises and scale singing. Phonation exercises, as well as intoned voicing exercises using open vowels with incrementally increasing loudness, may emphasize relaxation to reduce possible spasticity in the vocal cords. Faulty resonance may be caused by hypernasality, a paresis of the soft palate. Intonation and singing exercises may be used to redirect the air stream forward to escape through the mouth. Intonation exercises may use melodic and rhythmic cues, as well as accents and stress points, to train for correct prosodic patterns in verbal utterances.

In VIT, the parameters shared by voice and speech production are most easily visible and utilized to enhance voice rehabilitation. One could say that when using VIT, the neurologic music therapist acts like a good voice coach or choir conductor. Voice disorders can have physiological reasons, be due to brain damage or illness, or have sociocultural or psychological reasons. Malformations of the vocal tract, the resonant cavities, or the respiratory system may cause hoarseness, lack of breath control, or abnormal timbre. Brain damage may directly afflict the brain centers responsible for the muscle control of the vocal apparatus. Throat cancer or vocal nodes can affect voice production. Cultural expectations may lead to the use of abnormal speech patterns (e.g., by associating feminine speech with very high-pitched registers). Psychological trauma may also cause abnormal loudness/softness or pitch control.

Examples of VIT exercises may involve singing through pitch ranges —similar to vocal warm-ups—to improve abnormally narrow pitch range during speaking, dynamic modulations of loudness in tone production to enhance loudness control, breathing and intoning exercises to improve breath control and diaphragmatic breathing, or vocal intonation exercises to regulate timbre (e.g., to reduce nasality). Breathing and singing, combined with relaxation exercises, can help reduce hoarseness. Accompanying vocal exercises on instruments such as the piano can significantly enhance the therapeutic exercises by offering preparatory time cues for start/stop; supporting the voice with another sound source; regulating tension and relaxation in the patient; enhancing cues relative to loudness, pitch, and rhythm; and motivating the patient to engage in and work on appropriate vocalization through musical intonation.

The science of voice production has made enormous strides in understanding the physiological mechanisms involved in the vocal and respiratory control systems. The technology of studying and imaging the vocal tract has made considerable progress since the mid-1990s. These new medical insights allow music to become a much more focused intervention technique to improve vocal control and the health of the voice and respiratory system. Many professional vocalist-musicians, in addition to patients with voice disorders, are beneficiaries of these new medical insights and treatment techniques.

8.6 Oral Motor and Respiratory Exercises (OMREX)

Oral motor and respiratory exercises (OMREX) refer to the use of musical materials and exercises, mainly through sound vocalization and playing of wind instruments, to enhance articulatory control and respiratory strength and function of the speech apparatus. OMREX techniques may be applied in developmental disorders, dysarthria, muscular dystrophy, and other disorders affecting speech motor control and respiratory function. Haas and Distenfeld (1986) have shown that rhythmic entrainment of respiratory function through music is possible. OMREX is specifically designed to work on articulatory control and associated functions rather than on voice quality, which is emphasized in vocal intonation therapy. However, some overlap between VIT and OMREX may exist in the training of respiratory function because the distinctions between proper mechanisms for voice production and articulation are not always clear-cut; both functions are interdependent and may influence each other.

Playing wind instruments such as flutes, kazoos, slide whistles, or tin whistles can strengthen and build awareness of the speech muscle apparatus at the same time it strengthens respiratory control and cardiopulmonary functions. The blowing mechanisms of wind instruments can easily be adapted to facilitate sound production for clients. Other exercises may include sound production of different speech phonemes, vowels, and consonants. These exercises can be shaped within musical materials by adding melodic and rhythmic elements to enhance intonation. The musical context can vary from speech rhymes to *Sprechgesang* to actual vocalization exercises through singing. Speech sounds can be practiced in isolation or in patterns of sound combinations.

It is important to remember that the primary goal in articulation exercises focuses on intelligibility and sufficient distinction rather than correct sound production. OMREX adds several important rationales to articulation and respiratory control exercises. Rhythm and music can regulate appropriate rates of production and repetition to enhance the exercise effect on control mechanisms and strength. Singing encourages prolonged voicing and accesses different pitch systems. Rhythm adds a time structure that creates predictability to facilitate motor planning and motor execution.

8.7 Developmental Speech and Language Training through Music (DSLM)

Developmental speech and language training through music (DSLM) is designed to utilize musical, as well as related materials to enhance and facilitate speech and language development in children with developmental speech and language delays. These delays can have several known etiologies, such as neurological disorders affecting speech and language function, different degrees of mental retardation, medical conditions that constrain the child's normal environmental input, or disease-related issues of speech production. Many times, however, speech and language delays are not easily connected to diagnostic categories, making the understanding of causation and a diagnostic-based treatment selection a difficult task. Minimal neural dysfunctions in the areas of cognition and perception, not clearly detectable through medical or neuropsychological assessments, are frequently suspected to underlie these syndromes. Psychological factors may play a negative role in slowed or impeded speech and language development. Some delays appear—in retrospect—purely as a developmental stage that the child simply outgrows, considered a normal deviation within a wide developmental spectrum of behavior functions. Some of these delays respond favorably to treatment, while others seem to remediate themselves within a developmental context.

In light of the wide spectrum of possible causes and large variety of manifestations of such developmental delays, an effective therapeutic technique is needed that accesses the cognitive and motor functions underlying speech and language in a broad, integrative, and global fashion (unlike some of the more specialized techniques addressing distinct diagnostic issues in speech production, neurological encoding, or voice and respiratory control). Music provides an excellent resource of materials and experiences to address speech and language development in a holistic manner. Children learn developmentally how to speak and sing in close tandem. Both singing and speaking are aural forms of communication. Music can incorporate song and speech, chanting and rhyming, in a very structurally cohesive way.

Furthermore, music elicits physical response. Speech and movement are closely related in children: Movement often serves as the impellant action to initiate speech and is also an integral accompaniment to speech in the early stages of language development (Lutia 1966). Musical experiences can encourage and facilitate verbal and physical expression through the combined structure of speaking, singing, and moving.

Performance on musical instruments can add another dimension in auditory communication and physical engagement. Excellent resources for DSLM have been assembled especially by the early childhood music education approaches of Orff and Kodaly. Many of these musical experiences, originally aimed at early musical development, can easily be adapted to emphasize cognitive and motor development through developmental music activities. Furthermore, concept development—an underlying fundamental cognitive function of language development—in such areas as numbers, letters, sounds, motions, colors, shapes, and animate beings (humans, animals), can be creatively translated and taught through musical activities.

Therapeutic music experiences in DSLM may range from simply singing or playing music to a severely developmentally disabled child, connecting sounds or actions with words to elicit some auditory and physical response, to complex exercises of writing songs, initiating vocalizations through singing, or learning numbers and shapes through performance exercises on musical instruments. All therapeutic music exercises have to be aligned with developmental scales of normal speech and language in order to be able to engage the child at the appropriate level and help to move functions to the next developmental level. Knowledge in such areas as first word acquisition, stages of sentence development (one-word sentences, different stages of two-word sentences, etc.), concept development, types of vocabulary acquisition (e.g., nouns and adjectives before verbs), and length of expected utterances at developmental stages are critical in building creative and emotionally arousing, yet structurally and functionally precise and goal-directed, exercises and experiences.

The emotional context of facilitating speech and language development through music cannot be overrated. Emotional context is a critical factor in effective learning, psychologically as well as neurologically. The motivational content of DSLM, based on the affective arousal quality of a music-facilitated therapeutic exercise, may be a critical factor in enhancing speech and language development.

8.8 Therapeutic Singing (TS)

Therapeutic singing (TS) refers to an unspecific use of singing activities—either in groups or between client and therapist—to facilitate initiation, development, and articulation in speech and language, as well as to increase functions of the respiratory apparatus, used with a variety of neurological or developmental speech and language dysfunctions (Jackson et al. 1997). The broad range of therapeutic goals for this technique indicates that TS addresses a wide spectrum of functions in a more general and undifferentiated way.

TS can incorporate and support the goals of other, more specific therapeutic techniques. For example, the goals and accomplishments in training units such as rhythmic speech cuing, oral motor and respiratory exercises (OMREX), and vocal intonation therapy (VIT) can be followed and reinforced by TS exercises, which allow the client to practice all exercise elements in an applied and integrated manner, focusing not on the specific exercises, but on the musical outcome. As such, TS has a very practical and enhancing effect, letting the client put all elements of speech production together within an applied musical focus. The practice of the combination of elements of speech production, required simultaneously in an undifferentiated manner to create a musical product, can serve as an important reinforcer of therapy, as well as a milestone in assessing the client's ability to utilize therapeutic techniques. The supportive role of TS in an applied and integrated manner may be extended to other techniques, such as musical speech stimulation or even melodic intonation therapy, not by taking its place as the primary intervention, but as a separate technique in support of the other, adding an important applied focus to enhance learning and recovery.

TS may, in a different therapeutic setting, be a reinforcing and supporting technique for speech and language development and initiation. Similar in role to the other techniques, TS presents a trade-off: It incorporates all elements of speech and language more comprehensively, yet less specifically. As such, the inclusion of TS in the therapy process warrants consideration of its most effective place in the timing of therapy. At certain stages or intervals, a change in therapeutic focus that is more applied, integrated, and emotionally focused may provide the more beneficial intervention. It may also help to summarize and cap developmental and therapeutic stages before a new stage is entered. TS, in its clear focus on the musical product, is a very success-oriented technique, thus providing an important motivational input in tandem with functional enhancements to the client.

Another arena of application for TS can be in medical settings, where it can play a beneficial role in providing physical exercises based on engagement of the respiratory tract, cardiopulmonary functions, and the speech motor apparatus. Applications can range from use in surgical units to treatment of respiratory and cardiopulmonary dysfunctions such as asthma or emphysema. In a medical unit, TS may be one of the first techniques for physical strengthening the client can undertake after some medical interventions (e.g., surgery) because of the limited physical involvement necessary. In therapy for respiratory diseases, TS may provide one of the more effective training outlets, because the patient can engage in TS for fairly long durations, thereby increasing the effectiveness of the exercise. The patient may also be highly motivated in participating in TS because of the emotional (and possibly social) context music may provide. Motivation is an important component in successful rehabilitation.

8.9 Symbolic Communication Training through Music (SYCOM)

In cases of complete loss of expressive language or a dysfunctional or absent functional language development, alternative communication systems need to be developed and provided for the client. Visual symbol systems, sign language, computerized speech systems, and many other systems and technologies have been developed. In severe loss of language, however, appropriate uses and an understanding of the meaning and the rules of communication are frequently affected as well. Providing an expressive substitute system does not mean the client understands how to use it appropriately to communicate effectively. This area of language is usually referred to as the pragmatics of language.

Proper pragmatic use of language is a prerequisite for the effective use of expressive communication systems, including normal speech. Music and speech share, among many other elements, the auditory modality to communicate. Music also has analogies to phonology, prosody, morphology, and syntax in spoken language. Music does not have explicit semantic meaning. However, within its rule structure and its associated extramusical meanings (e.g., expressing sorrow, sadness, happiness), it can simulate communication behavior. Rules of communication thus can be effectively simulated and rehearsed in musical exercises (e.g., through improvisatory performance exercises using structured instrumental or vocal improvisation). These exercises can effectively be used to train structural communication behavior such as dialoguing, using questions and answers, listening and responding, appropriate speech gestures, appropriate timing of initiation and responding, initiating and terminating communication, appropriate recognition of the other communicant's message, and so on.

In further development of symbolic communication training through music (SYCOM), music can be utilized to express emotional communication. SYCOM uses music as a nonverbal language system that is sensorily structured, requires social awareness, has strong affective saliency, evolves in real time, and thus can effectively simulate communication structures in social interaction patterns. Within such a role, SYCOM can be also used in conjunction with teaching alternative communication systems to build an enhanced understanding of the rules, function, and meaning of language interaction in general with other people.

8.10 NMT and Hearing Impairment

Many of the techniques that we have discussed could be used in adapted forms for interventions with hearing-impaired persons. Rhythmic speech cuing, vocal intonation therapy, therapeutic singing, oral motor and respiratory exercise, and symbolic communication and developmental speech and language training through music can all be applied in effective ways. Applications of these techniques focus on four goal areas: (a) auditory training, (b) speech development, (c) language development, and (d) social skills development (Gfeller 1999; Gfeller et al. 1997). Pitched and nonpitched percussion can be used to train auditory perception, especially in the early stages of auditory training, in four areas: sound detection, discrimination, identification, and comprehension. The wider frequency, timbre, and amplitude spectrum of musical instruments may facilitate sound awareness. Also, tactile stimulation can be paired with auditory stimulation to access additional perceptual channels.

Speech development can be enhanced by free vocalization or imitation exercises, as well as more structured singing exercises using TS, RSC, VIT, and OMREX. These can help in articulation exercises, intelligibility, developing proper prosody (rhythm, pitch), and voice control (pitch, loudness) (Gfeller 1999; Darrow and Starmer 1986; Bang 1980). Exercises in DSLM can help encourage language development in terms of concept and vocabulary, use of expression employing language skills, conversational rules, and spontaneous interaction in communication. SYCOM can further facilitate the exposure to language models by using an alternative aural communication system to train all the pragmatic aspects of language use, nonverbal expression, and appropriate communication behaviors for social skills development.

In summary, NMT techniques can enhance auditory, speech, language, and social functions in hearing-impaired persons by effectively accessing processes shared by music and speech, including common acoustical parameters, auditory perception, vocal production mechanisms, and auditory and cognitive elements in an aural communication system.

9

Neurologic Music Therapy in Cognitive Rehabilitation

JAMES C. GARDINER

It is fitting for two entities as dynamic as neurologic music therapy and cognitive rehabilitation to join together, complement one another, and produce a powerful force for improving mental abilities. This chapter will (a) showcase the latest principles of cognitive rehabilitation, founded on clinical experience and research (e.g., Prigatano 1999; Cicerone et al. 2000; Raskin and Mateer 2000); (b) present neurologic music therapy (NMT) principles as applied to cognitive rehabilitation through the transformational design model (TDM) (Thaut 2000); (c) define the various NMT techniques used for cognitive rehabilitation; and (d) offer an example of how attention can be improved through musical attention control training (MACT).

9.1 Principles of Cognitive Rehabilitation

9.1.1 Introduction

Rimmele and Hester (1987) define cognitive rehabilitation as "procedures designed to provide patients with the cognitive and perceptual skills necessary to perform tasks or solve problems which are currently difficult, but which were within their capabilities before injury" (353). Cicerone and his colleagues (2000) add that cognitive rehabilitation is "based on assessment and understanding of the patient's brain-behavioral deficits" (1596–1597).

179

According to histories by Boake (1989) and Prigatano (1999), cognitive rehabilitation began in the early twentieth century. Prior to that time, most neurological injuries resulted in death, either from the blow to the head or from a resulting infection. J. Hughlings Jackson has been credited with focusing neurology during the late nineteenth century on the process of recovery, which was believed to happen largely through compensation. Concentrated efforts at rehabilitating neurological injuries began in Germany and the United States during World War I. Shepherd Ivory Franz developed quantitative methods for assessing outcomes after neurological injuries, and Karl S. Lashley emphasized that motivation and the complexity of the brain's structure are important variables to consider during rehabilitation.

During World War II, cognitive rehabilitation efforts developed in England, Scotland, the Soviet Union, and the United States. Kurt Goldstein, trained in both neurology and psychiatry, worked in Germany and the United States. He is credited with offering holistic, practical, and humane approaches to neurological rehabilitation. A. R. Luria, a Russian neuropsychologist with vast experience treating neurological injuries among Russian soldiers, insisted on a thorough assessment of brain functions before beginning rehabilitation. He emphasized that extensive practice is needed for retraining, introduced the idea of plasticity of the brain, and believed that motivation is a vital component of the rehabilitation process.

After World War II, interest in cognitive rehabilitation waned until the late 1960s, when neurological rehabilitation units were established in Tel Aviv and Los Angeles. During the 1970s and 1980s, cognitive rehabilitation programs grew into lucrative commercial enterprises. Computerized programs for improving brain function emerged, and were often hailed as a panacea for neurological injury. By the late 1990s, however, the popularity of specialty rehabilitation programs and computerized training began to wane. Funding sources for cognitive rehabilitation diminished as a result of managed health care and research evidence showing that computerized interventions were not necessarily effective treatments.

Many professionals contributed to the scientific and clinical knowledge in the field over the last two decades of the twentieth century: Yehuda Ben-Yishay, who is considered the pioneer of outpatient cognitive rehabilitation; Muriel Lezak, who has made monumental contributions to the assessment of neurological disorders; George Prigatano, who has brilliantly articulated the emotional effects of neurological injury and the use of psychotherapy in neurological rehabilitation; Catherine Mateer and McKay Moore Sohlberg, who have provided a model for understanding and treating attention disorders; Barbara Wilson, Alan Baddeley, and Rick Parenté, who have illuminated the area of memory; and Keith Cicerone, who completed the formidable task of summarizing the research on cognitive rehabilitation and providing practice standards and guidelines for the field. As a result of excellent leadership, continued research, and learning experiences from clinical practice, cognitive rehabilitation is now in a stage of early maturity, with principles, standards, and guidelines that are promising for both practitioners and their clients.

9.1.2 General Principles

9.1.2.1 Foundation Principles

9.1.2.1.1 Research-Based Cognitive rehabilitation needs to be founded on sound neuropsychological principles and based on outcome research (Cicerone et al. 2000; Prigatano 1999). Cicerone and his colleagues have provided the most comprehensive review of the cognitive rehabilitation research literature available to date. They focused on remediation of attention; visual-spatial skills, language, memory, and executive functioning; and on multimodal and comprehensive-holistic cognitive rehabilitation programs to establish practice standards, practice guidelines, and practice options for cognitive rehabilitation.

9.1.2.1.2 Effectiveness and Limitations Several reviews of cognitive rehabilitation research (Rimmele and Hester 1987; Gordon and Hibbard 1992; Wilson 2000; Cicerone et al. 2000) concluded that rehabilitation has a measurable impact on a person's cognitive abilities, psychological adjustment, and ability to function independently. However, Rimmele and Hester noted that rehabilitation does not necessarily result in productive employment and that "comprehensive rehabilitation efforts usually do not result in a complete recovery of pre-morbid functioning" (380).

9.1.2.1.3 Plasticity It is important to recognize that the brain has the ability to reorganize after an injury in order to accomplish tasks by using new neural strategies (Goodwin 1989; Loring 1999). According to Almli and Finger (1992), there are two possible explanations for this recovery of function: neuronal sparing (prevention of damaged nerve cells from dying) and neuronal reorganization (building new strategies for accomplishing tasks). Plasticity provides a rationale for proceeding with cognitive retraining.

9.1.2.1.4 Assessment Successful cognitive rehabilitation depends on a comprehensive assessment of all cognitive factors, including attention, spatial, memory, language, executive functioning, and psychosocial adjustment (Lezak 1995; Raskin and Mateer 2000; Prigatano 1999).

9.1.2.2 Treatment Principles

9.1.2.2.1 Immediacy Cognitive treatment is best when delivered as soon after the neurological injury as possible. Early intervention helps prevent dysfunctional patterns (e.g., lowered self-esteem, isolation, anger, depression, and a downward trend in cognitive abilities) from forming (Kay 1993).

9.1.2.2.2 Shaken Sense of Self The first issue that needs attention in neurological rehabilitation is the person's disrupted identity. After a neurological injury or illness with its accompanying cognitive losses, the following questions may emerge: Who am I? Why am I different? Why can't I do the things I did before? Why do people treat me differently? What will happen to me? Will I regain my former abilities? Effective cognitive rehabilitation needs to help the person reestablish a sense of self in a way that assists him or her in achieving stability. In order to engage the patient in cognitive rehabilitation, the clinician first needs to consider the client's subjective experience (Prigatano 1999) and lead the person to a state of acceptance. Only after a person has accepted her or his condition will cognitive rehabilitation be successful.

9.1.2.2.3 Self-awareness Rehabilitation needs to deal with disorders of self-awareness (Prigatano 1999; Bennett et al. 1998). Many neurological disorders include a lack of awareness of cognitive and behavioral changes. In order to improve functioning in this area, there are three levels of awareness that need to be addressed: (a) intellectual awareness (knowledge that one's performance has changed), (b) emergent awareness (knowing that the problem is now occurring), and (c) anticipation awareness (knowledge that the difficulty could occur in the near future). Achieving these levels of awareness will help the person prevent future problems with cognitive and behavioral functioning (Bennett et al. 1998).

9.1.2.2.4 Interactions among Physical, Cognitive, and Emotional Functioning Kay (1993) introduced the idea that physical, psychological, and cognitive functions influence each other to produce changes in each area, as well as changes in the functional abilities of the person. For example, a neurological injury may produce pain, which may lower cognitive functioning and produce depression, which in turn exacerbates the pain. This state of being calls on professionals to keep a holistic picture and to provide psychological support for clients with neurological injuries.

9.1.2.2.5 Treat Emotional Factors A key principle in neurological rehabilitation, according to Prigatano (1999), is to be aware of and provide support for emotional reactions in clients, their families, and rehabilitation staff members. Thus, psychotherapy (including individual, relationship, and family) is an important component of cognitive rehabilitation.

9.1.2.2.6 *Begin with Basics* Gordon and Hibbard (1992) emphasize that treatment must be ordered in layers, beginning with the most basic skills such as attention and concentration, then progressing to more complex skills such as memory, verbal, language, visuospatial, executive function, and social behavior. To be effective, rehabilitation must not have a one-size-fits-all approach, but should start with the person's most basic skill that needs improvement and progress to develop more complex skills.

9.1.2.2.7 *Process-specific* Good cognitive rehabilitation efforts will be process-specific or directed at individual areas of cognitive functioning, such as attention, memory, or executive function (Bennett et al. 1998). Sohlberg and Mateer (1987) investigated three cognitive remediation approaches: functional adaptation, which facilitates functioning in a naturalistic environment; general stimulation, which facilitates general cognitive processing; and the process-specific approach, which focuses on individual areas of mental ability (such as attention, memory, executive function, etc.). Their results support the use of a process-specific approach to rehabilitation.

9.1.2.2.8 *Compensation* Wilson (2000) emphasizes that compensation (finding a new strategy for accomplishing mental tasks) is frequently necessary when recovery from a neurological injury is not complete: "One of the major goals of cognitive rehabilitation is to enable people to compensate for their particular problems" (242). Compensation involves teaching clients to (a) use strategies to reach goals in alternative ways, (b) use remaining skills more effectively, and (c) change the environment to eliminate the need for the damaged cognitive function.

9.1.2.2.9 *Education* Educating persons about the nature and the effects of neurological injuries is an important part of cognitive rehabilitation (Kay 1993; Prigatano 1999; Mateer 2000). Cognitive rehabilitation needs to include information and education about understanding and predicting symptoms and their resolution for clients and their families.

9.1.2.2.10 *Family Involvement* One of the key factors in the success of cognitive rehabilitation is having a strong support system. It is vital to include family members and significant others in cognitive rehabilitation. Because the impact of a neurological injury or illness extends from the patient to his or her family, friends, coworkers, employer, and others, those persons need to be supported, educated, and recruited to be part of the rehabilitation team (Kay 1993; Prigatano 1999).

9.1.3 Outcome Principles

9.1.3.1 Generalization Outcome studies have shown that the effects of training in the clinic or laboratory do not necessarily carry over into the real world. Thus, generalization is an important factor, and all cognitive rehabilitation training needs to be generalized into the natural environment (Prigatano 1999; Mateer 2000; Bennett et al. 1998). Gordon and Hibbard (1992) recommend that training be conducted in diverse settings with plenty of repetition, and that the clients be taught to understand the underlying mechanisms of their cognitive successes and failures and how they operate in various everyday settings.

9.1.3.2 Gradual Return to Responsibilities Whenever possible, it is important for the client to return to duties and responsibilities gradually, with plenty of support from the family, treatment team, and employer (Kay 1993).

9.1.3.3 Evaluation The treatment efficacy of each cognitive rehabilitation effort needs to be carefully evaluated, not only to discover the effectiveness of the treatment offered, but also to add to the scientific knowledge of the field of cognitive rehabilitation (Prigatano 1999; Raskin and Mateer 2000).

9.1.4 Principles of Attention Rehabilitation

9.1.4.1 Neuroanatomy Studies of the neuroanatomy of attention (Mirsky et al. 1991) reveal that attentional capacities are supported by a complex neurological system that receives support from the brain stem, frontal lobes, limbic system, temporal lobes, and parietal lobes. Thus, rehabilitation efforts need to be directed toward many areas of the brain and to be multimodal.

9.1.4.2 Model of Attention Functions Mateer (2000) and Sohlberg and Mateer (1989) provide the most widely accepted clinical model of attention. They divide attention into the following categories:

1. Focused: the ability to "respond discretely to specific…stimuli"
2. Sustained: the "ability to maintain a consistent behavioral response during continuous and repetitive activity"
3. Selective: the skill to "maintain a behavioral or cognitive set in the face of…competing stimuli"
4. Alternating: the ability to "shift focus of attention and move between tasks"
5. Divided: the ability to "respond simultaneously to multiple tasks" (Mateer 2000, 79)

9.1.4.3 Rehabilitation Potential While the attention system is particularly vulnerable to injury, "this system also appears to be one that can be modified with targeted intervention" (Mateer 2000, 86; Cicerone et al. 2000; Rimmele and Hester 1987; Sohlberg and Mateer 1987; Ben-Yishay et al. 1987).

9.1.4.4 Foundation Skill Attention is a foundation skill that is necessary for good memory, executive function, communication, and executive control (Bennett et al. 1998). Attention training appears to generalize to other tasks (Rimmele and Hester 1987).

9.1.4.5 Timing Specific attention rehabilitation is recommended during postacute rehabilitation, but not in acute care (Cicerone et al. 2000).

9.1.4.6 Variety and Complexity Cicerone and his colleagues (2000) summarize the evidence demonstrating that cognitive rehabilitation improves attention functioning. They recommend that interventions "include training with different stimulus modalities, levels of complexity, and response demands. The intervention should include therapist activities such as monitoring subjects' performance, providing feedback, and teaching strategies. Attention training appears to be more effective when directed at improving the subject's performance on more complex, functional tasks" (1600).

9.1.4.7 Therapist Involvement Cognitive therapists need to be involved with attention rehabilitation, monitoring progress, giving feedback, and teaching strategies. Stand-alone use of computers or other machines is not recommended for rehabilitating attention skills (Cicerone et al. 2000; Weber 1990).

9.1.5 Principles of Memory Rehabilitation

9.1.5.1 Neuroanatomy Recent research studies with brain-injured persons show that various regions of the brain are involved with the regulation of memory (Tranel and Damasio 2002; Markowitsch 2000). They include the following:

> the early association cortices, the higher-order association cortices of the temporal, frontal and occipital regions, and the limbic-related cortices of the temporal lobe. At subcortical level, the roster includes the hippocampus proper, the amygdala, the basal forebrain nuclei and projection system, the thalamus and hypothalamus, and neurotransmitter nuclei in the brainstem. Also, the evidence suggests that structures critical for the learning and memory of nondeclarative knowledge include the primary somatomotor cortices, the neostriatum, some thalamic nuclei and the cerebellum (Tranel and Damasio 2002, 46).

9.1.5.2 Model of Memory Functioning Memory theorists have included several elements in their models of memory functioning:

1. Sensory memory saves information in near-perfect form for a very short time, to "hold information for selection and processing by the working memory system (Parenté and Anderson-Parenté 1989, 56).
2. Working memory gives the ability to hold and manipulate information (Mateer et al. 1987; Parenté and Anderson-Parenté 1989; Schacter et al. 2000; Baddeley 2002).
3. Semantic memory provides access to a "wide range of organized information, including facts, concepts, and vocabulary" (Schacter et al. 2000, 632).
4. Episodic memory stores and retrieves information about personal experiences (Schacter et al. 2000).
5. Procedural memory gives the ability to learn motor and mental skills (Schacter et al. 2000).
6. Prospective memory initiates "a specific action at a future designated time" (Sohlberg et al. 1992, 129).

9.1.5.3 Conditions for Memory Training Before commencing, memory rehabilitation therapists must consider the nature of the patient's memory loss, other cognitive abilities, physical difficulties, social status, emotional state, and readiness for treatment (Tate 1997, Laaksonen 1994). Memory remediation is most effective with persons who have mild impairment, are fairly independent in functioning, and are motivated to continue using compensation strategies (Cicerone et al. 2000).

9.1.5.4 Foundations for Memory Training Sensory memory training begins with basic sensory skills in order to provide a foundation for improved memory (Parenté and Anderson-Parenté 1989). Attention training is used to provide a foundation for better memory skills (Sohlberg and Mateer 1989; Parenté and Anderson-Parenté 1989; Kapur and Graham 2002).

9.1.5.5 Severe Memory Impairment For persons with severe memory impairment, cognitive rehabilitation will not likely restore memory functioning (Cicerone et al. 2000; Rimmele and Hester 1987). Persons with severe memory deficits can benefit from environmental restructuring and compensation strategies (Wilson 2000).

9.1.5.6 Emotions Memory and emotional functioning are closely linked in the brain (Markowitsch 2000). Thus, in order to be effective, interventions with memory need to include an emotional component.

9.1.5.7 Compensation Strategies Memory compensation strategies have proven effective (Cicerone et al. 2000). Prosthetic memory aids are often used to compensate for memory loss, including checklists, notebooks, electronic devices, recorders, and computers (Parenté and Anderson-Parenté 1989). Notebooks have been shown to be the most effective strategy in compensating for memory loss (Zencius et al. 1990). Strategy training can produce long-term improvement in memory skills (Berg et al. 1991).

9.1.5.8 Error-free Training Memory impairment can produce isolation and withdrawal from others, out of fear of making mistakes. Thus, the therapist should provide error-free opportunities for persons to learn memory strategies. These strategies have proven highly effective for teaching memory skills (Wilson 2002; Wilson and Evans 1996; Wilson et al. 1994).

9.1.5.9 Domain-specific training with memory remediation replicates the demands of the real-world setting where the skills will later be used (Parenté and Anderson-Parenté 1989).

9.1.6 Principles of Executive Function Rehabilitation

9.1.6.1 Definition Executive function refers to a person's ability to "formulate goals; to initiate behavior; to anticipate the consequences of actions; to plan and organize behavior according to spatial, temporal, topical, or logical sequences; and to monitor and adapt behavior to fit a particular task or context" (Cicerone et al. 2000, 1605).

9.1.6.2 Anatomical Correlates It is generally accepted that executive function is controlled primarily from the frontal lobes of the brain.

9.1.6.3 Process Assessment A detailed process analysis of the subject's problem-solving difficulty is necessary in order to propose a plan of action to improve executive functioning (Goldstein and Levin 1987).

9.1.6.4 Outcome Effectiveness The best studies provide strong evidence that executive control skills improve as a result of formal problem-solving strategy training (Cicerone et al. 2000).

9.1.6.5 Strategies for Improving Executive Function A typical strategy for improving executive function involves "moving from simple structured activities with significant external cuing and support to more complex, multistep activities in which external support is gradually reduced and internal support or self-direction is enhanced" (Raskin 2000, 124). Other strategies that have proven effective for improving executive functioning include verbal self-instruction, self-questioning, and self-monitoring, as well as the following:

1. Self-awareness checklists can effectively improve problem-solving skills (Burke et al. 1991).

2. Self-prediction, self-instruction, and error-monitoring training have been helpful (Cicerone and Giacino 1992; Cicerone and Wood 1987).

3. The generation of an alternative solutions approach to problem-solving training has proven successful, not only for improving immediate problem-solving skills, but also for generalizing to new situations (Foxx et al. 1989).

4. External cues, including verbal mediation cues, have proven to be effective for helping persons learn to initiate appropriate social behaviors (Evans et al. 1998; Sohlberg et al. 1988; Raskin 2000).

5. Remedial actions should focus on both clinical and real-world activities (Goldstein and Levin 1987).

6. Compensation strategies, such as environmental modification, cuing systems, alarms, scheduling systems, and lists are often helpful (Raskin 2000).

7. Executive control can be improved by training underlying mental abilities, such as attention (Raskin 2000).

8. Behavior modification can be used to improve executive functions (Raskin 2000).

9. Direct retraining of executive control skills involves breaking down the deficient behavior into component parts, working through a hierarchy from easy to difficult behaviors for the person. The client is taught to analyze problems, divide tasks into smaller steps, look for possible solutions that are goal-directed, analyze the possible solutions, analyze multiple pieces of information simultaneously, and draw inferences (Raskin 2000).

9.1.7 Principles of Psychosocial Rehabilitation

9.1.7.1 Introduction   While cognitive rehabilitation initially focused primarily on mental abilities such as attention, perception, memory, and executive control, since the mid-1980s rehabilitation specialists have added emphasis to psychosocial factors in rehabilitation. Gordon and Hibbard (1992), Kay (1993), and Prigatano (1999) believe that the person's altered sense of self needs attention from professionals. They proposed psychotherapy as a mediating force for successful rehabilitation.

9.1.7.2 Model   Kay (1993) provides a helpful model of the interactions among physical, neurological, cognitive, and psychological factors in mediating functional outcomes after mild traumatic brain injuries. He proposes that rehabilitation professionals educate patients and their families about symptoms, assist in managing a gradual process of improvement, involve the family or significant other in treatment, validate the subjective experience of the patient, help "reestablish the shaken sense of self" (83), and treat the emotional problems at the same time as the cognitive difficulties.

9.1.7.3 Group treatment is recommended for dealing with many psycho-social difficulties, including lack of social skills, communication problems, and emotional problems (Guzik 1987).

9.1.7.4 Social Skills Training Giles and Clark-Wilson (1993) provide a comprehensive outline of methods for improving social skills after neurological injury. They advocate breaking behaviors into small components for attention in therapy, using behavioral techniques and role-playing, giving feedback from the group and leaders, and adapting the behaviors into real-life settings.

9.1.7.5 Nonverbal Communication Training Giles and Clark-Wilson (1993) stress the importance of remediating nonverbal communication in facial expression, gaze, gesture, posture and orientation, interpersonal space, proximity, physical contact, language-free elements of speech, and appearance.

9.1.7.6 Conversational Skills In teaching social interaction abilities, Giles and Clark-Wilson (1993) advocate helping clients build skills in social routines, attracting attention, initiating conversations, maintaining dialogue, listening, questioning, responding, and closing conversations.

9.1.7.7 Dealing with Emotions Depression is common with neurological injury and can be treated with medications, psychotherapy, cognitive therapy, behavioral interventions, grief management, group psychotherapy, and family interventions (Prigatano 1999, Raskin and Stein 2000). Other common emotional difficulties associated with neurological injury include anxiety, posttraumatic stress (Hovland and Raskin 2000), irritability, and anger (Hovland and Mateer 2000). Anger and frustration can be managed through environmental controls, cognitive behavior therapy, teaching coping strategies, and self-monitoring.

9.1.7.8 Psychotherapy Principles Sohlberg (2000) emphasizes the need for psychotherapy after neurological injury, proposing the use of cognitive therapy, multimodal approaches, behavior modification, and group psychotherapy. She emphasizes reconciling perceptions of past, present, and future abilities while searching for residual strengths. She proposes a five-step process of behavior modification: (1) identify the target problem, (2) generate a list of options, (3) have the patient select the most appropriate option, (4) give training and support for implementing the strategy, and (5) encourage independence in managing the problem.

Psychosocial interventions need to involve not only counseling, but also modeling, behavioral rehearsal, treatment contracting, and full, nonjudgmental acceptance by the therapist. The following guidelines for psychotherapy are offered by Cicerone et al. (1997): establish a well-defined treatment focus, set proximal goals, use mediating goals, conduct comprehension checks, and teach goal setting (21–22).

Prigatano (1999) views psychotherapy as "a useful component of neuropsychological rehabilitation for *some* patients after brain injury" (201). One of the key purposes of psychotherapy in neurological rehabilitation is to help the person explore and arrive at a renewed sense of self. It helps the person "understand and cope with reality" (206). It builds into his or her life the important values of love, play, and work (contributing), so that he or she can feel fulfilled. With neurological injury, each person is embarking on a hero's journey to discover who he or she is now and how he or she can learn to be the best person possible. Guidelines for psychotherapy include the following: go slowly, be a consultant, assist in sharpening the person's perspective on reality, recognize the complexity of the person's behavior, focus on the present, keep a problem-solving perspective, deal with the person's emotions slowly and honestly, help the person align with natural human responses, share the emotional responsibility for working with the brain dysfunction, and help the person find meaning in his or her neurological disorder.

9.1.7.9 Family Intervention   Prigatano (1999) considers it vital to work with family members who are involved in neurological rehabilitation. Psychotherapy assists families in meeting their needs. Working with the family is like helping deliver a baby; it may be a slow and painful process with no way to speed it along. At times the psychotherapist may need to give specific advice to help the family through the process. Practical guidelines include recognizing that the family is hurting; entering their field of view; hearing them out; helping them through their denial; helping them get their needs met; helping them deal with their anger; establishing good relationships with the family; not rushing into psychotherapy; offering individual psychotherapy for family members if needed; helping them establish the values of love, play, and work; and having both the patient and the family be part of the rehabilitation team.

9.2 Principles of Cognitive Rehabilitation as Applied to Neurologic Music Therapy (NMT)

9.2.1 Introduction

There are many principles and guidelines that cognitive rehabilitation and NMT share. These commonalities add to the compatibility between the two disciplines, and provide potential for unlimited creativity and the power to produce benefits for the clients who receive cognitive training through NMT. Table 9.1 summarizes how NMT, through the transformational design model (TDM), merges with cognitive rehabilitation to provide musical applications designed to improve mental abilities.

9.2.1.1 Research-based Cognitive rehabilitation and NMT have both grown into viable treatment modalities because of their reliance on evidence-based treatment approaches (see Cicerone et al. 2000 and chapters 4 and 6 of this volume). Working together, cognitive rehabilitation and NMT are founded on the scientific bases of neurology, neurologic music therapy, and neuropsychology, combined with the principles of music production (Lucia 1987).

9.2.1.2 Plasticity Another principle shared by NMT and cognitive rehabilitation is the belief that the brain can reorganize and shift functions after an injury. Sacks (1998) provides numerous examples of music's power to reorganize the brain.

9.2.1.3 Assessment Just as successful cognitive rehabilitation depends on a comprehensive assessment of all cognitive factors, including attention, spatial, memory, language, executive functioning, and psychosocial adjustment, so NMT cannot be conducted until physical conditions, cognitive abilities, and musical skills and preferences are evaluated.

9.2.1.4 Begin with Basics Frequently, cognitive treatment must be ordered in layers, beginning with the most basic skills, such as attention and concentration, then progressing to more complex skills, such as memory, verbal, language, visuospatial, executive function, and social behavior. NMT is fully compatible with this concept. Attention and perception training allows the therapist to train basic skills and then progress to more complex abilities, such as memory training or executive function training.

9.2.1.5 Generalization Because the effects of cognitive training in the clinic do not necessarily carry over into the real world, generalization is an important factor. NMT, through the transformational design model (Thaut 2000), emphasizes generalization into the natural environment through homework assignments and exercises that are as lifelike as possible.

9.2.1.6 Variety and Complexity Cicerone and his colleagues (2000) recommend that cognitive interventions for attention "should include training with different stimulus modalities, levels of complexity, and response demands. The intervention should include therapist activities such as monitoring subjects' performance, providing feedback, and teaching strategies" (1600). NMT provides such needed complexity for the

TABLE 9.1 Application of the Transformational Design Model to Cognitive Rehabilitation

Area of Cognitive Functioning	Assessment	Treatment Goal	Treatment Strategy	NMT Approach	Transfer
Attention	Digit Span Forward	Improve: Focus	Attention Process Training	Attention and Perception Training:	Homework Exercises
	Digit Span Backward	Selective Attention		Musical Sensory Orientation Training (MSOT)	
	Trail Making Test A	Sustained Attention		Musical Neglect Training (MNT)	
	Trail Making Test B	Alternating Attention		Auditory Perception Training (APT)	
	Letter-Number Sequencing	Divided Attention		Musical Attention Control Training (MACT)	
Memory	Wechsler Memory Scale-III	Improve: Recall	Repetition	Memory Training:	Homework Exercises
		Recognition	Association	Musical Mnemonics Training (MMT)	
		Compensation	Compensation	Associative Mood and Memory Training (AMMT)	

		Improve:	Goal Setting	Executive Functions Training: Homework
Executive Function	Wisconsin Card Sort Test	Goal Setting	Goal Setting	
	Delis-Kaplan Executive Function System	Planning	Planning	Musical Executive Function Training (MEFT) Exercises
	Function System	Organization	Organization Skill Training	
	Mazes	Execution	Initiation	
	TinkerToy Test	Adjustment	Problem Solving	
Psychosocial	Clinical Interview	Improve: Acceptance	Contribution To Life	Psychosocial Behavior Training: Homework
	Minnesota Multiphasic	Emotions	Psychotherapy	Music Psychotherapy and Counseling (MPC) Exercises
	Personality Inventory 2	Stress Management	Relaxation	
	Symptom Checklist 90-R	Communication	Communication Training	
	Beck Depression Inventory	Social Skills	Social Skills Training	
	Rorschach Inkblot	Relationships	Relationships Training	

rehabilitation setting: "The simultaneous stimuli of rhythm, melody, timbre, and tempo require an integrated response, unlike many stimulus-response tasks" (Purdie 1997, 211).

9.2.1.7 Therapist Involvement   It has been established that cognitive therapists need to be involved face-to-face with their clients in rehabilitation, rather than relying on computers or other mediating devices to conduct treatment. The practices of neurologic music therapists are compatible with this principle, in that NMT is conducted in a face-to-face setting.

9.2.1.8 Attention Functions   Knox and his associates (Knox and Jutai 1996; Knox et al. 2003) have been foremost in the investigation of using music to improve attention. Their studies have demonstrated that alternating attention can be improved with music therapy. Morton et al. (1990) demonstrated that music improved capacities for attention and decreased distractibility. The NMT approach to improving attention is research-based and includes a variety of attention and perception training approaches (see Table 9.1).

9.2.1.9 Memory Functioning   Neurologic music therapy is heavily involved in improving memory functioning, through musical mnemonics training and associative mood and memory training. The research literature on music and memory gives ample evidence that music plays a strong role in memory (see, for example, Wallace 1994; Levitin and Cooke 1996; Morton et al. 1990; Tomaino 1998; Carruth 1997; Gingold and Abravanel 1987; Iwanaga and Ito 2002).

9.2.1.10 Self-awareness   Since rehabilitation deals with disorders of self-awareness, NMT can provide excellent experiences for the client to gain knowledge of present abilities and limitations. Musical executive function training (MEFT), for example, causes clients to look at their performance and, when in a group setting, receive feedback from peers. This facilitates self-awareness and helps the person develop anticipation and avoid future problems.

9.2.1.11 Emotional Treatment Factors   A key principle in neurological rehabilitation, emotional support for clients, their families, and rehabilitation staff members, is another concept closely shared with NMT. Music can "reach the 'inner self' and function as a source of emotional support, as the patient deals with the trauma of the disease" (Purdie 1997, 212). Bever (1988) adds that, "The key to the emotional power of music is that it stimulates cognitive operations which unlock our private feelings" (175). Purdie reviewed the available studies on music therapy in neurorehabilitation and extracted several principles that apply to cognitive and emotional rehabilitation for neurological disorders:

1. Music can provide "environmental enrichment by stimulating inter-active participation and nonverbal communication and thereby facilitating cognitive and behavioral change" (210).
2. Music can arouse attention, and thus actively engage attention and memory systems.
3. "Music provides multiple layers of information, and thereby stimulates more than one level of attention" (211).
4. Music serves as a "stimulus for psychological adjustment to neurological disorder" (211).
5. "Music can reach the 'inner self' and function as a source of emotional support, as the patient deals with the trauma of the disease" (212).
6. Psychotherapy and life review can be supported with music, which can be used as a compensatory technique.
7. Music encourages socialization and improves emotional empathy.
8. "Music therapy is used as a form of nonverbal psychotherapy" (212).

9.2.1.12 Shaken Sense of Self   As an issue that needs attention in neurological rehabilitation, disrupted personal identity, is an area that is readily accessed through NMT with musical psychotherapy and counseling (MPC): "Music acts as a mnemonic or reminder, recalling the person to his former self, forming a lifeline through apathy, amnesia, or dementia" (Sacks 1998, 13).

As part of recovery from disrupted personal identity, Prigatano (1999) advocates using the hero's journey to help the person find her or his new role in life. Similar to this process is the song story (Hiller 1989), which is a musical technique to assist survivors of neurological injury in dealing with extreme emotional reactions. The method "provides an opportunity for the client to experience an integrated framework of imagery, language, music and lyrics, each offering a message of hope and caring in a holistic, symbolic manner" (20).

In summary, the principles of cognitive rehabilitation and NMT are closely aligned and have potential for providing powerful interventions with persons experiencing neurological injuries or illnesses.

9.3 Cognitive Rehabilitation and the Transformational Design Model (TDM)

The transformational design model, as outlined in chapter 6, provides a five-step framework for the union of traditional cognitive rehabilitation and music therapy approaches. In step 1, the scientific nature of the TDM relies on clinical research and practices of cognitive rehabilitation to assess the cognitive abilities of the patients, so that interventions can be based on needs. Clear, realistic goals for treatment outcomes are set in step 2 of the

TDM. With goals clearly established, traditional cognitive rehabilitation approaches can be outlined (step 3). Until this point, music has not entered the picture. Step 4 of the TDM introduces neurologic music therapy interventions designed to enhance the traditional cognitive rehabilitation approaches given in step 3. Finally, in step 5, the therapeutic interventions and changes accomplished with neurologic music therapy need to be transferred into everyday situations. This can normally be accomplished through homework exercises that will apply to the patient's everyday life. Table 9.1 outlines NMT as it is applied to cognitive rehabilitation. The following sections will define and explain the standardized clinical techniques used when NMT is applied to cognitive rehabilitation.

9.3.1 Auditory Attention and Perception Training

9.3.1.1 Musical Sensory Orientation Training (MSOT) This technique uses live or recorded music to stimulate arousal and recovery of wake states and to facilitate meaningful responsiveness and orientation to time, place, and person. In more advanced recovery or developmental stages, active engagement in simple musical exercises increases vigilance and trains basic attention maintenance with emphasis on quantity rather than quality of response (Ogata 1995). It includes sensory stimulation, arousal orientation, and vigilance and attention maintenance.

9.3.1.2 Musical Neglect Training (MNT) MNT includes active performance exercises on musical instruments that is structured in time, tempo, and rhythm, and is in appropriate spatial configurations, to focus attention to a neglected or inattended visual field. A second application type consists of receptive music listening to stimulate hemispheric brain arousal while engaging in exercises addressing visual neglect or inattention (Hommel et al. 1990).

9.3.1.3 Auditory Perception Training (APT) APT includes auditory perception and sensory integration. It is composed of musical exercises to discriminate and identify different components of sounds (e.g., time, tempo, duration, pitch, timbre, rhymic patterns, and speech sounds). It involves integration of different sensory modalities (visual, tactile, and kinesthetic) during active musical exercises, such as playing from symbolic or graphic notation, using tactile sound transmission, or integrating movement to music (Bettison 1996; Gfeller et al. 1997; Heaton et al. 1988).

9.3.1.4 Musical Attention Control Training (MACT) MACT includes structured active or receptive musical exercises involving precomposed performance or improvisation in which musical elements cue different musical responses to practice focused, sustained, selective, divided, and alternating attention functions.

9.3.2 Memory Training

9.3.2.1 Musical Mnemonics Training (MMT) In the areas of echoic, procedural, and declarative memory, MMT includes musical exercises addressing various memory encoding and decoding/recall functions. Immediate recall of sounds or sung words using musical stimuli addresses echoic functions. Musical stimuli are used as mnemonic devices or memory templates (e.g., in songs, rhymes, or chants). The exercises facilitate learning of nonmusical information by sequencing and organizing the information into temporally structured patterns or chunks (Deutsch 1982; Gfeller 1983; Wallace 1994; Claussen and Thaut 1997; Maeller 1996; Wolfe and Hom 1993).

9.3.2.2 Associative Mood and Memory Training (AMMT) Musical mood-induction techniques are used (a) to produce mood-congruent states to facilitate memory recall, (b) to access associative mood and memory networks to direct specific memory access, and (c) to enhance learning and memory function through inducing positive emotional states in the learning and recall process (Bower 1981).

9.3.3 Executive Function Training

9.3.3.1 Musical Executive Function Training (MEFT) This technique includes improvisation and composition exercises presented individually or in groups to practice executive function skills such as organization, problem solving, decision making, reasoning, and comprehension. The musical context provides important therapeutic elements, such as performance products in real time, temporal structure, creative processes, affective content, sensory structure, or social interaction patterns.

9.3.4 Psychosocial Behavior Training

9.3.4.1 Music Therapy and Counseling (MPC) MPC employs guided music listening, musical role playing, and expressive improvisation or composition exercises. It uses musical performance to address issues of mood control, affective expression, cognitive coherence, reality orientation, and appropriate social interaction to facilitate psychosocial functions. The techniques are based on models derived from affect modification, associative network theory of mood and memory, social learning theory, classical and operant conditioning, and mood vectoring based on isoprinciple techniques (selecting musical stimuli that match the patient's mood as a therapeutic starting point before attempting to modulate mood states in desired directions) (Millard and Smith 1989; Unkefer and Thaut 2002; Blood et al. 1999; Sutherland et al. 1982; Teasdale and Spencer 1984).

9.4 Rehabilitation of Attention Using the Transformational Design Model

This final section will illustrate how the transformational design model can be used to develop a plan to rehabilitate attention skills for a person with a neurological injury. As presented in chapter 6, the TDM provides an opportunity to develop music therapy techniques that are based on brain research and principles of brain injury rehabilitation. The following treatment plans will show in practical format how the music therapist and cognitive rehabilitation specialist can collaborate to achieve improvement in attention skills. For an overview of the process of NMT with attention rehabilitation, see Table 9.2.

9.4.1 Assessment

In order to effectively assess attention skills, a qualified psychologist will need to be consulted, and standardized tests will need to be used. All types of attention will need to be assessed, including focused, selective, sustained, alternating, and divided. Lezak (1987, 1995) and Bennett et al. (1998) propose several tests as effective for assessment of attention. Ability to *focus* attention can be assessed with the Digit Span (forward). *Selective* attention can be assessed with Digit Span (backward), the Delis-Kaplan Executive Function System (D-KEFS) Color-Word Interference Test—Inhibition, and the Digit Vigilance Test. Selected tests for *sustained* attention include Digit Span (forward), Digit Symbol, Symbol Digit Modalities Test, and Trail-making Test (part A). *Alternating* attention can be assessed using the Trail-making Test (part B), Paced Auditory Serial Addition Test (PASAT), and three tests from the D-KEFS: Verbal Fluency Test—Category Switching, Design Fluency—Switching, and Color-Word Interference Test—Inhibition/Switching. Finally, *divided* attention can be assessed with the Letter-Number Sequencing Test from the Wechsler Memory Scale-III.

9.4.2 Treatment Goals

Once the assessment of attention has been completed, specific treatment goals are established. The goal outcomes need to be observable, and can be based on improvement on neuropsychological tests and reports from objective observers or significant others, and from self reports. Examples of treatment goals are "The client will improve his score on the Letter-Number Sequencing Test by five or more points" and "The client's husband will report that she has increased her reading concentration time by more than 15 minutes."

TABLE 9.2 Application of the Transformational Design Model to the Rehabilitation of Attention

Assessment	Treatment Goal	Treatment Strategy	NMT Approach	Transfer to the Real World
Test:	Improve:		Musical Attention Control Training (MACT):	
Digit Span Forward	Focus	Attention Process Training	NMT Application on Focused Attention (NMT-MACT-FOC)	Homework Exercises
Digit Span Backward	Selective Attention	Attention Process Training	NMT Application on Selective Attention (NMT-MACT-SEL)	Homework Exercises
Trail Making Test A	Sustained Attention	Attention Process Training	NMT Application on Sustained Attention (NMT-MACT-SUS)	Homework Exercises
Trail Making Test B	Alternating Attention	Attention Process Training	NMT Application on Alternating Attention (NMT-MACT-ALT)	Homework Exercises
Letter-Number Sequencing	Divided Attention	Attention Process Training	NMT Application on Divided Attention (NMT-MACT-DIV)	Homework Exercises

9.4.3 Cognitive Rehabilitation Strategies

The first step in cognitive rehabilitation is to educate clients and their families about the nature of attention and how it can be improved. In order to make positive changes, clients need to understand the nature of the changes that neurological injuries/diseases have brought to their lives. They also need to develop hope that changes are possible and to learn what they can do to accomplish those changes in their lives. Appendices A and B are handouts used to educate clients and their significant others about attention and how they can improve their attention skills.

The second stage in cognitive rehabilitation of attention abilities is direct training. If the practitioner is to choose the most comprehensive and carefully researched approach to rehabilitating attention skills, it will likely be attention process training (Mateer 2000; Sohlberg and Mateer 1987, 1989; Bennett et al. 1998). Mateer describes attention process training as "a group of hierarchically organized tasks designed to exercise sustained, selective, alternating, and divided attention" (81). The treatment tasks include audiotapes for detection of number targets; number manipulation exercises; audiotapes with background noise to train selective attention; exercises for addition/subtraction flexibility, before/after, and odd/even number flexibility; simultaneous sequencing exercises; set-dependent activities; card sorting; and dual tasks requiring responses to both visual and auditory information (Sohlberg and Mateer 1987). In addition to training basic attention skills, the attention process training program has a feature of generalization, whereby clients use daily logs to record attention mistakes and attention successes.

9.4.4 Neurologic Music Therapy: Musical Attention Control Training (MACT)

Musical attention control training uses the same structure as attention process training, in that it trains the clients in focusing, selecting, sustaining, alternating, and dividing attention. MACT is based on research findings from cognitive rehabilitation (e.g., Mateer 2000; Sohlberg and Mateer 1987, 1989; Bennett et al. 1998). Five MACT applications illustrate the use of music therapy with attention.

9.4.4.1 NMT-MACT-FOC
This exercise, which is conducted in a group setting, helps clients focus their attention, then and initiate a musical event to help other persons focus their attention. Details on how to conduct NMT-MACT-FOC are presented in appendix C.

9.4.4.2 NMT-MACT-SEL
MACT for selective attention skills involves using music to help each client maintain focus while being bombarded with competing stimuli. Each person in the group treatment setting has

the opportunity to receive training in selective attention and to provide the competing stimuli. Appendix D provides full details for conducting NMT-MACT-SEL.

9.4.4.3 NMT-MACT-SUS One of the most vital elements of attention is the ability to sustain focus in order to complete a task. Because rhythm is the trainer of attention in the brain, sustained rhythmic patterns are used to help clients develop sustained attention (also called concentration). The MACT exercise presented in appendix E engages each client in sustained rhythm practice. The exercise also encourages creativity, since each client creates a rhythm for the other clients to use as they practice sustained attention.

9.4.4.4 NMT-MACT-ALT Alternating attention is another key skill that allows a person to shift focus among two or more stimuli. Therapists can use MACT techniques to train alternating attention by having clients shift among various stimuli at command. As in other attention training techniques, MACT uses rhythms to teach alternating attention skills. See appendix F for details on using NMT-MACT-ALT.

9.4.4.5 NMT-MACT-DIV To treat divided attention, in a group setting clients are taught to attend to two stimuli simultaneously and follow instructions from both. The instructions for using NMT-MACT-DIV are presented in appendix G.

9.4.4.6 Transfer of Attention Training to the Real World Training in cognitive skills needs to be applicable to everyday experiences. Unless the skills are practiced in realistic settings, they will not benefit the client. Mateer (2000) and her colleagues incorporate generalization during the early stages of cognitive rehabilitation. MACT also builds in generalization through homework assignments. After completing training in MACT, clients are given assignments that are similar to those used in the clinic, but are designed to use at home. See appendix H for a sample of homework assignments used with clients engaged in MACT.

9.5 Summary

This chapter has presented an integration of the principles of cognitive rehabilitation and how they are applied to neurologic music therapy through the transformational design model. The qualified reader is invited to enter the world of evidence-based scientific treatment of neurological diseases and disorders, apply the principles of cognitive rehabilitation to neurologic music therapy, and improve the cognitive abilities of his or her clients.

Appendix A
Attention

Definition

Attention is the ability to direct one's awareness to a thought, object, person, or event in one's environment without being distracted.

The Nature of Attention

1. Attention is a system that requires the cooperation of many areas of the brain.
2. Attention is the foundation of memory, language, spatial skills, executive control, and other mental functions.

Elements of Attention

1. **Focus**—the ability to direct one's mind to a particular thing.
    Example: You are in a room full of people talking, and the telephone rings. You are able to hear the phone and answer it.
2. **Select**—the ability to avoid distractions as you focus on one thing.
    Example: You tune out a loud noise on the street as you talk on your cell phone.
3. **Sustain**—the ability to hold attention over time (also called concentration).
    Example: You are reading, and can stay focused on the book for an hour.
4. **Shift**—the ability to switch attention back and forth from one thing to another.
    Example: You are cooking, and shift your attention back and forth from a pan on the stove to a dish you are mixing on the counter.
5. **Divide**—the ability to sustain attention between two different things.
    Example: While driving, you look at the road ahead, as well as the side roads, where someone may be entering the highway.

Rehabilitation of Attention

1. Attention and concentration are frequently impaired when the brain is injured.
2. Attention and concentration are areas that respond well to rehabilitation.

Appendix B
Improving Attention and Concentration Skills

I. **BECOME AWARE OF YOUR ATTENTION PROBLEMS**

  A. Take a look at the *results* of your attention deficits. How, when, and where do they cause problems?
  B. Learn to observe your deficits as they happen.
  C. Anticipate situations when your deficits will operate, and stop your problem before it happens.

II. **TAKE RESPONSIBILITY FOR IMPROVING YOUR ATTENTION**

  A. Keep a mentally active lifestyle.
  B. Use *music* in your life.
    1. Listen to inspiring music.
    2. Learn to play a musical instrument.
  C. Avoid watching TV, unless it is a game show that challenges your mind.
  D. Play *games* as often as possible: card games, video games, or computer games (limit video and computer games to one hour or less each day).
  E. Work with puzzles: jigsaw, crossword, and word search.
  F. Do exercises for your attention.
    1. While riding as a passenger in a car, look at roadside signs, read them quickly, look away, try to recite what was on the sign, and then look back before the sign passes.
    2. Look at words, look away, try to spell them backward, then look back to check on yourself. Start with two-letter words, then gradually increase the length of the words you choose.
  G. Go to a library or bookstore to find books of puzzles, math, games, and problem solving.
  H. Volunteer to help others who have attention and concentration difficulties. Be a reading tutor for an illiterate adult, tutor an elementary school student in arithmetic, or work with developmentally disabled persons.

III. **LEARN TO LIVE IN THE HERE AND NOW**

Appendix C
Neurologic Music Therapy (NMT) Cognitive Rehabilitation Application: NMT-MACT-FOC

General Cognitive Area
 Targeted: Attention
Specific Cognitive Skill
 Targeted: Focus
NMT Technique Utilized: Music attention control training (MACT)
Outcome Goal: Each participant will be able to focus his or
                              her attention on a given stimulus.
Clientele Description: People with neurological injury or illness.
Session Type: Group (2–15 people)
Equipment Needed: A variety of rhythm instruments in
                              containers ready for easy distribution to
                              the group, such as autoharp, guitar, or
                              piano.

Step-by-Step Procedure:

1. The leader chooses a musical instrument that will draw the attention of the other group members.
2. She or he plays an introduction to a song in a way that gains their attention.
3. After gaining their attention, the leader stops and discusses the process, including the part of the brain that allowed them to focus (temporal), and how they were able to effectively shut off other stimuli and to focus on the leader.
4. Each group member is given the opportunity to choose an instrument, gain the attention of the rest of the group, and discuss the process experienced as he or she attracted attention to himself or herself.

Appendix D
Neurologic Music Therapy (NMT)
Cognitive Rehabilitation Application:
NMT-MACT-SEL

General Cognitive Area Targeted:	Attention
Specific Cognitive Skill Targeted:	Ability to select a stimulus to the exclusion of competing stimuli.
NMT Technique Utilized:	Music attention control training (MACT)
Outcome Goal:	Each participant will be able to successfully select a stimulus from the environment, stay focused on that stimulus, respond appropriately, and exclude input from competing stimuli.
Clientele Description:	People with neurological injury or illness.
Session Type:	Group (2–15 people)
Equipment Needed:	A variety of percussion instruments.

Step-by-Step Procedure:

1. The group is seated in a circle.
2. Rhythm instruments are distributed to the group.
3. Two people are chosen from the group—a leader and a "heckler."
4. Using drums or other rhythm instruments, the group leader plays a simple, sustained rhythm.
5. The group members are invited to join with the rhythm.
6. The heckler, who is given a loud, distinct instrument, attempts to disrupt the rhythm by playing a rhythm that is contrary to that of the leader.
7. The leader ends the rhythm.
8. Other group members are given the opportunity to be the leader and the heckler.
9. The group discusses the experience from three angles: being a group member, being a heckler, and being a leader.

Appendix E
Neurologic Music Therapy (NMT)
Cognitive Rehabilitation Application:
NMT-MACT-SUS

General Cognitive Area Targeted:	Attention
Specific Cognitive Skill Targeted:	Sustain
NMT Technique Utilized:	Music attention control training (MACT)
Outcome Goal:	Each participant will be able to continue focusing his or her attention on a given stimulus.
Clientele Description:	People with neurological injury or illness.
Session Type:	Group (2–15 people)
Equipment Needed:	A variety of percussion instruments in containers ready for easy distribution to the group; such as autoharp, guitar, or piano.

Step-by-Step Procedure:

1. Using a drum or other rhythm instrument, the group leader plays a simple, sustained rhythm.
2. The group members are invited to join with the rhythm.
3. The leader ends the rhythm by counting down—"5,4,3,2,1"—and then stops.
4. Each group member is given the opportunity to introduce a rhythm to the group, lead the group in producing the rhythm, and stop the group with whatever cue he or she devises.

Appendix F
Neurologic Music Therapy (NMT)
Cognitive Rehabilitation Application:
NMT-MACT-ALT

General Cognitive Area Targeted:	Attention
Specific Cognitive Skill Targeted:	Alternating attention
NMT Technique Utilized:	Music attention control training (MACT)
Outcome Goal:	Each participant will be able to alternate focusing his or her attention back and forth between two stimuli.
Clientele Description:	People with mild-to-moderate brain injury or brain illness.
Session Type:	Group (2–15 people)
Equipment Needed:	A variety of percussion instruments, autoharp, guitar or piano

Step-by-Step Procedure:

1. Arrange the group in a horseshoe shape and pass out rhythm instruments.
2. Have two leaders sit facing the group.
3. Leader #1 will teach rhythm pattern #1.
4. Leader #2 will teach rhythm pattern #2.
5. Leader #1 will start the group and lead it through a few bars of the rhythm, then stop. Without missing a beat, leader #2 will lead the group with his or her rhythm, then stop after a few bars. Leader #1 will then begin again. They will switch back and forth until both leaders stop.

Appendix G
Neurologic Music Therapy (NMT)
Cognitive Rehabilitation Application:
NMT-MACT-DIV

General Cognitive Area Targeted:	Attention
Specific Cognitive Skill Targeted:	Divided attention
NMT Technique Utilized:	Music attention control training (MACT)
Outcome Goal:	Each participant will be able to divide his or her attention between two stimuli.
Clientele Description:	People with neurological injury or illness.
Session Type:	Group (2–15 people)
Equipment Needed:	A variety of percussion instruments.

Step-by-Step Procedure:

1. Seat the group in a horseshoe pattern, and pass out rhythm instruments.
2. Appoint two people with adequate control ability to sit at the head of the group as leaders.
3. Leader #1 will start and stop the group. She or he will decide on a signal system, teach the group the signals, and start and stop the group numerous times during the session.
4. Leader #2 will set the rhythm and continue playing, regardless of what the rest of the group does.
5. The group will divide attention between the two leaders, following the rhythm set by leader #1 while starting and stopping according to leader #2's instructions.

Appendix H
Homework Assignments for Attention

Focus: Survey the room around you and consider everything that competes for your attention (radio, TV, other people, wind noise, pictures, fan, etc.). Choose one thing and focus your attention on that. Then choose another object or process to focus on. Keep moving your attention around until you have focused on at least ten things.

Sustain: Find one or more rhythm instruments (your hands to clap, your fingers to click, spoons, sticks, a cardboard box, a drum, maracas, etc.). Decide on a rhythm, perform it, and try to keep it up as long as you can. Use a clock or timer to keep track of how long you can sustain your rhythm. Do this exercise with a friend or group of friends to make it more fun.

Practice living in the here and now by talking yourself through everything you do. For example, suppose you are sitting in your living room and need to get a pair of scissors from the kitchen. Say to yourself, "I am placing my feet solidly on the floor, standing up, turning toward the kitchen, walking, opening the drawer, reaching for the scissors, closing the drawer, turning toward the living room, walking, turning, standing in front of the chair, and sitting down." Do this aloud if you are alone. If other people are in the room, say it in your mind. For a fun and more powerful approach, sing or whistle your way through the above exercise.

For the next three exercises, you will need two musical sound sources, such as a radio, CD or cassette player, or TV.

Select: Play two songs at once. Stay focused on one song while you ignore the other one.

Alternate: Play two songs at the same time. Listen to one for a few seconds and tune out the other one. Then switch your attention to the other song while you tune out the first one. Keep changing back and forth between the two songs.

Divide: Listen to two songs at once. Both should include words. After the songs have ended, try to write down the words to each of the songs.

Variation: Listen to two newscasts at the same time. After listening to them for five minutes, turn them off and write down what you can remember from each.

217

References

Aiello, R. 1994. Music and language: Parallels and contrasts. In R. Aiello (Ed.), *Musical Perceptions*, 40–63. New York: Oxford University Press.

Albert, M., Sparks, R., and Helm, N. 1973. Melodic intonation therapy for aphasics. *Archives of Neurology*, 29, 130–131.

Almli, C.R., and Finger, S. 1992. Brain injury and recovery of function: Theories and mechanisms of functional reorganization. *Journal of Head Trauma Rehabilitation*, 7, 70–77.

An, K., Bejjani, F.J. 1990. Analysis of upper-extremity performance in athletes and musicians. *Hand Clinics*, 6(3), 393–403.

Andrews, G., Craig, A., and Feyer, A.M. 1983. Stuttering: A review of research findings and theories circa 1982. *Journal of Speech and Hearing Disorders*, 48, 226–246.

Apel, W. 1981. *Harvard Dictionary of Music*. Cambridge, MA: Belknap Press of Harvard University Press.

Aschersleben, G., and Prinz, W. 1995. Synchronizing actions with events: The role of sensory information. *Perception and Psychophysics*, 57, 305–317.

Avanzini, G., Faienza, C., Minciacchi, D., Lopez, L., and Majono, M. (Eds.). 2003. *The Neurosciences and Music. Annals of the New York Academy of Sciences*, 999. New York: New York Academy of Sciences.

Baddeley, A.D. 2002. The psychology of memory. In A.D. Baddeley, M.D. Kopelman, and B.A. Wilson (Eds.), *The Handbook of Memory Disorders*, 2nd ed., 3–15. Chichester, UK: Wiley.

Bang, C. 1980. A world of sound and music. *Journal of the British Association for Teachers of the Deaf*, 4, 1–10.

Basso, A., Capitani, E., and Vignolo, L.A. 1979. Influence of rehabilitation on language skills in aphasic patients. *Archives of Neurology*, 36, 190–196.

Baur, B., Uttner, I., Ilmberger, J., et al. 2000. Music memory provides access to verbal knowledge in a patient with global amnesia. *Neurocase*, 6, 415–421.

Beale, E.M.L. 1988. *Introduction to Optimization*, edited by L. Mackley. New York: Wiley.

Belin, P., Van Eeckhout, P., Zilbovicius, M., et al. 1996. Recovery from nonfluent aphasia after melodic intonation therapy. *Neurology*, 47, 1504–1511.

Bellaire, K., Yorkston, K.M., and Beukelman, D.R. 1986. Modification of breath patterning to increase naturalness of a mildly dysarthric speaker. *Journal of Communication Disorders*, 19, 271–280.

219

Bennett, T., Raymond, M., Malia, K., et al. 1998. Rehabilitation of attention and concentration deficits following brain injury. *Journal of Cognitive Rehabilitation*, 16, 8–13.

Ben Yishay, Y., Piasetsky, L., and Rattock, J. 1987. A systematic method for ameliorating disorders in basic attention. In M. Meier, A. Benton, and L. Diller (Eds.), *Neuropsychological Rehabilitation*. New York: Guilford.

Ben Yishay, Y., Rattock, J., Ross, B., et al. 1980. A remedial module for the systematic amelioration of basic attentional disturbances in head trauma patients. In Y. Ben Yishay (Ed.), *Working Approaches to Remediation of Cognitive Deficits in Brain Damaged Persons*. New York: New York University Medical Center.

Berg, I.J., Koning-Haanstra, M., and Deelman, B.G. 1991. Long-term effects of memory rehabilitation: A controlled study. *Neuropsychological Rehabilitation*, 1, 97–111.

Berlin, C.I. 1976. On: *Melodic intonation therapy for aphasia*, by R.W. Sparks and A.L. Holland. *Journal of Speech and Hearing Disorders*, 41, 298–300.

Berlyne, D.E. 1971. *Aesthetics and Psychobiology*. New York: Appleton-Century- Crofts.

Bernstein, L. 1976. *The Unanswered Question: Six Talks at Harvard*. Cambridge, MA: Harvard University Press.

Bettison, S. 1996. The long-term effects of auditory training on children with autism. *Journal of Autism and Developmental Disorders*, 26, 361–375.

Bever, T.G. 1988. A cognitive theory of emotion and aesthetics in music. *Psychomusicology*, 7, 165–175.

Bhogal, S.K., Teasell, R., Foley, N.C., et al. 2003. Rehabilitation of aphasia: More is better. *Topics in Stroke Rehabilitation*, 10(2), 66–76.

Blood, A.J., Zatorre, R.J., Bermudez, P., and Evans, A.C. 1999. Emotional responses to pleasant and unpleasant music correlate with activity in paralimbic brain regions. *Nature Neuroscience*, 2(4), 382–387.

Boake, C. 1989. A history of cognitive rehabilitation of head-injured patients, 1915 to 1980. *Journal of Head Trauma Rehabilitation*, 4, 1–8.

Bonakdarpour, B., Eftekharzadeh, A., and Ashayeri, H. 2003. Melodic intonation therapy with Persian aphasic patients. *Aphasiology*, 17, 75–95.

Bonnel, A.M., Faita, F., Peretz, I., et al. 2001. Divided attention between lyrics and tunes of operatic songs: Evidence for independent processing. *Perception & Psychophysics*, 63(7), 1201–1213.

Boucher, V., Garcia, J.L., Fleurant, J., et al. 2001. Variable efficacy of rhythm and tone in melody-based interventions: Implications of the assumption of a right-hemisphere facilitation in non-fluent aphasia. *Aphasiology*, 15, 131–149.

Bower, G.H. 1981. Mood and memory. *American Psychologist*, 36(2), 129–148.

Bregman, A.S. 1990. *Auditory scene analysis: The Perceptual Organization of Sound*. Cambridge, MA: MIT Press.

Brown, S.H., Thaut, M.H., Benjamin, J., et al. 1993. Effects of rhythmic auditory cueing on temporal sequencing of complex arm movements. *Proceedings of the Society for Neuroscience*, 227.2.

Buonomano, D.V. 2000. Decoding temporal information: A model based on short-term synaptic plasticity. *Journal of Neuroscience*, 20(3), 1129–1141.

Buonomano, D.V., Hickmott, P.W., and Merzenich, M.M. 1997. Context-sensitive synaptic plasticity and temporal-to-spatial transformations in hippocampal slices. *Proceedings of the National Academy of Sciences of the United States of America*, 94(19), 10403–10408.

Buonomano, D.V., and Merzenich, M.M. 1995. Temporal information transformed into a spatial code by a neural network with realistic properties. *Science*, 267(5200), 1028–1030.

Burke, W.H., Zencius, A.H., Wesolowski, M.D., et al. 1991. Improving executive function disorders in brain-injured clients. *Brain Injury*, 5, 241–252.

Buetefisch, C., Hummelsheim, H., Denzler, P., et al. 1995. Repetitive training of isolated movements improves the outcome of motor rehabilitation of the centrally paretic hand. *Journal of the Neurological Sciences*, 130, 59–68.

Cadalbert, A., Landis, T., Regard, M., et al. 1994. Singing with and without words: Hemispheric asymmetries in motor control. *Journal of Clinical and Experimental Neuropsychology*, 16(5), 664–670.

Caligiuri, M.P. 1989. The influence of speaking rate on articulatory hypokinesia in Parkinsonian dysarthria. *Brain and Language*, 36, 1493–1502.

Carruth, E.K. 1997. The effects of singing and the spaced retrieval technique on improving face-name recognition in nursing home residents with memory loss. *Journal of Music Therapy*, 34, 165–186.

Casseday, J.H., and Covey, E. 1995. Mechanisms for analysis of auditory temporal patterns in the brainstem of echolocating bats. In E. Covey, H.L. Hawkins, and R.F. Port (Eds.), *Neural Representations of Temporal Patterns*. New York: Plenum Press.

Chan, A.S., Ho, Y.C., and Cheung, M.C. 1998. Music training improves verbal memory. *Nature*, 396, 128.

Chen, Y., Ding, M., and Kelso, J.A.S. 2001. Origins of timing errors in human sensorimotor coordination. *Journal of Motor Behaviors*, 33, 3–8.

Chomsky, N. 1980. *Rules and Representations*. New York: Columbia University Press.

Cicerone, K.D., Dahlberg, C., Kalmar, K., et al. 2000. Evidence-based cognitive rehabilitation: Recommendations for clinical practice. *Archives of Physical Medicine and Rehabilitation*, 81, 1596–1615.

Cicerone, K.D., Fraser, R.T., and Clemmons, D.C. (Eds.). 1997. *Counseling Interactions with Traumatically Brain Injured Clients*. Boca Raton, FL: St. Lucie.

Cicerone, K.D., and Giacino, J.T. 1992. Remediation of executive function deficits after traumatic brain injury. *NeuroRehabilitation*, 2, 12–22.

Cicerone, K.D., and Wood, J.C. 1987. Planning disorder after closed head injury: A case study. *Archives of Physical Medicine and Rehabilitation*, 68, 111–115.

Clark, C., and Chadwick, D. 1980. *Clinically Adapted Instruments for the Multiply Handicapped*. St Louis, MO: Magnamusic-Baton.

Claussen, D., and Thaut, M.H. 1997. Music as a mnemonic device for children with learning disabilities. *Canadian Journal of Music Therapy*, 5, 55–66.

Clynes, M. (Ed). 1982. *Music, Mind, and Brain: The Psychology of Music*. New York: Plenum Press.

Cohen, N. 1988. The use of superimposed rhythm to decrease the rate of speech in a brain-damaged adolescent. *Journal of Music Therapy*, 25, 85–93.

Colcord, R.D., and Adams, M.R. 1979. Voicing duration and vocal SPL changes associated with stuttering reduction during singing. *Journal of Speech and Hearing Research*, 22(3), 468–479.

Collins, J.J. 1995. The redundant nature of locomotor optimization laws. *Journal of Biomechanics*, 28(3), 251–267.

Cook, P.R. 1999. *Music, Cognition, and Computerized Sound: An Introduction to Psychoacoustics*. Cambridge, MA: MIT Press.

Costa-Giomi, E. 2003. Young children's harmonic perception. *Annals of the New York Academy of Sciences*, 999, 477–484.

Coull, J.T., Vidal, F., Nazarian, B., et al. 2004. Functional anatomy of the attentional modulation of time estimation. *Science*, 303, 1506–1508.

Cowles, A., Beatty, W.W., Nixon, S.J., et al. 2003. Musical skill in dementia: A violinist presumed to have Alzheimer's disease learns to play a new song. *Neurocase*, 9, 493–503.

Critchley, M. and Henson, R.A. (Eds.) 1977. *Music and the Brain: Studies in the Neurology of Music*. Springfield, IL: C.C. Thomas.

Cross, P., McLellan, M., Vomberg, E., et al. 1984. Observations on the use of music in rehabilitation of stroke patients. *Physiotherapy Canada*, 36, 197–201.

Crystal, D. 1980. *Introduction to Language Pathology*. Baltimore, MD: University Park Press.

Crystal, H., Grober, E., and David, M. 1989. Preservation of musical memory in Alzheimer's disease. *Journal of Neurology, Neurosurgery, and Psychiatry*, 52, 1415–1416.

Darrow, A.A., and Cohen, N. 1991. The effect of programmed pitch practice and private instruction on the vocal reproduction accuracy of hearing-impaired children: Two case studies. *Music Therapy Perspectives*, 9, 61–65.

Darrow, A.A., and Starmer, G.J. 1986. The effect of vocal training on the intonation and rate of hearing-impaired children's speech: A pilot study. *Journal of Music Therapy*, 23, 194–201.

De Goede, C.J.T., Keus, S.H.J., Kwakkel, G., et al. 2001. The effects of physical therapy in Parkinson's disease: A research synthesis. *Archives of Physical Medicine and Rehabilitation*, 82, 509–515.

De Stewart, B.J., Willemse, S.C., Maassen, B.A., et al. 2003. Improvement of voicing in patients with Parkinson's disease by speech therapy. *Neurology*, 60(3), 498–500.

Deutsch, D. 1979. Language and music as communication: A discussion. *Music Educators Journal*, 65, 68–71.

Deutsch, D. 1982. Organizational processes in music. In M. Clynes (Ed.), *Music, Mind and Brain*, 119–131. New York: Plenum Press.

Dewey, J. 1934. *Art as Experience.* New York: Minton, Balch.

Dowling, W.J., and Harwood, D.L. 1986. *Music Cognition.* Orlando, FL: Academic Press.

Drake, C., Jones, M.R., and Baruch, C. 2000. The development of rhythmic attending in auditory sequences: Attunement, referent period, focal attending. *Cognition*, 77, 251–288.

Düchting, H. 2002. *Paul Klee: Painting and Music.* Munich: Prestel.

Dworkin, J.P., and Abkarian, G.G. 1996. Treatment of phonation in a patient with apraxia and dysarthria secondary to severe closed head injury. *Journal of Medical Speech Language Pathology*, 4, 105–115.

Dworkin, J.P, Abkarian, G.G., and Johns, D.F. 1988. Apraxia of speech: The effectiveness of a treatment regimen. *Journal of Speech and Hearing Disorders*, 53, 280–294.

Effenberg, A.O., and Mechling, H. 1998. Bewegung horbar machen-Warum? Zur Zukunftsperspektive einer systematischen Umsetzung von Bewegung in Klaenge. *Psychologie und Sport*, 5, 28–38.

Elliot, B., Grove, J.R., and Gibson, B. 1988. Timing of the lower limb drive and throwing limb movement in baseball pitching. *International Journal of Sport Biomechanics*, 4, 59–67.

Elliott, B. 1982. *Guide to the Selection of Musical Instruments with Respect to Physical Ability and Disability.* St. Louis, MO: MMB Music.

Epstein, D. 1985. Tempo relations: A cross cultural study. *Music Theory Spectrum*, 7, 34–71.

Evans, J.J., Emslie, H., and Wilson, B.A. 1998. External cueing systems in the rehabilitation of executive impairments of action. *Journal of the International Neuropsychological Society*, 4, 399–408.

Feltner, M., and Dapena, J. 1986. Dynamics of the shoulder and elbow joints of the throwing arm during a baseball pitch. *International Journal of Sport Biomechanics*, 2(4), 235–259.

Fernandez del Olmo, M., and Cudeiro, J. 2003. The timing in Parkinson's disease: Effects of a rehabilitation programme based on rhythmic sound cues. *Proceedings of the Society for Neuroscience*, 734.2.

Fetters, L., and Holt, K.G. 1990. Efficiency of human movement: Biomechanical and metabolic aspects. *Pediatric Physical Therapy*, 2, 155–159.

Fleisig, G.S., Barrentine, S.W., Escamilla, R.F., and 1996. Biomechanics of overhand throwing with implications for injuries. *Sports Medicine*, 21(6), 421–437.

Fodor, J. 1975. *The Language of Thought.* New York: Crowell.

Fodor, J. 1983. *The Modularity of Mind: An Essay on Faculty Psychology.* Cambridge, MA: MIT Press.

Foster, N.A., and Valentine, E.R. 2001. The effect of auditory stimulation on autobiographical recall in dementia. *Experimental Aging Research*, 27, 215–228.

Foxx, R.M., Martella, R.C., and Marchand-Martella, N.E. 1989. The acquisition, maintenance, and generalization of problem-solving skills by closed head-injury adults. *Behavior Therapy*, 20, 61–76.

Frassinetti, F., Bolognini, N., and Ladavos, E. 2002a. Enhancement of visual perception by cross-modal visual-auditory interaction. *Experimental Brain Research*, 147, 332–343.

Frassinetti, F., Pavani, F. and Ladavos, E. 2002b. Acoustical vision of neglected stimuli: Interaction among spatially convergent audio-visual inputs in neglect patients. *Journal of Cognitive Neuroscience*, 14, 62–69.

Freedland, R.L., Festa, C., Sealy, M., et al. 2002. The effects of pulsed auditory stimulation on various gait measurements in persons with Parkinson's disease. *Neurorehabilitation*, 17, 81–87.

Freeman, J.S., Cody, F.W., and Schady, W. 1993. The influence of external timing cues upon the rhythm of voluntary movements in Parkinson's disease. *Journal of Neurology, Neurosurgery and Psychiatry*, 56, 1078–1084.

Fries, P., Reynolds, J.H., Rorie, A.E., et al. 2001. Modulation of oscillatory neuronal synchronization by selective visual attention. *Science*, 291, 1560–1563.

Galaretta, M., and Hestrin, S. 2001. Spike transmission and synchrony detection in networks of GABAergic interneurons. *Science*, 292, 2295–2299.

Galloway, H.F. 1975. Music and the speech handicapped. In R.M. Graham (Comp.), *Music for the Exceptional Child*, 15–47. Reston, VA: Music Educators National Conference.

Gaser, C., and Schlaug, G. 2003. Brain structures differ between musicians and non-musicians. *Journal of Neuroscience*, 23(27), 9240–9245.

Gaston, E.T. (Ed.). 1968. *Music in Therapy*. New York: Macmillan.

Georgiou, N., Iansek, R., Bradshaw, J.L., et al.1993. An evaluation of the role of internal cues in the pathogenesis of Parkinsonian hypokinesia. *Brain*, 116, 1575–1587.

Gfeller, K.E. 1983. Musical mnemonics as an aid to retention with normal and learning disabled students. *Journal of Music Therapy*, 20, 179–189.

Gfeller, K.E. 1999. Music therapy in the treatment of sensory disorders. In W.B. Davis, K.E. Gfeller, and M.H. Thaut, *An Introduction to Music Therapy: Theory and Practice*, 2nd ed. Boston: McGraw-Hill.

Gfeller, K.E., and Baumann, A.A. 1988. Assessment procedures for music therapy with hearing-impaired children: Language development. *Journal of Music Therapy*, 25, 192–205.

Gfeller, K.E., and Darrow, A.A. 1987. Music as a remedial tool in the language education of hearing-impaired children. *The Arts in Psychotherapy*, 14, 229–235.

Gfeller, K.E., and Schum, R. 1994. Requisites for conversation: Engendering world knowledge. In N. Tye-Murray (Ed.), *Let's Converse: A "How-to" Guide to Develop and Expand Conversational Skills of Children and Teenagers Who Are Hearing Impaired*. Washington, DC: Alexander Graham Bell Association for the Deaf.

Gfeller, K.E., Woodworth, G., Robin, D.A., et al. 1997. Perception of rhythmic and sequential pitch patterns by normally hearing adults and adult cochlear implant users. *Ear and Hearing*, 18, 252–260.

Giles, G.M., and Clark-Wilson, J. 1993. *Brain Injury Rehabilitation: A Neurofunctional Approach*. London: Chapman & Hall.

Gillam, R.B., Marquardt, T.P., and Martin, F.N. 2000. *Communication Sciences and Disorders: From Science to Clinical Practice*. San Diego: Singular Publishing Group.

Gingold, H., and Abravanel, E. 1987. Music as a mnemonic: The effects of good- and bad-music settings on verbatim recall of short passages by young children. *Psychomusicology*, 7, 25–39.

Glassman, R.B. 1999. Hypothesized neural dynamics of working memory: Several chunks might be marked simultaneously by harmonic frequencies within an octave band of brain waves. *Brain Research Bulletin*, 50, 77–93.

Glover, H., Kalinowski, J., Rastatter, M., et al. 1996. Effect of instruction to sing on stuttering frequency at normal and fast rates. *Perceptual and Motor Skills*, 83, 511–522.

Goldfarb, R., and Bader, E. 1979. Espousing melodic intonation therapy in aphasia rehabilitation: A case study. *International Journal of Rehabilitation Research*, 2, 333–342.

Goldstein, F.C., and Levin, H.S. 1987. Disorders of reasoning and problem-solving ability. In M.J. Meier, A.L. Benton, and L. Diller (Eds.), *Neuropsychological Rehabilitation*, 327–354. New York: Guilford.

Goodwin, D.M. 1989. *A Dictionary of Neuropsychology*. New York: Springer-Verlag.

Gordon, W.A., and Hibbard, M.R. 1992. Critical issues in cognitive remediation. *Neuropsychology*, 6, 361–370.

Grady, C.L., Furey, M.L., Pietrini, P., et al. 2001. Altered brain functional connectivity and impaired short-term memory in Alzheimer's disease. *Brain*, 124, 739–756.

Gregory, D. 2002. Music listening for maintaining attention of older adults with cognitive impairments. *Journal of Music Therapy*, 39(4), 244–264.

Guzik, J. 1987. Group treatment approaches to cognitive and social needs. In P.A. Morse (Ed.), *Brain Injury: Cognitive and Prevocational Approaches to Rehabilitation*, 121–144. New York: Tiresias Press.

Haas, F., Distenfield, S., and Axen, K. 1986. Effects of perceived music rhythm on respiratory patterns. *Journal of Applied Physiology*, 61, 1185–1191.

Halpern, A.R. 1992. Musical aspects of auditory imagery. In D. Reisberg (Ed.), *Auditory Imagery*, 1–26. Hillsdale, NJ: Erlbaum.

Halpern, A.R. and O'Connor, M. 2000. Implicit memory for music in Alzheimer's disease. *Neuropsychology*, 14, 391–397.

Hammen, V.L., and Yorkston, K.M. 1996. Speech and pause characteristics following speech rate reduction in hypokinetic dysarthria. *Journal of Communication Disorders*, 29, 429–445.

Hammen, V.L., Yorkston, K.M., and Minifie, F.D. 1994. Effects of temporal alterations on speech intelligibility in Parkinsonian dysarthria. *Journal of Speech and Hearing Research*, 37, 244–253.

Haneishi, E. 2001. Effects of a music therapy voice protocol on speech intelligibility, vocal acoustic measures, and mood of individuals with Parkinson's disease. *Journal of Music Therapy*, 38(4), 273–290.

Hanslick, E. 1854. *Vom Musikalisch-Schönen*. Leipzig: Weigel.

Harrington, D.L., and Haaland, K.Y. 1999. Neural underpinnings of temporal processing: A review of focal lesion, pharmacological, and functional imaging research. *Reviews in Neuroscience*, 10, 91–116.

Harris, C.M., and Wolpert, D.M. 1998. Signal-dependent noise determines motor planning. *Nature*, 194, 780–784.

Hary, D., and Moore, P. 1987. Synchronizing human movement with an external clock source. *Biological Cybernetics*, 56, 305–311.

Haslam, C., and Cook, M. 2002. Striking a chord with amnesic patients: Evidence that song facilitates memory. *Neurocase*, 8, 453–465.

Hassan, M.A., and Thaut, M.H. 1999. Autoregressive moving average modeling for finger tapping with an external stimulus. *Perceptual and Motor Skills*, 88, 1331–1346.

Hatsopoulos, N.G., and Warren, W.H. 1996. Resonance tuning in rhythmic arm movements. *Journal of Motor Behavior*, 28(1), 3–14.

Hausdorf, J.M., Schaasma, J.D., Balash, Y., et al. 2003. Impaired regulation of stride variability in Parkinson's disease subjects with freezing of gait. *Experimental Brain Research*, 149, 187–194.

Healey, E.C., Mallard, A.R., and Adams, M.R. 1976. Factors contributing to the reduction of stuttering during singing. *Journal of Speech and Hearing Research*, 19, 475–480.

Heaton, P. 2003. Pitch memory, labeling, and disembedding in autism. *Journal of Child Psychiatry and Psychology*, 44, 543–551.

Heaton, P., Hermelin, B., and Pring, L. 1988. Autism and pitch processing: A precursor for savant musical ability? *Music Perception*, 15, 291–305.

Heaton, P., Hermelin, B., and Pring, L. 1999. Can children with autistic spectrum disorders perceive affect in music? An experimental investigation. *Psychological Medicine*, 29, 1405–1410.

Heaton, P., Pring, L., and Hermelin, B. 2001. Musical processing in high functioning children with autism. *Annals of the New York Academy of Sciences*, 930, 443–444.

Hebb, D.O. 1949. *The Organization of Behavior: A Neuropsychological Theory*. New York: Wiley.

Hebert, S., Racette, A., Gagnon, L., et al. 2003. Revisiting the dissociation between singing and speaking in expressive aphasia. *Journal of Neurology*, 126(8), 1838–1851.

Helfrich-Miller, K.R. 1984. Melodic intonation therapy with developmentally apraxic children. *Seminars in Speech and Language*, 5, 119–126.

Helfrich-Miller, K.R. 1994. A clinical perspective: Melodic intonation therapy for developmental apraxia. *Clinics in Communication Disorders*, 4(3), 175–182.

Hermelin, B., O'Connor, N., and Lee, S. 1997. Musical inventiveness of five idiots-savants. *Psychological Medicine*, 17(3), 685–694.

Hermelin, B., O'Connor, N., Lee, S., et al. 1989. Intelligence and musical improvisation. *Psychological Medicine*, 19(2), 447–457.

Hiller, P.U. 1989. Song story: A potent tool for cognitive and affective relearning in head injury. *Cognitive Rehabilitation*, 7, 20–23.

Hitch, G.J., Burgess, N., Towse, J.N., et al. 1996. Temporal grouping effects in immediate recall: A working memory analysis. *Quarterly Journal of Experimental Psychology: A, Human Experimental Psychology*, 49, 116–139.

Ho, Y.C., Cheung, M.C., and Chan, A.S. 2003. Music training improves verbal but not visual memory: Cross-sectional and longitudinal explorations in children. *Neuropsychology*, 17, 439–450.

Hodges, D.A. (Ed.). 1999. *Handbook of Music Psychology*, 4th ed. San Antonio, TX: IMR Press.

Hommel, M., Peres, B., Pollak, P., et al. 1990. Effects of passive tactile and auditory stimuli on left visual neglect. *Archives of Neurology*, 47, 573–576.

Hovland, D., and Mateer, C.A. 2000. Irritability and anger. In S.A. Raskin and C.A. Mateer (Eds.), *Neuropsychological Management of Mild Traumatic Brain Injury*, 187–212. New York: Oxford University Press.

Hovland, D., and Raskin, S.A. 2000. Anxiety and posttraumatic stress. In S.A. Raskin and C.A. Mateer (Eds.), *Neuropsychological Management of Mild Traumatic Brain Injury*, 171–186. New York: Oxford University Press.

Howe, T.E., Lovgreen, B., Cody, F.W., et al. 2003. Auditory cues can modify the gait of persons with early-stage Parkinson's disease: A method for enhancing Parkinsonian walking performance. *Clinical Rehabilitation*, 17, 363–367.

Hummelsheim, H. 1999. Rationales for improving motor function. *Current Opinion in Neurology*, 12, 697–701.

Hund-Georgiadis, M., and von Cramon, D.Y. 1999. Motor-learning-related changes in piano players and non-musicians revealed by functional magnetic-resonance signals. *Experimental Brain Research*, 125, 417–425.

Hurt, C.P., Rice, R.R., McIntosh, G.C., et al. 1998. Rhythmic auditory stimulation in gait training for patients with traumatic brain injury. *Journal of Music Therapy*, 35, 228–241.

Ikegaya, Y., Aaron, G., Cossart, R., et al. 2004. Synfire chains and cortical songs: Temporal modules of cortical activity. *Science*, 302, 559–564.

Imada, T., Watanabe, M., Mashiko, T., et al. 1997. The silent period between sounds has a stronger effect than the interstimulus interval on auditory evoked magnetic fields. *Electroencephalography and Clinical Neurophysiology*, 102, 37–45.

Iwanaga, M., and Ito, T. 2002. Disturbance effect of music on processing of verbal and spatial memories. *Perceptual and Motor Skills*, 94, 1251–1258.

Jackendoff, R., and Lehrdahl, F. 1982. Grammatical parallels between music and language. In M. Clynes (Ed.), *Music, Mind, and Brain*, 83–118. New York: Plenum Press.

Jackson, S.A., Treharne, D.A., and Boucher, J. 1997. Rhythm and language in children with moderate learning disabilities. *European Journal of Disorders of Communication*, 32, 99–108.

Jakobson, L.S., Cuddy, L.L., and Kilgour, A.R. 2003. A key to musicians' superior memory. *Music Perception*, 20, 307–313.

Janata, P., Tillmann, B., and Bharucha, J.J. 2002. Listening to polyphonic music recruits domain-general attention and working memory circuits. *Cognitive Affective Behavioral Neuroscience*, 2, 121–140.

Jeffery, D.R., and Good, D.C. 1995. Rehabilitation of the stroke patient. *Current Opinion in Neurology*, 8, 62–68.

Jeng, S., Holt, K.G., Fetters, L., et al. 1996. Self-optimization of walking in nondisabled children and children with spastic hemiplegic cerebral palsy. *Journal of Motor Behavior*, 28(1), 15–27.

Jensen, U.S., Lewsi, B., Tranel., D et al. 2004. Emotion enhances long-term declarative memory. *Proceedings of the Society for Neuroscience*, 203–9.

Kant, I. 1790. *Kritik der Urteilskraft*. Berlin: Lagarde.

Kapur, N., and Graham, K.S. 2002. Recovery of memory function in neurological disease. In A.D. Baddeley, M.D. Kopelman, and B.A. Wilson (Eds.), *The Handbook of Memory Disorders*, 233–248. Chichester, UK: Wiley.

Kay, T. 1993. Neuropsychological treatment of mild traumatic brain injury. *Journal of Head Trauma Rehabilitation*, 8, 74–85.

Keith, R., and Aronson, A. 1975. Singing as therapy for apraxia of speech and aphasia: Report of a case. *Brain and Language*, 2, 483–488.

Kelso, J.A.S. 1995. *Dynamic Patterns: The Self-Organization of Human Brain and Behavior*. Cambridge, MA: MIT Press.

Kelso, J.A.S., and Tuller, B. 1984. A dynamical basis for action systems. In M.S. Gazzaniga (Ed.), *Handbook of Cognitive Neuroscience*, 319–356. New York: Plenum Press.

Kenyon, G.P., and Thaut, M.H. 2000. A measure of kinematic limb instability modulation by rhythmic auditory stimulation. *Journal of Biomechanics*, 33(10), 1319–1323.

Kenyon, G.P., and Thaut, M.H. 2003. Rhythm-driven optimization of motor control. *Recent Developments in Biomechanics*, 1, 29–47.

Kilgour, A.R., Jakobson, L.S., and Cuddy, L.L. 2000. Music training and rate of presentation as mediators of text and song recall. *Memory and Cognition*, 28, 700–710.

Killeen, P., and Weiss, N. 1987. Optimal timing and the Weber function. *Psychological Review*, 94, 455–468.

Klein, J.M., and Reiss Jones, M. 1996. Effects of attentional set and rhythmic complexity on attending. *Perception and Psychophysics*, 58, 34–46.

Klimesch, W., Doppelmayr, M., Russeger, H., et al. 1998. Induced alpha band power changes in the human EEG and attention. *Neuroscience Letters*, 244, 73–76.

Knox, R., and Jutai, J. 1996. Music-based rehabilitation of attention following brain injury. *Canadian Journal of Rehabilitation*, 9, 169–181.

Knox, R., Yokota-Adachi, H., Kershner, J., et al. 2003. Musical attention training program and alternating attention in brain injury: An initial report. *Music Therapy Perspectives*, 21, 99–104.

Koffka, K. 1935. *Principles of Gestalt Psychology*. New York: Harcourt, Brace.

Krauss, T., and Galloway, H. 1982. Melodic intonation therapy with language delayed apraxic children. *Journal of Music Therapy*, 19(2), 102–113.

Kraut, R. 1992. On the possibility of a determinate semantics for music. In M. Riess Jones and S. Holleran (Eds.), *Cognitive Bases of Musical Communciation*, 11–22. Washington, DC: American Psychological Association.

Kreitler, H., and Kreitler, S. 1972. *Psychology of the Arts*. Durham, NC: Duke University Press.

Kugler, P.N., and Turvey, M.T. 1987. *Information, Natural Laws, and Self-assembly of Rhythmic Movement*. Hillsdale, NJ: Erlbaum.

Laaksonen, R. 1994. Cognitive training methods in rehabilitation of memory. In A.L. Christensen and B.P. Uzzell (Eds.), *Brain Injury and Neuropsychological Rehabilitation: International Perspectives*, 125–132. Hillsdale, NJ: Erlbaum.

Langer, S. 1942. *Philosophy in a New Key: A Study in the Symbolism of Reason, Rite, and Art*. Cambridge, MA: Harvard University Press.

Large, E.W., Fink, P., and Kelso, J.A.S. 2002. Tracking simple and complex sequences. *Psychological Research*, 66, 3–17.

Large, E.W., and Jones, M.R. 1999. The dynamics of attending: How people track time-varying events. *Psychological Review*, 106, 119–159.

Lee, S.H., and Blake R. 1999. Visual form created solely from temporal structure. *Science*, 284, 1165–1167.

Levitin, D.J., and Cooke, P.R. 1996. Memory for musical tempo: Additional evidence that auditory memory is absolute. *Perception and Psychophysics*, 58, 927–935.

Lezak, M.D. 1987. Assessment for rehabilitation planning. In M.J. Meier, A.L. Benton, and L. Diller (Eds.), *Neuropsychological Rehabilitation*, 41–58. New York: Guilford.

Lezak, M.D. 1995. *Neuropsychological Assessment*, 3rd ed. New York: Oxford University Press.

Liepert, J., Graef, S., Uhde, I., et al. 2000. Training-induced changes of motor cortex representations in stroke patients. *Acta Neurologica Scandinavica*, 101(5), 321–326.

Loring, D.W. (Ed.). 1999. *INS Dictionary of Neuropsychology*. New York: Oxford University Press.

Lu, Z.L., Williamson, S.J., and Kaufman, L. 1992. Human auditory primary and association cortex have different lifetimes for activation traces. *Brain Research*, 572, 236–241.

Lucia, C.M. 1987. Toward developing a model of music therapy intervention in the rehabilitation of head trauma patients. *Music Therapy Perspectives*, 62, 34–39.

Luria, A.R. 1966. *Higher Cortical Functions in Man*, translated by B. Haigh. New York: Basic Books.

Luft, A.R., McOmbe-Waller, S., Whitall, J., et al. 2004. Repetitive bilateral arm training and motor cortex activation in chronic stroke: A randomized controlled trial. Journal of the American Medical Association, 292, 1853–1861.

Ma, Y., Nagler, J., Lee, M., et al. 2001. Impact of music therapy on the communication skills of toddlers with pervasive developmental disorder. *Annals of the New York Academy of Sciences*, 930, 445–447.

Maeller, D.H. 1996. Rehearsal strategies and verbal working memory in multiple sclerosis. Unpublished Master's thesis, Colorado State University.

Malherbe, V., Breniere, Y., and Bril, B. 1992. How do cerebral palsied children with hemiplegia control their gait? In M. Woollacott and F. Horak (Eds.), *Posture and Control Mechanisms*, vol. 2, 102–105. Eugene: University of Oregon Books.

Mandel, A.R., Nymark, J.R., Balmer, S.J., et al. 1990. Electromyographic feedback versus rhythmic positional biofeedback in computerized gait retraining with stroke patients. *Archives of Physical and Medical Rehabilitation*, 71, 649–654.

Mandler, G. 1984. *Mind and Body: Psychology of Emotional Stress*. New York: Norton.

Marieb, E.N. 1989. *Human Anatomy and Physiology*. Redwood City, CA: Benjamin/Cummings.

Markowitsch, H.J. 2000. Neuroanatomy of memory. In E. Tulving and F.I.M. Craik (Eds.), *The Oxford Handbook of Memory*. Oxford: Oxford University Press.

Mateer, C.A. 2000. Attention. In S.A. Raskin and C.A. Mateer (Eds.), *Neuropsychological Management of Mild Traumatic Brain Injury*, 73–92. New York: Oxford University Press.

Mateer, C.A., Sohlberg, M.M., and Crinean, J. 1987. Focus on clinical research: Perceptions of memory function in individuals with closed head injury. *Journal of Head Trauma Rehabilitation*, 2, 74–84.

Matzel, L.D., Held, F.P., and Miller, R.R. 1988. Information and expression of simultaneous and backward associations: Implications for contiguity theory. *Learning and Motivation*, 19, 317–344.

Mauritz, K.H. 2002. Gait training in hemiplegia. *European Journal of Neurology*, 9 (supp.1), 23–29; discussion, 53–61.

McDougall, W. 1908. *An Introduction to Social Psychology*. London: Methuen.

McIntosh, G.C., Brown, S.H., Rice, R.R., et al. 1997. Rhythmic-auditory motor facilitation of gait patterns in patients with Parkinson's disease. *Journal of Neurology, Neurosurgery and Psychiatry*, 62, 122–126.

McIntosh, G.C., Prassas, S.G., Kenyon, G., et al. 1998. Movement synchronization during rhythmic tracking: Period versus phase cuing. *Proceedings of the Society for Neuroscience*, 455.8.

McIntosh, G.C., Rize, R.R., Hurd, C.P., et al. 1998. Long-term training effects of rhythmic auditory stimulation on gait in patients with Parkinson's disease. *Movement Disorders*, 13 (Suppl 2), 212.

McMullen, P.T. 1999. The musical experience and affective/aesthetic responses: A theoretical framework for empirical research. In D.A. Hodges (Ed.), *Handbook of Music Psychology*, 387–400. San Antonio, TX: IMR Press.

Meck, W.H. 1996. Neuropharmacology of timing and time perception. *Brain Research: Cognitive Brain Research*, 3(3–4), 227–242.

Merriam, A.P. 1964. *The Anthropology of Music*. Evanston, IL: Northwestern University Press.

Merzenich, M.M., Schreiner, C., Jenkins, W., et al. 1993. Neural mechanisms underlying temporal integration, segmentation, and input sequence representation: Some implications for the origin of learning disabilities. *Annals of the New York Academy of Sciences*, 682, 1–22.

Meyer, L.B. 1956. *Emotion and Meaning in Music*. Chicago: University of Chicago Press.

Michon, J.A. 1967. *Timing in Temporal Tracking*. Soesterberg: Institute for Perception RVO-TNO.

Millard, K.A.O., and Smith, J.A. 1989. The influence of group singing therapy on the behavior of Alzheimer's disease patients. *Journal of Music Therapy*, 26, 58–70.

Miller, R.A., Thaut, M.H., McIntosh, G.C., and Rice, R.R. 1996. Components of EMG symmetry and variability in Parkinsonian and healthy elderly gait. *Electroencephalography and Clinical Neurophysiology*, 101, 1–7.

Mirsky, A.F., Anthony, B.J., Duncan, C.C., et al. 1991. Analysis of the elements of attention: A neuropsychological approach. *Neuropsychology Review*, 2, 109–145.

Mitra, S., Riley, M.A., and Turvey, M.T. 1997. Chaos in human rhythmic movement. *Journal of Motor Behavior*, 29, 195–198.

Molinari, M., Leggio, M.G., DeMartin, M., et al. 2003. The neurobiology of rhythmic motor entrainment: A neurorehabilitation perspective. *Annals of the New York Academy of Sciences*, 999, 313–321.

Molinari, M., Thaut, M.H., Gioia, C., et al. 2001. Motor entrainment to auditory rhythm is not affected by cerebellar pathology. *Proceedings of the Society for Neuroscience*, 950.2.

Morris, G.S., Suteerawattananon, M., Etnyre, B.R., et al. 2004. Effects of visual and auditory cues on gait in individuals with Parkinson's disease. *Journal of the Neurological Sciences*, 219, 63–69.

Morton, L.L., Kershner, J.R., and Siegel, L.S. 1990. The potential for therapeutic applications of music on problems related to memory and attention. *Journal of Music Therapy*, 26, 58–70.

Mottron, L., Peretz, I., and Menard, E. 2000. Local and global processing of music in high-functioning persons with autism: Beyond central coherence? *Journal of Child Psychology and Psychiatry*, 41, 1057–1065.

Mueller, G.E., and Schumann, F. 1894. Experimentelle Beiträge zur Untersuchung des Gedächtnisses. *Zeitschrift für Psychologie*, 6, 81–190, 257–339.

Mueller, K., Schmitz, F., Schnitzler, A., et al. 2000. Neuromagnetic correlates of sensorimotor synchronization. *Journal of Cognitive Neuroscience*, 12, 546–555.

Naeser, M.A., and Helm-Estabrooks, N. 1985. CT scan lesion localization and response to melodic intonation therapy with nonfluent aphasia cases. *Cortex*, 21, 203–223.

Nagasaki, H. 1989. Asymmetric velocity and acceleration profiles of human arm movements. *Experimental Brain Research*, 74, 319–326.

Natke, U., Donath, T.M., and Kalveram, K.T. 2003. Control of voice fundamental frequency in speaking versus singing. *Journal of the Acoustical Society of America*, 113(3), 1587–1593.

Nelles, G., Jentzen, W., Jueptner, M., et al. 2001. Arm-training induced brain plasticity in stroke studied with serial positron emission tomography. *Neuroimage*, 13 (6, pt. 1), 1146–1154.

Nudo, R.J., Wise, B.M., Sifuentes, F., et al. 1996. Neural substrates for the effects of rehabilitative training on motor recovery after ischemic infarct. *Science*, 272(5269), 1791–1794.

Ogata, S. 1995. Human EEG responses to classical music and simulated white noise: Effects of a musical loudness component on consciousness. *Perceptual and Motor Skills*, 80, 779–790.

Overy, K. 2000. Dyslexia, temporal processing and music: The potential of music as an early learning aid for dyslexic children. *Psychology of Music*, 28, 218–229.

Overy, K., Nicolson, R.I., Fawcett, A.J., et al. 2003. Dyslexia and music: Measuring musical timing skills. *Dyslexia*, 9(1), 18–36.

Overy, K., Norton, A.C., Ozdemir, E., et al. 2004. Activation of the left anterior inferior frontal gyrus after melodic intonation therapy in a Broca's aphasia patient. *Proceedings of the Society for Neuroscience*, 595.7.

Pacchetti, C., Aglieri, R., Mancini, F., et al. 1998. Active music therapy and Parkinson's disease: Methods. *Functional Neurophysiology*, 10, 1–7.

Pacchetti, C., Mancini, F., Aglieri, R., et al. 2000. Active music therapy in Parkinson's disease: An integrative method for motor and emotional rehabilitation. *Psychosomatic Medicine*, 62, 386–393.

Paltsev, Y.I., and Elner, A.M. 1967. Change in the functional state of the segmental apparatus of the spinal cord under the influence of sound stimuli and its role in voluntary movement. *Biophysics*, 12, 1219–1226.

Pantev, C., Ross, B., Fujioka, T., et al. 2003. Music and learning-induced cortical plasticity. *Annals of the New York Academy of Sciences*, 999, 438–450.

Parenté, R., and Anderson-Parenté, J.K. 1989. Retraining memory: Theory and application. *Journal of Head Trauma Rehabilitation*, 4, 55–65.

Parenté, R., and Herrmann, D. 1996. *Retraining Cognition: Techniques and Applications*. Gaithersburg, MD: Aspen.

Parncutt, R. 1994. A perceptual model of pulse salient and metrical accent in musical rhythm. *Music Perception*, 11, 409–464.

Parsons, L.M., and Thaut, M.H. 2001. Functional neuroanatomy of the perception of musical rhythm in musicians and nonmusicians. *Neuroimage* 13, 925 (abs.).

Pascual-Leone, A. 2001. The brain that plays music and is changed by it. *Annals of the New York Academy of Sciences*, 930, 315–329.

Pascual-Leone, A., Cohen, L.G., Dang, N., et al. 1993. Acquisition of fine motor skills in humans is associated with the modulation of cortical motor outputs. *Neurology*, 43(supp. 2), A157.

Pascual-Leone, A., Nguyet, D., Cohen, L.G., et al. 1995. Modulation of muscle responses evoked by transcranial magnetic stimulation during the acquisition of new fine motor skills. *Journal of Neurophysiology*, 74, 1037–1045.

Patel, A. 2003. Rhythm in language and music: Parallels and differences. *Annals of the New York Academy of Sciences*, 999, 140–143.

Patel, A., Gibson, E., Ratner, J., et al. 1998. Processing syntactic relations in language and music: An event-related potential study. *Journal of Cognitive Neuroscience*, 10, 717–733.

Peirce, C.S. 1931–1935. *Collected Papers*, edited by C. Hartshorne and P. Weiss, vols. 1–6. Cambridge, MA: Belknap Press of Harvard University Press.

Penhune, V.B., Zatorre, R.J., and Evans, A. 1998. Cerebellar contributions to motor timing: A PET study of auditory and visual rhythm reproduction. *Journal of Cognitive Neuroscience*, 10, 752–765.

Peretz, I., and Kolinsky, R. 1993. Boundaries of separability between melody and rhythm in music discrimination: A neuropsychological perspective. *Quarterly Journal of Experimental Psychology*, A46, 301–325.

Perkins, W.H. 2001. Stuttering: A matter of bad timing. *Science*, 294(5543), 786.

Peterson, D.A., McIntosh, G.C., and Thaut, M.H. 2004. Differential predictions in spectral EEG plasticity with verbal versus music-facilitated learning strategies. *Proceedings of the Society for Neuroscience*, 766–16.

Peterson, D.A., and Thaut, M.H. 2002. Delay modulates spectral correlates in the EEG of nonverbal auditory working memory. *Neuroscience Letters*, 328, 17–20.

Pilon, M.A., McIntosh, K.W., and Thaut, M.H. 1998. Auditory versus visual speech timing cues as external rate control to enhance verbal intelligibility in mixed spastic-dysarthric speakers: A pilot study. *Brain Injury*, 12, 793–803.

Pizzamiglio, L., Perani, D., Cappa, S.F., et al. 1998. Recovery of neglect after right hemispheric damage: H2(15)O positron emission tomographic activation study. *Archives of Neurology*, 55(4), 561–568.

Platel, H., Price, K., Baron, J.C., et al. 1997. The structural components of music perception. *Brain*, 120, 229–243.

Plenger, P.M., Breier, J.I., Wheless, et al. 1996. Lateralization of memory for music: Evidence from the intracarotid sodium amobarbital procedure. *Neuropsychologia*, 34, 1015–1018.

Plutchik, R. 1962. *The Emotions: Facts, Theories, and a New Model*. New York: Random House.

Popovici, M. 1995. Melodic intonation therapy in the verbal decoding of aphasics. *Revue Roumaine de Neurologie et Psychiatrie*, 33, 57–97.

Prassas, S., Thaut, M., McIntosh, G., et al. 1997. Effect of auditory rhythmic cuing on gait kinematic parameters of stroke patients. *Gait and Posture*, 6, 218–223.

Premack, D. 2004. Is language the key to human intelligence? *Science* (5656), 318–319.

Pressing, J. 1999. The referential dynamics of cognition and action. *Psychological Review*, 106, 714–747.

Pressing, J., and Jolley-Rogers, G. 1997. Spectral properties of human cognition and skill. *Biological Cybernetics*, 76, 339–347.

Prigatano, G.P. 1999. *Principles of Neuropsychological Rehabilitation*. New York: Oxford University Press.

Purdie, H. 1997. Music therapy in neurorehabilitation: Recent developments and new challenges. *Critical Reviews in Physical and Rehabilitation Medicine*, 9, 205–217.

Rainey, D.W., and Larsen, J.D. 2002. The effect of familiar melodies on initial learning and long-term memory for unconnected text. *Music Perception*, 20, 173–186.

Ramig, L.O., Bonitati, C.M., Lemke, J.H., et al. 1994. Voice treatment for patients with Parkinson disease: Development of an approach and preliminary efficacy data. *Journal of Medical Speech-Language Pathology*, 2, 191–209.

Rao, S.M., Mayer, A.R., and Harrington, D.L. 2001. The evolution of brain activation during temporal processing. *Nature Neuroscience*, 4, 317–323.

Raskin, S.A. 2000. Executive functions. In S.A. Raskin and C.A. Mateer (Eds.), *Neuropsychological Management of Mild Traumatic Brain Injury*, 113–133. New York: Oxford University Press.

Raskin, S.A., and Mateer, C.A. (Eds.). 2000. *Neuropsychological Management of Mild Traumatic Brain Injury*. New York: Oxford University Press.

Raskin, S.A., and Stein, P.N. 2000. Depression. In S.A. Raskin and C.A. Mateer (Eds.), *Neuropsychological Management of Mild Traumatic Brain Injury*, 157–170. New York: Oxford University Press.

Rauschecker, J.P. 2001. Cortical plasticity and music. *Annals of the New York Academy of Sciences*, 930, 330–336.

Repp, B.H. 1999. Detecting deviations from metronomic timing in music: Effects of perceptual structure on the mental timekeeper. *Perception and Psychophysics*, 61, 529–548.

Richards, C.L., Malouin, F., Bedard, P.J., et al. 1992. Changes induced by L-dopa and sensory cues on the gait of Parkinsonian patients. In M. Woollacott and F. Horak (Eds.), *Posture and Control Mechanisms*, vol. 2, 126–129. Eugene: University of Oregon Books.

Riess Jones, M. 1992. Attending to musical events. In M.R. Jones and S. Holleran (Eds.), *Cognitive Bases of Musical Communication*, 91–110. Washington, DC: American Psychological Association.

Riess Jones, M., Boltz, M., and Kidd, G. 1982. Controlled attending as a function of melodic and temporal context. *Perception and Psychophysics*, 32, 211–218.

Riess Jones, M., and Ralston, J.T. 1991. Some influences of accent structure on melody recognition. *Memory and Cognition*, 19, 8–20.

Rimmele, C.T., and Hester, R.K. 1987. Cognitive rehabilitation after traumatic head injury. *Archives of Clinical Neuropsychology*, 2, 353–384.

Roberts, S., Eykholt, R., and Thaut, M.H. 2000. Analysis of correlations and search for evidence of deterministic chaos in rhythmic motor control by the human brain. *Physical Review E*, 62, 2597–2607.

Robertson, I.H. 1999. Setting goals for cognitive rehabilitation. *Current Opinion in Neurology*, 12, 703–708.

Robertson, I.H., Mattingley, J.M., Rorden, C., et al. 1998. Phasic alerting of neglect patients overcomes their spatial deficit in visual awareness. *Nature*, 395, 169–172.

Robertson, I.H., Nico, D., and Hood, B. 1995. The intention to act improves unilateral neglect: Two demonstrations. *Neuroreport*, 17, 246–248.

Rosenbaum, R.S., Furey, M.L., Horwitz, C.L. et al. 2004. Altered communication between emotion-related brain regions support short-term memory in Alzheimer's disease. *Proceedings of the Society for Neuroscience*, 203–8.

Rossignol. S., and Melvill Jones, G. 1976. Audiospinal influences in man studied by the H-reflex and its possible role in rhythmic movement synchronized to sound. *Electroencephalography and Clinical Neurophysiology*, 41, 83–92.

Rossini, P.P., Caltagirone, C., Castriota-Scanderberg, A., et al. 1998. Hand motor cortical area reorganization in stroke: A study with fMRI, MEG, and TCS maps. *Neuroreport*, 9(9), 2141–2146.

Sacks, O. 1998. Music and the brain. In C.M. Tomaino (Ed.), *Clinical Applications of Music in Neurologic Rehabilitation*, 1–18. St. Louis, MO: MMB Music.

Saffran, J.R. 2003. Musical learning and language development. *Annals of the New York Academy of Sciences*, 999, 397–401.

Safranek, M.G., Koshland, G.F., and Raymond, G. 1982. The influence of auditory rhythm on muscle activity. *Physical Therapy*, 2, 161–168.

Sakai, K., Hikosaka, O., Miyauchi, S., Nielsen, M., et al. 1999. Neural correlates for short term rhythm memory. *Proceedings of the Society for Neuroscience*, 494.12.

Salvino, L.W., and Cawley, R. 1994. Smoothness implies determinism: A method to detect it in time series. *Physical Review Letters*, 73, 1091–1094.

Sanes, J.N., Demartin, M., Weckel, J., and Thaut, M.H. 2001. Brain activation patterns for producing symmetrically and asymmetrically synchronized movement rhythms. *Neuroimage*, 13, 1249 (abs.).

Sarnthein, J., von Stein, A., Rappelsberger, P., et al. 1997. Persistent patterns of brain activity: An EEG coherence study of the positive effect of music on spatial-temporal reasoning. *Neurology Research*, 19, 107–116.

Schacter, D.L., Wagner, A.D., and Buckner, R.L. 2000. Memory systems of 1999. In E. Tulving and F.I.M. Craik (Eds.), *The Oxford Handbook of Memory*, 627–643. Oxford: Oxford University Press.

Schauer, M.L., and Mauritz, K.H. 2003. Musical motor feedback (MMF) in walking of hemiparetic stroke patients: Randomized trials of gait improvement. *Clinical Rehabilitation*, 17, 713–722.

Schauer, M.L., Steingrueber, W., and Mauritz, K.H. 1996. Die Wirkung von Musik auf die Symmetrie des Gehens von Schlaganfallpatienten auf dem Laufband. *Biomedizinische Technik*, 41, 291–296.

Schellenberg, E.G. 2001. Music and nonmusical abilities. *Annals of the New York Academy of Sciences*, 930, 355–371.

Schenker, H. 1935. *Der freie Satz*. Vienna: Universal Editions.

Schlaug, G., and Chen, C. 2001. The brain of musicians: A model for functional and structural adaptation. *Annals of the New York Academy of Sciences*, 930, 281–299.

Schmahmann, J.D. (Ed.). 1997. *The Cerebellum and Cognition*. San Diego: Academic Press.

Schneck, D. 1990. *Engineering Principles of Physiological Function*. New York: New York University Press.

Sears, W. 1968. Processes in music therapy. In E.T. Gaston (Ed.), *Music in Therapy*, 30–44. New York: Macmillan.

Seashore, C.E. 1938. *Psychology of Music*. New York: McGraw-Hill.

Serafine, M.L. 1988. *Music as Cognition: The Development of Thought in Sound*. New York: Columbia University Press.

Shane, H.C., and Darley, F.L. 1978. The effect of auditory rhythmic stimulation on articulatory accuracy in apraxia of speech. *Cortex*, 14(3), 444–450.

Shaw-Miller, S. 2002. *Visible Deeds of Music*. New Haven, CT: Yale University Press.

Shuter-Dyson, R., and Gabriel, C. 1981. *The Psychology of Musical Ability*, 2nd rev ed. London: Methuen.

Singer, W. 1999. Neuronal synchrony: A versatile code for the definition of relations? *Neuron*, 24: 49–65, 11–125.

Singer, W. 1993. Synchronization of cortical activity and its putative role in information processing and learning. *Annual Review of Physiology*, 55, 349–374.

Sloboda, J.A. 1985. *The Musical Mind: The Cognitive Psychology of Music*. Oxford: Oxford University Press.

Smith, A., and Denny, M. 1990. High-frequency oscillations as indicators of neural control mechanisms in human respiration, mastication, and speech. *Journal of Neurophysiology*, 63, 745–758.

Smith, E.E., Jonides, J., Marshuetz, C., et al. 1998. Components of verbal working memory: Evidence from neuroimaging. *Proceedings of the National Academy of Sciences of the United States*, 95, 876–882.

Snyder, B. 2000. *Music and Memory*. Cambridge, MA: MIT Press.

Sohlberg, M.M. 2000. Psychotherapy approaches. In S.A. Raskin and C.A. Mateer (Eds.), *Neuropsychological Management of Mild Traumatic Brain Injury*, 137–156. New York: Oxford University Press.

Sohlberg, M.M., and Mateer, C.A. 1987. Effectiveness of an attention-training program. *Journal of Clinical and Experimental Neuropsychology*, 9, 117–130.

Sohlberg, M.M., and Mateer, C.A. 1989. *Attention Process Training*. Puyallup, WA: Association for Neuropsychological Research and Development.

Sohlberg, M.M., Sprunk, H., and Metzelaar, K. 1988. Efficacy of an external cuing system in an individual with severe frontal lobe damage. *Cognitive Rehabilitation*, 6, 36–41.

Sohlberg, M.M., White, O., Evans, E., et al. 1992. Background and initial case studies into the effects of prospective memory training. *Brain Injury*, 6, 129–138.

Son, G.R., Therrien, B., and Whall, A. 2002. Implicit memory and familiarity among elders with dementia. *Journal of Nursing Scholarship*, 34, 263–267.

Sparks, R.W., and Deck, J.W. 1994. Melodic intonation therapy. In R. Chapey (Ed.), *Language Intervention Strategies in Adult Aphasia*, 368–386. Baltimore: Williams & Wilkins.

Sparks, R.W., Helm, N., and Albert, M. 1974. Aphasia rehabilitation resulting from melodic intonation therapy. *Cortex*, 10, 313–316.

Sparks, R.W., and Holland, A.L. 1976. Method: Melodic intonation therapy for aphasia. *Journal of Speech and Hearing Disorders*, 41, 298–300.

Sparrow, W.A. 1983. The efficiency of skilled performance. *Journal of Motor Behavior*, 15, 237–261.

Stephan, K.M., Thaut, M.H., Wunderlich, G., et al. 2002a. Conscious and subconscious sensorimotor synchronization: Prefrontal cortex and the influence of awareness. *Neuroimage*, 15, 345–352.

Stephan, K.M, Thaut M.H., Wunderlich, G., et al. 2002b. Cortico-cerebellar circuits and temporal adjustments of motor behavior. *Proceedings of the Society for Neuroscience*, 462.8.

Stewart, L., Walsh, V., Frith, U., and Rothwell, J. 2001. Transcranial magnetic stimulation produces speech arrest but not song arrest. *Annals of the New York Academy of Sciences*, 930, 433–435.

Stravinsky, I. 1935. *Chroniques de ma vie*. Paris: Denoël and Steele.

Sutherland, G., Newman, B., and Rachman, S. 1982. Experimental investigations of the relations between mood and intrusive unwanted cognitions. *British Journal of Medical Psychology*, 23, 149–150.

Sutton, K. 1984. The development and implementation of a music therapy physiological measures test. *Journal of Music Therapy*, 21, 160.

Tallal, P., Miller, S., and Fitch, R.S. 1993. Neurological basis of speech: A case of the preeminence of temporal processing. *Annals of the New York Academy of Sciences*, 682, 27–47.

Tate, R.L. 1997. Beyond one-bun, two-shoe: Recent advances in the psychological rehabilitation of memory disorders after acquired brain injury. *Brain Injury*, 11, 907–918.

Teasdale, J.D., and Spencer, P. 1984. Induced mood and estimates of past success. *British Journal of Clinical Psychology*, 23, 149–150.

Teasell, R.W., Bhogal, S.K., Foley, N.C., et al. 2003. Gait retraining post-stroke. *Topics in Stroke Rehabilitation*, 10(2), 34–65.

Tecchio, F., Salustri, C., Thaut, M.H., et al. 2000. Conscious and preconscious adaptation to rhythmic auditory stimuli: A magnetoencephalographic study of human brain responses. *Experimental Brain Research*, 135, 222–230.

Temple, E., Poldrack, R.A., Protopapas, A., et al. 2000. Disruption of the neural response to rapid acoustic stimuli in dyslexia: Evidence from functional MRI. *Proceedings of the National Academy of Sciences of the United States*, 97, 13907–13912.

Thaut, M.H. 1985. The use of auditory rhythm and rhythmic speech to aid temporal muscular control in children with gross motor dysfunction. *Journal of Music Therapy*, 22, 108–128.

Thaut, M.H. 1988. Measuring musical responsiveness in autistic children: A comparative analysis of improvised musical tone sequences of autistic, normal and mentally retarded individuals. *Journal of Autism and Developmental Disorders*, 18, 561–571.

Thaut, M.H. 2000. *A Scientific Model of Music in Therapy and Medicine*. San Antonio: Institute for Music Research/University of Texas San Antonio Press.

Thaut, M.H. 2003. Neural basis of rhythmic timing networks in the human brain. *Annals of the New York Academy of Sciences*, 999, 364–373.

Thaut, M.H., Hurt, C.P., Dragan, D., et al. 1998a. Rhythmic entrainment of gait patterns in children with cerebral palsy. *Developmental Medicine and Child Neurology*, 40, 15.

Thaut, M.H., and Kenyon, G.P. 2003. Rapid motor adaptations to subliminal frequency shifts in syncopated rhythmic sensorimotor synchronization. *Human Movement Science*, 22, 321–338.

Thaut, M.H., Kenyon, G.P., Hurt, C.P., et al. 2002a. Kinematic optimization of spatiotemporal patterns in paretic arm training with stroke patients. *Neuropsychologia*, 40, 1073–1081.

Thaut, M.H., Kenyon, G.P., Schauer, M.L., et al. 1999. The connection between rhythmicity and brain function: Implications for therapy of movement disorders. *IEEE Engineering in Medicine and Biology*, 18, 101–108.

Thaut, M.H., and Mahraun, D. 2004. The influence of music and rhythm on a sustained attention task in children with autism. Submitted for publication.

Thaut, M.H., and McIntosh, G.C. 1999. Music therapy in mobility training with the elderly: A review of current research. *Care Management Journals*, 1(1), 71–74.

Thaut, M.H., McIntosh, G.C., and Rice, R.R. 1997. Rhythmic facilitation of gait training in hemiparetic stroke rehabilitation. *Journal of the Neurological Sciences*, 151, 207–212.

Thaut, M.H., McIntosh, G.C., Rice, R.R., et al. 1993. The effect of auditory rhythmic cuing on stride and EMG patterns in hemiparetic gait of stroke patients. *Journal of Neurologic Rehabilitation*, 7, 9–16.

Thaut, M.H., McIntosh, G.C., Rice, R.R., et al. 1996. Rhythmic auditory stimulation in gait training for Parkinson's disease patients. *Movement Disorders*, 11(2), 193–200.

Thaut, M.H., McIntosh, K., McIntosh, G.C., et al. 2001. Auditory rhythm enhances movement and speech motor control in patients with Parkinson's disease. *Functional Neurology*, 16, 163–172.

Thaut, M.H., Miller, R.A., and Schauer, L.M. 1998b. Multiple synchronization strategies in rhythmic sensorimotor tasks: Phase vs period correction. *Biological Cybernetics*, 79, 241–250.

Thaut, M.H., Miltner, R., Lange, H.W., et al. 1999. Velocity modulation and rhythmic synchronization of gait in Huntington's disease. *Movement Disorders*, 14(5), 808–819.

Thaut, M.H., and Peterson, D.A. 2002. Plasticity of neural representations in auditory memory for rhythmic tempo: Trial dependent EEG spectra. *Proceedings of the Society for Neuroscience*, 373.8.

Thaut, M.H., and Peterson, D.A. 2003. The role of theta and alpha EEG synchronization in verbal learning with a musical template. *Proceedings of the Society for Neuroscience*, 194.21.

Thaut, M.H., Schicks, W., McIntosh, G.C., et al. 2002b. The role of motor imagery and temporal cuing in hemiparetic arm rehabilitation. *Neurorehabilitation & Neural Repair*, 16, 115.

Thaut, M.H., Tian, B., and Azimi, M. 1998c. Rhythmic finger tapping to cosine wave modulated metronome sequences: Evidence of subliminal entrainment. *Human Movement Science*, 17, 839–863.

Thulborn, K.R., Carpenter, P.A., and Just, M.A. 1999. Plasticity of language-related timing cues as external rate control to enhance verbal intelligibility in mixed brain function during recovery from stroke. *Stroke*, 30(4), 749–754.

Tomaino, C.M. 1998. Music and memory: Accessing residual function. In C.M. Tomaino (Ed.), *Clinical Applications of Music in Neurologic Rehabilitation*, 19–27. St Louis, MO: MMB Music.

Trainor, L.J., Shahin, A., and Roberts, L.E. 2003. Effects of musical training on the auditory cortex in children. *Annals of the New York Academy of Sciences*, 999, 506–513.

Tranel, D., and Damasio, A.R. 2002. Neurobiological foundations of human memory. In A.D. Baddeley, M.D. Kopelman, and B.A. Wilson (Eds.), *The Handbook of Memory Disorders*. Chichester, UK: Wiley.

Trehub, S.E. 2003. Toward a developmental psychology of music. *Annals of the New York Academy of Sciences*, 999, 402–413.

Unkefer, R.F., and Thaut, M.H. (Eds.). 2002. *Music Therapy in the Treatment of Adults with Mental Disorders*. St. Louis, MO: MMB Music.

Uno, Y., Kawato, M., and Suzuki, R. 1989. Formation and control of optimal trajectory in human multijoint arm movements. *Biological Cybernetics*, 61, 89–101.

Verwey, W.B. 2001. Concatenating familiar movement sequences: The versatile cognitive processor. *Acta Psychologica*, 106, 69–95.

Vorberg, D., and Wing, A.M. 1996. Modeling variability and dependence in timing. In H. Hewyer and S.W. Keele (Eds)., *Handbook of Perception and Action*, 181–262. New York: Academic Press.

Vos, P.G., and Helsper, E.L. 1992. Tracking simple rhythms: On-beat versus offbeat performance. In F. Macar, W.J. Friedman, and V. Pouthas (Eds.), *Time, Action, and Cognition: Towards Bridging the Gap*, 287–299. Dordrecht: Kluwer Academic Publishers.

Wallace, W.T. 1994. Memory for music: Effect of melody on recall of text. *Journal of Experimental Psychology: Learning, Memory, Cognition*, 20, 1471–1485.

Wambaugh, J.L., and Martinez, A.L. 2000. Effects of rate and rhythm control treatment on consonant production accuracy in apraxia of speech. *Aphasiology*, 14(8), 851–871.

Warren, J.D., Warren, J.E., Fox, N.C., et al. 2003. Nothing to say, something to sing: Primary progressive dynamic aphasia. *Neurocase*, 9, 140–153.

Wartenberg, T.E. (Ed.). 2002. *The Nature of Art*. Fort Worth, TX: Harcourt College.

Watson, J.B. 1925. *Behaviorism*. New York: Norton.

Weber, A.M. 1990. A practical clinical approach to understanding and treating attentional problems. *Journal of Head Trauma Rehabilitation*, 5, 73–85.

Wespatat, V., Tennigkeit, F., and Singer, W. 2004. Phase sensitivity of synaptic modifications in oscillating cells of rat visual cortex. *Journal of Neuroscience*, 24, 9067–9075.

Whitall, J., McCombe, W.S., Silver, K.H., et al. 2000. Repetitive bilateral arm training with rhythmic auditory cueing improves motor function in chronic hemiparetic stroke. *Stroke*, 31, 2390–2395.

Whybrew, W. 1962. Measurement and Evaluation in Music. Dubuque, IA: Brown.

Wilk, K.E., Meister, K., Fleisig, G., et al. 2000. Biomechanics of the overhead throwing motion. *Sports Medicine and Arthroscopy Review*, 8(2), 124–134.

Williams, S.M. 1993. Perceptual principles of sound grouping. In G.M. Nielson and D. Bergeron (Eds.), *Visualization '93: The Proceedings of SIGGRAPH 93. An Introduction to Data Sonification*, 4.66–4.91. Los Alamitos, CA: IEEE Computer Society Press.

Wilson, B.A. 2000. Compensating for cognitive deficits following brain injury. *Neuropsychology Review*, 10, 233–243.

Wilson, B.A. 2002. Management and remediation of memory problems in brain-injured adults. In A.D. Baddeley, M.D. Kopelman, and B.A. Wilson (Eds.), *The Handbook of Memory Disorders*, 655–682. Chichester, UK: Wiley.

Wilson, B.A., Baddeley, A., Evans, J., et al. 1994. Errorless learning in the rehabilitation of memory impaired people. *Neuropsychological Rehabilitation*, 4, 307–326.

Wilson, B.A., and Evans, J.J. 1996. Error free learning in the rehabilitation of individuals with memory impairments. *Journal of Head Trauma Rehabilitation*, 11, 54–64.

Wimpory, D., Chadwick, P., and Nash, S. 1995. Brief report: Musical interaction therapy for children with autism. An evaluative case study with two-year follow-up. *Journal of Autism and Developmental Disabilities*, 25(3), 231–248.

Wolfe, D.E., and Hom, C. 1993. Use of melodies as structural prompts for learning and retention of sequential verbal information by preschool students. *Journal of Music Therapy*, 30, 100–118.

Wolff, P.H. 2002. Timing precision and rhythm in developmental dyslexia. *Reading and Writing*, 15, 179–206.

Wundt, W.M. 1874. *Grundzüge der physiologichen Psychologie*. Leipzig: Engelmann.

Yamadori, A., Osumi, Y., Masuhara, S., et al. 1977. Preservation of singing in Broca's aphasia. *Journal of Neurology, Neurosurgery and Psychiatry*, 40(3), 221–224.

Yorkston, K.M., and Beukelman, D.R. 1981. Ataxic dysarthria: Treatment consequences based on intelligibility and prosodic considerations. *Journal of Speech and Hearing Disorders*, 46, 398–404.

Yorkston, K.M., Hammen, V.L., Beukelman, D.R., et al. 1990. The effect of rate control on the intelligibility and naturalness of dysarthric speech. *Journal of Speech and Hearing Disorders*, 55, 550–560.

Zatorre, R.J., and Peretz, I. (Eds.). 2001. *The Biological Foundations of Music. Annals of the New York Academy of Sciences*, 930. New York: New York Academy of Sciences.

Zencius, A., Wesolowski, M.D., and Burke, W.H. 1990. A comparison of four memory strategies with traumatically brain-injured clients. *Brain Injury*, 4, 33–38.

Index

Beck Depression Inventory, 193
behavior modification, 189
Ben-Yishay, Yehuda, 180
Berlyne, D. E., 4, 5, 19–23, 27, 36, 117
Boethius, 29–30
boundary conditions, 97
brain
    amygdala, 76, 185
    auditory-motor pathway in, 141–142
    basal ganglia, 48–49, 51–52, 65–66, 142
    brain stem. *See* brain stem.
    Brodman area, 223
    cerebellum. *See* cerebellum.
    cingulum, 49, 50, 52
    cortex. *See* cortex.
    gyrus, 46, 51, 72
    hippocampus, 48, 76, 185
    hypothalamus, 185
    inferior colliculus, 47
    insula, 48
    lesions. *See* lesions, brain.
    midbrain, 52, 53
    neurons. *See* neurons.
    plasticity of. *See* plasticity, brain.
    putamen, 48, 51
    rhythm and, 45–57
    subcortical cell ensembles, 46–48
    thalamus, 48–50, 142, 169, 185
    traumatic injury to. *See* traumatic brain
        injury.
    Wernicke's area, 166, 168
brain stem
    arousal of, 138
    attention and, 184
    CPGs in, 89
    memory and, 185
    rhythmic motion and, 47, 79
    temporality and, 48
Broca's aphasia, 68–69, 166
Brownian motion, 44
Byrd, William, 165

C

cadence, 63, 66, 143–145, 162
call-and-response patterns, 73
cardiopulmonary functions
    arousal and, 20
    OMREX and, 173
    therapeutic singing and, 176
    TIMP and, 155
    walking and, 110

central pattern generators (CPGs), 89
central sensory code hypothesis, 45
cerebellum
    cognition and, 58
    direct resonance hypothesis and, 49
    duration and, 52
    memory and, 53, 185
    meter and, 52
    pattern discrimination and, 52
    perception and, 58
    rhythmic movement and, 142
    synchronization and, 48–51
    tempo and, 52
cerebral palsy, 67, 140
Chomsky, Noam, 2, 10, 33–34
chronos, 16
chunking, 74–75, 123, 197
Cicerone, Keith, 181
cingulum, 49, 50, 52
clinical research models, 119, 124–125
cluttering, 70, 170
coefficient of variation, 92
cognition. *See also* perception.
    aesthetics and, 26
    concept development and, 174
    definition of, 36
    emotion and, 182–183, 194–195
    improvisation and, 122–123
    Kant on, 35–36
    mood and, 122
    in motor rehabilitation, 141
    neuroanatomy of, 33–37, 50, 54, 58
    NMT and, 126–131, 190–201, 207–215
    rehabilitation of, 74–81, 128–130,
        179–201
    research on, 37–38, 73–74, 180–181
    rhythm and, 54–55
    R-SMM and, 119–125
    synchronization and, 54
    TDM and, 132–133, 191–193,
        195–201
collative variables, 21
Color-Word Interference Tests, 198
communication
    association in, 2–3
    attention and, 185
    definition of, 1
    improvisation and, 122–123
    in psychosocial rehabilitation, 189
    R-SMM and, 119–124
    rules of, 177
    symbol systems of, 68